ACRL Publications in Librarianship no. 34

Nonprint Media in Academic Libraries

Edited by

PEARCE S. GROVE

American Library Association

Chicago 1975

The Audiovisual Committee of the Association of College and Research Libraries is a divisional subcommittee of the Audiovisual Committee of the American Library Association

Library of Congress Cataloging in Publication Data

Grove, Pearce S. 1930–
Nonprint media in academic libraries.

(ACRL publications in librarianship; no. 34)
Bibliography: p.
1. Libraries—Special collections—Non-book materials. 2. Libraries, University and college. I. Title. II. Series: Association of College and Research Libraries. ACRL publications in librarianship; no. 34.
Z674.A75 no. 34 [Z688.N6] 025.17′7 74–23972
ISBN 0–8389–0153–0

Printed in the United States of America
Second printing, October 1976

Contents

Foreword

As current chairperson of the Audiovisual Committee of the Association of College and Research Libraries, I am pleased to see the completion of this work.

This guide not only satisfies the need of academic librarians for information on the selection, classification, and cataloging of nonprint materials at a time when libraries are beginning to give more attention to content rather than to format, but it also signals the appearance of another of the Audiovisual Committee's products.

In tracing the uncomplicated but long incubation period for this little volume, credit must be given to those who have labored hard on its behalf. Any omissions of credit can be attributed to the writer's ignorance and not to her intent. As part of the official record then, recognition must be given to Ruth Christensen, under whose capable leadership the antecedent of the present volume was completed: a work entitled *Guidelines for Audio-Visual Services in Academic Libraries*, edited by Ralph Emerick and published by the American Library Association in 1968.

The earlier *Guidelines* served as a spur to the Audiovisual Committee to attempt a more ambitious work; consequently, an enlarged and a more comprehensive project was planned under the leadership of the next chairperson, Mr. A. P. Marshall. It was under his leadership that much of the work for the present volume was accomplished, but as the committee chairpersonship passed from Mr. Marshall to Dr. Herman L. Totten, so did the responsibility for the continuation and the nurturing of the project. During the energetic pursuance of this task, Dr. Totten brilliantly assigned the editorship for the present volume to Mr. Pearce S. Grove, to whom the major portion of the credit must be given for its completion.

The current chairperson merely happens to be the midwife at the time of this book's publication. It could not have happened without the perseverance of so many, without the pain and hard work on the part of its contributors, and without the help and guidance of the Association of College and Research Libraries and the American Library Association.

Mary B. Cassata, *Chairperson*
ACRL Audiovisual Committee

Acknowledgments

This manuscript has emerged through an array of committees to be published. Members of the American Library Association have rendered genuine encouragement, which was needed at times, while Association of College and Research Libraries' Audio-visual Committee members have given generously of their time and talent. Many of them are authors or coauthors of chapters whose contribution is easily recognized. Pioneering efforts of others are delineated in her introductory remarks by Dr. Mary B. Cassata, who mentions Dr. Herman L. Totten, A. P. Marshall, Mrs. Ruth M. Christensen, and Ralph Emerick. Others to whom acknowledgments are due include Sister Ellen Huff, an inspiration to her younger colleagues, and Miss D. Nora Gallagher, an early advocate of library responsibility for multimedia formats. Authors represented in this volume who went far beyond their specific assignments to assist with additional aspects of the manuscript are Mrs. Evelyn G. Clement and Wolfgang M. Freitag.

Critics who made invaluable suggestions are Dr. Robert Steele, Boston University School of Communications; David Hall of the Rogers and Hammerstein Archives of Recorded Sound, New York Public Library; William Shank, Music Librarian at the City University of New York; Miss Judy L. Rose, Reference Librarian at the California State College at Los Angeles; and

Calvin J. Boyer, Graduate School of Library Science, Indiana University.

Special acknowledgment is due Dr. Edward G. Holley, Dean, Graduate School of Library and Information Science at the University of North Carolina and Chairman of the ACRL Publications Committee. In his latter capacity, he and each of his committee members—Dr. Kenneth G. Peterson, University of Virginia; Mr. Richard D. Johnson, the Honnold Library for the Claremont Colleges; and Dr. Dale Barker, University of Miami (Florida)—read an early draft of the manuscript giving invaluable assistance to its accuracy, clarity, and editorial style. Their enthusiastic reception spurred the editor on to complete, enlarge, and further refine each chapter. Dr. Holley, an accomplished author and devoted academician, has been both a constant source of inspiration and a leveling agent, for we otherwise might have become overly enamored with the role of nonprint formats in the libraries of tomorrow.

Through the understanding of my immediate supervisor, Dr. Gail Shannon, and Dr. James Sublette, Eastern New Mexico University Graduate Dean, sufficient time, travel, and a modest research grant were made available to this project. They have been loyal friends and colleagues whose interest in scholarship among their faculty is acknowledged.

Creative attempts by administrators must undoubtedly be traceable to the support of their staffs. In this case no doubt exists, for the devotion of Miss Becky Barnett, Mrs. Linda Honeyfield, Miss Pennie Carrasco, and Mrs. Winifred White has been paramount to everything undertaken. However, only one person shares the full burden and joy of this writing and that is my Library Office Manager, Mrs. June Rankin. Without her constant devotion, little beyond administrative routines would be possible—certainly no manuscript of this magnitude. Therefore, Mrs. Rankin shares equally in any contribution this volume may render.

Although each chapter author is responsible for a specific portion of the book, the editor has in most instances altered significantly the original chapter manuscripts. It was usually possible to do so in concert with the authors, coauthors, critics, and readers. Nevertheless, the final responsibility for the entire volume is mine.

Introduction

The recent completed report of the Carnegie Commission on Higher Education, *The Fourth Revolution: Instructional Technology in Higher Education,* stated that

> the library, by whatever name, should occupy a central role in the instructional resources of educational institutions. Its personnel should be available not only for guidance to materials held in the collections of the campus, but should also, when qualified by subject-matter expertise, be utilized as instructors. We also believe that nonprint information, illustration, and instructional software components should be maintained as part of a unified informational-instructional resource that is cataloged and stored in ways that facilitate convenient retrieval as needed by students.

The commission's report echoes the joint *Standards for School Media Programs* which strongly recommends the unification of print and nonprint media in "media centers." The center, according to Burns, "will house all learning materials and accompanying services, putting audiovisual and printed resources under an allegedly more favorable single administrative organization and providing easier access for individual or group study." The recommendations of these individuals, task forces, and commissions concur that all resources for academic endeavor, regardless of format, should be under the direction of a central library facility and made readily available to all students and members of the faculty.

Let the reader therefore understand that a basic premise for this volume is the assumption that librarians and media specialists will accept media in all formats and integrate them not only for the benefit of present users but for the even larger number of potential users as well.

Although a variety of media, even multi-media, are now available to academic libraries in the United States and virtually every library now contains these materials in some formats, few professional publications exist to aid librarians in their selection, care, and use. We hope that our words will serve as a guide for administrators and students, as well as librarians and audiovisual specialists responsible for the development, organization, and service of nonprint media collections. Although each chapter is an integral part of the entire volume, each could also stand as a separate treatise for a librarian seeking information on judicious selection, prudent acquisition, useful classification, and accurate cataloging of a specific form of media. It is important, however, to keep in mind that this volume, while several years in the making, cannot incorporate all the most recent developments in the nonprint media field. However, chapter authors have presented the results of literature searches, research in progress, procedures of existing programs, and their own recommendations for collection development and effective utilization. These are offered as initial guides for the most effective and efficient handling of nonprint media in institutions of higher education.

Nonprint media, although only recently gaining recognition equal to that of printed materials, is by no means a recent phenomena. The shadow show, popular for over two thousand years in the Orient, is a forerunner to modern communication. The projection of shadows with body and hand actions which conveyed sophisticated messages and delighted audiences throughout Asia was probaly the first application of educational technology. While many significant advances were made in the creative use of visual projections, man, in his desire to preserve and transmit information, attempted to transfer his subject matter to clay, bark, stone, and cloth. Thus, representational images became widely understood and used within and between cultures.

What is currently available to academicians is presented in this volume by specialists in separate chapters that deal with specific media formats. A more comprehensive coverage of cataloging and classification of nonprint media is given by the editor in his chapter on this topic. A chronological treatment is utilized to strengthen its historic and encyclopedic value. It also serves, as do the chapters on selection and standards, as a supplement to all other chapters.

The vast quantities of nonprint media produced locally (thus eluding national responsibilities of copyright and bibliography) compound the problem and thwart all attempts to render nonprint media produced in one public or private institution available to potential users in another. Yet, the elaborate network of journals, indexes, abstracts, publishers' tools, university presses, and depository collections remains devoted almost exclusively to material in a print format. Robert Broadus, in his chapter on the selection and acquisition of nonprint media, examines the reference works that are currently available to guide those who are to deal effectively with collection development.

Cooperation in these matters can no longer be restricted to the concerns of a single nation, thus current realities compel those in professional organizations directly concerned to assume an international perspective. Working through their organizations and standards groups such as the American National Standards Institute (ANSI) and its subgroups, e.g. PH5 and Z39, those responsibile for the bibliographic control of nonprint media may gain official and professional association with their counterparts in other countries. The International Standards Organization (ISO) is one of the vitally important world forums whereby agreements may be reached for the benefit of mankind. The United States Bureau of Standards at the national level and United Nations Educational, Scientific, and Cultural Organization (UNESCO) at the international level have also made significant contributions to procedures for improved access to information in several formats. Evelyn Clement, a doctoral candidate at Indiana University and Chairman, Department of Library Service at Memphis State University, reviews the progress which can be claimed to date with the intention of documenting both accomplishments and the need for further research, study, and professional deliberation at all geographic and institution levels. Her chapter, devoted to standards for nonprint media in academic institutions, discusses both national and international agencies concerned with the development of standards for nonprint media, its equipment and service. Mrs. Clement has both directed and participated in United States Office of Education (USOE) institutes, National Center for Educational Statistics (NCES) conferences and American Library Association (ALA) committees devoted to the standardization of procedures for library and audiovisual personnel.

Sound recordings, available commercially for over seventy years, are still elusive to the collector who seeks to systematically acquire those most appropriate to his needs or those of his institution's clientele. Gerald Gibson, formerly sound recordings librarian from Eastman's distinguished Sibley Music Library, was chosen in response to recommendations by his colleagues in music librarianship to present the historical development and current status of sound recording collections in U.S. academic libraries. During the preparation of this manuscript, Mr. Gibson accepted the position of Music Librarian, Music Section, Descriptive Cataloging Division on the staff of the Library of Congress. He has been assisted in his chapter by David Hall, head of Rodgers and Hammerstein Archives of Recorded Sound, and William Shank of the City University of New York.

Coauthors Dennis Fields and Tony Schulzetenberg of Saint Cloud State College were chosen to develop the chapter on filmstrips, a learning resource often overlooked by academic librarians although it has proven to be a valuable format for information in both elementary and secondary schools for more than a half a century. The filmstrip combines favorable aspects of slides and motion picture film for the benefit of individual users as well as teacher-oriented learning programs. Fields and Schulzetenberg have had experience with filmstrips in library and audiovisual service centers and combine their talents to give a historical perspective to the development, use, care, and availability of filmstrips in college and university libraries.

Harvard University slide librarian Wolfgang Frietag, curator of an extensive collection and advocate of more bibliographic attention to slides, initiated the chapter on this media format. Simultaneously, though independently, Betty Jo Irvine, slide librarian at Indiana University, was involved in a research project of similar import. Their expertise was combined in the chapter on slides to provide academic librarians both intellectual background and practical procedures for the organization and development of slide collections.

Although films remain one of the most expensive media resources, their value to the learning process is unquestioned. Expanding collections of 8- and 16mm films both commercially and locally produced footage are found on ever increasing numbers of college and university campuses. Although no clear pattern of use, location, administration, or organization exists, authors Dwight Burlingame, Saint Cloud State College librarian, and Herbert Farmer of the University of Southern California, Department of Cinema, combine different backgrounds to bring forth recommended procedures and practices favored by those professional associations most directly concerned. Film rental collections developed during the last thirty years, a unique phenomenon among educational institutions, offer efficient and inexpensive service to schools, clubs, libraries, and other educationally oriented groups. Immediate access to large numbers of costly films for relatively small rental fees necessitates the development of precise bibliographic reference works and handling procedures that may be widely understood. Burlingame and Farmer relate the details of film collecting essential for administrators and collection supervisors who are considering the beginning or the expansion of a film acquisition program in their academic institutions.

Pictures, photographs, and prints are dealt with in a single chapter by Joanne Harrar, assistant library director at the University of Georgia, who chose this topic because of her feeling that it is a significant aspect of nonprint media that seldom receives the recognition it deserves by librarians. While archivists, art departments, historians, and many faculty members often acquire collections of this material, it is usually unorganized and inaccessible to the general student body and faculty of colleges and universities. In libraries where these information formats are valued, collections are available for campus-wide use. Joanne Harrar relates her own experience and that obtained from curators of other photograph, picture, and print collections in academic libraries and museums.

That maps are an enigma to librarians is suggested by coauthors Alberta Koerner, map librarian at the University of Michigan, and Mary Galneder of the map library at the University of Wisconsin, who were so pleased to have maps treated as nonprint media that they agreed to do the extensive research necessary to develop a comprehensive manuscript on maps for a chapter in this volume. Through a review of the literature and personal observations as curators of two large university library collections, the authors addressed themselves to the selection, acquisition, cataloging, and administration of maps in academic libraries.

Although other nonprint media such as videotape and transparencies are not treated as separate formats in this volume, it should not be construed that the committee felt they deserve little attention. While some may be adequately dealt with in several of the chapters in this volume others require more experience and research than is currently available to librarians. This publication is based largely on the personal observation and successful practice of pioneer librarians of a rather recent vintage who view the organization, care, and presentation of information, regardless of format, as their responsibility. It is, however, the authors' intention also to present the contributions of others through reviews of the literature.

To further assist the librarian, media specialist, and administrator, Mary Cassata of the State University of New York at Buffalo compiled an extensive bibliography which includes some references cited in individual chapters as well as other writings suggested by the authors of each chapter and the compiler's own search for appropriate references.

Microforms have increased the availability and storage capacity of libraries. They include microfiche, microfilm, and microcard formats of information, each possessing certain advantages and disadvantages for librarians and library users. However, it has been decided to omit microforms from this publication because of the state of current research, experimentation, and discussions now in progress. Recent research reports and state-of-the-art publications seem to adequately provide what is currently known on the topic. Representatives from the National Microfilm Association who were consultants to the publication have encouraged the editor and the ACRL Audiovisual Committee to state their position that microforms should be treated as nonprint media in a subsequent publication, but agree this volume should be issued without a chapter about them. The ACRL Publications Committee and editor of this publication agree with the committee that microforms are indeed nonprint media.

The Bibliographic Organization of Nonprint Media

Pearce S. Grove

Pearce S. Grove is Library Director and Chairman, Department of Library Science, Eastern New Mexico University.

The organization and systematic grouping of the components of knowledge have challenged philosophers throughout history. The need to organize things for methodical shelving and retrieval may be traced as far back as 2700 B.C. in Egypt and Crete, when according to Richardson, "the putting of like kinds of works into boxes together" and a classification of objects, if not of object records, was practiced.[1] Although the Babylonians were probably the first people to establish libraries, about 1700 B.C., the organization of knowledge into theoretical systems is believed to have been the discovery of the Greeks. Babylonians and Egyptians organized their clay tablets and papyrus rolls in the general form of classified subject catalogs.

Aristotle is reported by Strabo to be the first man to classify books.[2] His concept of the hierarchy was used by his successors as a basis for the classification of knowledge. Tyrannion, the grammarian, is believed to have excelled in the classification of books and, about 80 B.C., he reclassified and recataloged the library that had once belonged to Aristotle.

Dorothy Mae Norris dismissed the development of libraries and their catalogs during the first ten centuries of the Christian Era with the assumption that little was accomplished.[3] She devoted herself to a history of cataloging and cataloging methods from 1100 to 1850. During this period, a wealth of knowledge concerning the organization of materials, structure of library catalogs, and glossary of common terminology was established.

The English nobleman, Francis Bacon, drew on the philosophical writings of his predecessors to evolve a system for the organization of all knowledge. It is said that "Francis Bacon denied the circulation of the blood, didn't understand the work of Galileo, rejected Gilbert on magnetism, and Copernicus on the sun," and, "Like any philosopher who distrusts abstraction, Bacon was driven by his inductive method to the use of classification as an instrument for ordering the world . . . ."[4] Bacon's belief in the unity of knowledge for use was based on cognitive thought. His influence is seen in a host of practical philosophers such as Panizzi, Cutter, Dewey, Charles Martel, J. C. M. Hanson, Hulme, Kaiser, H. E. Bliss, Ranganathan, J. D. Brown, Osborn, Berwick Sayers, Brunet, and Seymour Lubetsky. These men have evolved and refined complex systems for the organization of knowledge, primarily in print format.

A library "perfect in all ways" was presented to Henry III by the learned Lacroix du Maine in 1583.[5] This scheme to organize the king's library of ten thousand volumes appears to be the first use of a decimal classification system. Nearly three hundred years later in Boston, Nathaniel B. Shurtleff published a small manual entitled *A Decimal System for the Arrangement and Administration of Libraries,* which resembled that of du Maine.[6] The notation of both systems designated a fixed location for books, in contrast to Melvil Dewey's expansive decimal classification for the interfiling of books, which was first issued in 1876.

According to Kyly, "American librarians are in substantial agreement that books should be classified on the shelves in the order of subjects treated, rather than in that of arrangement by accession number, chronologically, alphabetically, by size, or by any other criteria."[7] In the latter part of the nineteenth century and first two decades of the twentieth century, librarians continued to accept and further develop the concept of the organization of book materials by subject content. This led to a similar pattern of organization for nonprint media.

EARLY TREATMENT

The U.S. Library of Congress map collection was begun shortly after the Civil War. The first picture collection organized for circulation to the U.S. public was opened at the Denver Public Library in 1889.[8] Paper prints, or contact prints, of motion pictures were deposited for copyright purposes at the Library of Congress as early as 1894, and nine years later a sound recording collection was established there. The Newark Public Library began circulating their collection of prints and framed pictures near the turn of the twentieth century.

Melvil Dewey, in an article on library pictures in 1906, suggested that

> Libraries are rapidly accepting the doctrine for which we have contended for many years, that what we call books have no exclusive rights in a library. The "library" has lost its etymologic meaning and means not a collection of books, but the central agency for disseminating information, innocent recreation, or, best of all, inspiration among the people. Whenever this can be done better, more quickly, or cheaply by a picture than a book, the picture is entitled to a place on the shelves and in the catalog.[9]

Dewey went on to note that the New York State Library had sixty thousand prints in 1906 and that lantern slides were becoming widely used as teaching aids in colleges and universities.

In 1910, Henry Evelyn Bliss outlined his classification system, a system of subject organization which eventually included nonprint media.[10] The first phonodisc collection outside the Library of Congress was founded at the St. Paul Public Library in 1914,[11] although phonodiscs were not actually circulated to the public until nine years later, when the Springfield, Massachusetts, Public Library began its service. During the intervening period, numerous articles began to appear in the professional literature reiterating the position taken earlier by Melvil Dewey.

Whether in response to suspicion or recognition of their value, librarians began to review and evaluate the mass media in 1914. This involvement coupled with public demand stimulated the collection of a wide variety of nonprint materials in libraries. Public libraries in large cities, such as Boston, Kansas City, New York, Chicago, and St. Louis, were developing extensive collections of pictures, photographs, post cards, and clippings in addition to other types of nonprint media in an effort to fulfill their expanding role as cultural centers of their communities. School classes were the major beneficiaries of these new services.

Although little discussion of their organization is given in the literature, each library was forced to establish its own scheme for the arrangement of these materials due to demands of the public for their circulation. C. W. Stokes reported an early classification and filing scheme in 1916 for a specialized collection of photographs. One year earlier, a statewide film exchange was proposed by the California state librarian, James Gillis, to aid "schools, clubs, societies and the like" in obtaining "industrial films and pictures treating educational and scientific subjects." Then, two years later, in response to an increased demand for better films, Thomas Edison decided to produce adaptations from favorite stories among "boys and young men readers," his first requirement being that these films should be "clean." In 1919, specific details of the organization and circulation of stereographs, lantern slides, and music records in the Kern County Library, Bakersfield, California, were reported by Julia G. Babcock.[12]

W. C. Berwick Sayers' *A Manual of Classification for Librarians and Bibliographers* appeared in 1926 "to explain how classification affects library methods, how it is applied to . . . illustrations . . . and maps. . . ."[13] A subsequent edition devoted a chapter to "prints, illustrations, lantern slides and negatives."

Margaret A. Klein, director of the Children's Bureau, U.S. Department of Labor, described a system used by government departments for filing visual materials with much of the work based on multicolored cards for filing different types of materials in different sections.[14] She described the distribution, stock, information, and photographic files which comprised the filing system for visual materials in government departments.

Complete Dewey decimal classification numbers were not accepted by all libraries for the organization of their nonprint material. Some utilized only the second line of the call number, the Cutter number, first set forth by Jacob Schwartz in 1871 to preserve an alphabetical order of authors. Charles A. Cutter developed the concept of letters and numbers as symbols to augment Melvil Dewey's classification scheme. The Cutter number was expanded by Kate E. Sanborn and work numbers added to give a unique number for a specific book. This book number, according to Dewey, was added to the class numbers to: (1) arrange books in order on the shelves; (2) provide a brief and accurate call number for each book; (3) locate a particular book on the shelf; (4) provide a symbol for charging books to borrowers; (5) facilitate the return of books to the shelves; (6) assist in quick identification of a book during inventories.[15] Although the title of Sanborn's pamphlet and emphasis of her list is on books, the so-called book number began to appeal to librarians who hesitated to utilize book classification numbers for nonprint material.

APPROACHES TO CATALOGING

M. Lanning Shane, audiovisual education consultant to the George Peabody College Demonstration School, expressed his belief in 1940 that audiovisual aids were really books of an unconventional sort and librarians, therefore, were best equipped to organize an efficient audiovisual service.[16] The problems of selection, purchase, classification, and cataloging were all familiar procedures to the librarian, though applied to "unfamiliar materials." Although certain visual aids had been a part of library collections for some time, he felt only "recently a few libraries have undertaken a more complete audiovisual program."

The term "media" appeared in the *Post-War Standards for Public Libraries* published by the American Library Association in 1943, and was used to encompass "books, periodicals, newspapers, pamphlets, maps, film, pictures, recordings, music scores, and similar material."[17] The term was meant to describe that "by which ideas are transmitted without oral aid . . ." and had a rightful place among the library's holdings.

Furthermore, British leadership in the organization of nonprint media was evident during a conference held at Chaucer House on April 20, 1944, "to meet the express desire on the part of a number of people that discussions should take place so that cataloging problems connected with these materials should be presented and some consideration given to the possibility of drafting rules to fit special circumstances."[18] Following a paper by M. Dean Smith of the British Broadcasting Corporation (BBC) Gramophone Library on "problems connected with cataloging in a gramophone library of national scope," the committee agreed that investigation should continue and it formed itself in "three groups, (a) gramophone records and music, (b) sound recordings and film, (c) illustrations, pictures, maps and plans."

In 1945, in an article entitled "Organization, Administration, Supervision, and Mechanical Facilities of Departments of Audio-Visual Aids," an analysis was made by Earl E. Sechriest for his doctoral dissertation at the University of Pittsburgh.[19] His recommendation for the organization of nonprint media in audiovisual centers was that "materials shall be classified according to a plan which divides the subject matter of the curriculum into ten main headings (these to be further divided and subdivided) to which a key number shall be given following the general pattern of the Dewey Decimal System. . . ."

Muriel L. Kemp, senior cataloger of the Worcester Free Public Library, was inspired by a card from Tufts College to experiment with a form card of 3" x 5" dimensions and subsequently make the "revolutionary decision . . . to use a 4" x 6" card" for a music record collection which was maintained separately from the book stock.[20] Kemp admitted "our work was well underway before the announcement by Andriot Index Service, Cincinnati, of printed catalog cards for phonograph records." The Worcester cataloger adapted form letters from the Enoch Pratt schedule and utilized the Barden scheme rather than Cutter numbers that seemed unnecessarily long. By October, 1947, one thousand discs were available to the residents of this Massachusetts community.

In 1948 a mimeographed manual entitled "Processing Audio-Visual Materials" was issued at Indiana University for library science courses.[21] A forerunner of numerous manuals on this topic, it carried this subtitle: "A Brief Outline for Cataloging, Processing, Housing and Circulating Films, Filmstrips, Slides, Stereographs, Recordings, Transcriptions, Maps, Charts, and Pictures." Two immediate problems posed were those of a scheme for classification and whether cards for nonbook materials would be interfiled in the catalog for books. It was pointed out that "arbitrary classification schemes to group all audiovisual materials according to subjects in the school curriculum have proven unsuccessful. . . ." Examples of ledgers, sample cards, mounting procedures, display instructions, and charging cards were given for further clarification and instruction.

Virginia Clarke announced, as a result of her scheme to organize and circulate books and nonbook material in the Demonstration School Library at North Texas State University, that there was just one place to look for materials. All cataloged materials were listed in one general catalog with one set of subject headings—regardless of material format—with every item assigned a call number or identifying symbol or word. The Demonstration School Library collection consisted of "approximately 15,000 books and 9,000 non-book materials."[22]

In the spring of 1949, Edith Scott of Ball State University gave an "account of a non-book cataloging program which is a description of procedures which are not standardized as yet."[23] Shortly afterward there appeared a brief account of "the attitude of British librarians toward visual materials" which was not "as pronounced as their attitude toward record libraries, since gramophone recording sales and record libraries were being pursued with enthusiasm and determination."[24] Dilla W. MacBean asserted that "audio-visual materials lend themselves to the same order, catalog, process, and circulation system" as do books. She also called for "the administering of the printed page, the motion picture, the slide, the filmstrip, the recording and radio program, and even the telecast."[25]

Another early handbook for the preparation of nonprint media was prepared by Bessie M. Daughtry at Florida State University in 1950. The twenty-page "guide to the preparation of films, filmstrips, slides, and records for the use in the Materials Center of the Library School, Florida State University," although descriptive of the procedures of a single institution, stands as an early "description of exactly how audio-visual materials are integrated with other kinds of materials in the library card catalog."[26] Utilizing a generous number of examples to clarify the policies and procedures, this guide reflects the author's library background and her desire to apply the best aspects of book processing to nonprint media. Daughtry suggested using 3″x 5″ catalog cards on colored stock for specific nonprint media formats; a current *Sears List of Subject Headings*;[27] a special format symbol and accession number which together form the call number; and an indication of grade level on the cards.

In 1951, academic librarians were given a cataloging description in Ira J. Peskind's article "The Organization of an Audio-Visual Unit in a Junior College Library."[28] He argued for the full acceptance of audiovisual material by academic librarians, setting the pace for junior and community colleges during the subsequent two decades. Peskind described his own program, giving background on what he considered essential physical characteristics, equipment, and material.

Unfortunately, as late as April 25, 1952, such a prominent library leader as Pierce Butler, pontificating upon the trials and tribulations of cataloging, described a cataloger as "a professional expert who organizes the book stock of the library in accordance with various incompatible principles."[29] This narrow description was promulgated in the same year that Richard Angell and David Haykin of the Library of Congress were conferring with the ALA Audio-Visual Board on the matter of subject headings utilized for LC motion picture and filmstrip cards.[30]

Colleges in the Pacific Northwest were surveyed in 1952 and the results reported in a study entitled "The Use and Administration of Audio-Visual Materials in Colleges in the Pacific Northwest."[31] This four-state study surveyed four-year colleges with enrollments of from 110 to 5,000 students regarding their audiovisual collections. Where audiovisual materials were cataloged, the cards were filed separately from the regular card catalog. Most of the schools rented their films from a central source and slides were kept in the individual departments in which they were made. While a lack of adequate space seemed to inhibit the actual practice, most of the respondents enthusiastically supported the concept of the library as a center for audiovisual aids.

In her introductory paragraph to "Cataloging of Nonbook Materials," Sister Mary Janet of Rosary College stated that "libraries may no longer be considered collections of books or their equivalent," but also as storehouses for such media as speech recordings, microfilms, films and filmstrips, slides, and flat pictures.[32] Sister Mary Janet viewed the relationship of book cataloging to that of nonprint media as the key to understanding the whole process of organizing information in all formats.

An extensive treatment of nonbook materials was offered by Evelyn Hensel, in which she cited forty-six references, providing an excellent review of the thinking in several professions up to 1953 and giving the library profession a concept of both archival and lending library approaches to the organization of nonprint media.[33] This was perhaps the first time that numerous references to archival practices for the organization of recordings and films were brought to the attention of librarians through their own professional literature.

C. Walter Stone stressed the principles of

> maximum decentralization of responsibility for materials selection and counseling . . . maximum decentralization of materials and equipment for preview and study in the library . . . maximum centralization of audio-visual equipment . . . central acquisition, processing, and a unified catalog . . . and the advisability to separate distribution from production responsibilities for the newer media.[34]

In 1955 the ALA Committee on Descriptive Cataloging approved "a few minor changes which the Library of Congress proposed for the preliminary edition of *Rules for Descriptive Cataloging in the Library of Congress, Phonorecords.*"[35] At a second meeting of the Audio-Visual Board, members of the Division of Cataloging and Classification were present to discuss a "proposed Joint AV Board-DDC Committee on the Bibliographic Control of Audio-

Visual Materials."[36] It was agreed that study of this topic was a proper function of the division, and that it would establish such a committee.

Special librarians were presented Beverly Hickok's experience in her article "Handling Visual Aid Material."[37] She pointed out that the Institute of Transportation and Traffic Engineering Library included slides, photographs, visual casts, and films which received general cataloging accession numbers, a set of cards, and cross references; classified maps; and display pictures arranged in cases by broad subject.

In 1957 John F. Harvey presented a paper entitled "Measuring Library Audio-Visual Activities."[38] About college libraries, it was based largely upon the results of a questionnaire sent by the ACRL Committee on Audio Visual Work in 1952 to 1,726 libraries and upon a second survey in 1955. The problems Harvey encountered were much the same as those that have historically plagued the library scientist in other areas of library operations. Careful attention to descriptions, comparisons with a suitable standard, the collection of proper data, and the establishment of purposes for audiovisual statistics were given as essential characteristics for the measurement of audiovisual services. Sampling techniques were endorsed when properly established beforehand, then analyzed and interpreted with skill and understanding. According to Harvey, this must be done with one ultimate objective—the improvement of library service.

H. R. Halvorsen praised the use of color-keyed cards for catalogs in his *Educational Screen and A-V Guide* article, "Colorful Card Catalog."[39] The most significant innovation in the Palo Alto Unified School District Instructional Materials Center Catalog had been the integration of all bibliographic records.

Last, commenting in 1965 on approaches to cataloging, Doris M. Carson wrote "The problem of cataloging nonbook material is not one of creating special rules but of adapting standard principles of cataloging to the special materials."[40] She observed that data will be found on the physical objects themselves for purposes of cataloging. Carson's determination to follow the standard rules for print media for such procedures as the choice of a main entry has yet to be accepted by many librarians and many more audiovisual specialists. Guides for the organization of media by the Library of Congress and American Library Association are utilized by the author in the advice given in her article cited above.

BIBLIOGRAPHIC CONTROL AND ORGANIZATION OF MEDIA

Classification methods utilized by art museums became the subject of a volume sponsored by the American Association of Museums and the Smithsonian Institution. *Museum Registration Methods,* issued in 1958, was a successful attempt "to provide much needed information about registration procedures and has helped to establish professional standards for all museums—large and small."[41] Ten years later a second edition appeared with two major parts—basic procedures and special information—the latter composed of seventeen articles by authorities in the field and related areas of specialization.

Authors of an article entitled "Developing an A-V Program in a Small College Library" found several advantages in centralizing nonprint services within their library.[42] These included the avoidance of scheduling conflicts, availability of a service desk, organization of materials for use in the form of a catalog, and proper storage for quick retrieval. They emphasized individual but simplified cataloging and classification for records, slides, films, and filmstrips. Later, in 1963, Shirley L. Hopkinson of San Jose State College devoted twenty-eight pages of her publication *The Descriptive Cataloging of Library Materials* to sample card forms for twelve different types of nonprint media.[43]

On May 3, 1960, Maurice F. Tauber and Oliver L. Lilley filed, as their grant report with the U.S. Office of Education (USOE), the "Feasibility Study Regarding the Establishment of an Educational Media Research Information Service."[44] This research endeavor stands as a landmark in the area of bibliographic control of nonprint media because of its early consideration of systems and standards to organize and provide access to these newer media and the research concerning them.

Another landmark report in newer educational media research was concluded and a USOE contract report filed on November 5, 1960.[45] This endeavor was the result of a conference on bibliographic control of newer media convened at Indiana University on October 5–7, 1960, by Margaret Rufsvold and Carolyn Guss. Leaders from a variety of subject disciplines and virtually all major organizations or publications directly concerned with newer educational media had been brought together to consider the report, "A Proposed Method for Establishing Bibliographic Control of the Newer Educational Media for the Purpose of Informing Teachers Concerning Available Materials and Their Educational Utility," which had been submitted by the coauthors to USOE on May 14, 1960.

Rufsvold and Guss were particularly concerned with current indexes, catalogs, and services that would make available information concerning audiovisual materials. They hoped to identify both the strengths and weaknesses of these various bibliographic sources as well as the interest and resources of suppliers for the purpose of modifying existing tools and services and, if needed, to bring about the creation of new methods for the control of nonprint media. They were also concerned with the proper diffusion of information to users and potential users of these newer but increasingly important information learning resources. Carolyn Guss also brought to the general attention of the education and library professions one concern of this conference in an article entitled "Toward a National Descriptive and Evaluative Cataloging Service for Newer Educational Media."[46]

Rufsvold and Guss had also conducted a research project on "Sources of Information about Newer Educational Media for Elementary and Secondary Education (1950–1960)" and filed their official report with a sponsoring U. S. Office of Education on April 20, 1960.[47] This successful attempt to locate "200 available separate lists, indexes, and services and annotating the 79 that met the criteria set up for the project . . . " led to subsequent publication of guides to newer media.

Carolyn I. Whitenack wrote her article "A National Catalog for A-V" in response to needs identified both by the Educational Media Council (EMC) and through the research work of Rufsvold and Guss.[48] An Educational Media Index in several parts was envisioned by the council utilizing a committee structure, subcontracts, and the cooperation of the Library of Congress, the Educational Film Library Association, and the National Educational Television Center. Whitenack said EMC would try "to keep the price of the master index and sub-catalogs within reach of educational consumers."

A grant was announced by USOE for a study by the University of Southern California's Department of Cinema: "The Feasibility of an Automated Cataloging Service for All Audio-Visual Material in an 8-County Southern California Area."[49] The two-year study involved experimental cataloging service and the inventory of materials now in schools, libraries, and other nonprofit institutions. The university's director of film distribution, Glenn McMurry, said the experiment was "to prove that the system we have developed at USC will work for a larger selection of audio-visual materials than we have in our own extensive library and for a much larger geographical area." After a five-year experience with USC's automated cataloging program, McMurry expressed hope that "USC's Systems Cataloging could work for the nation—with all the information on all of the educational films in the country stored at one point. . . ." This research endeavor led eventually to the National Information Center for Educational Media (NICEM), which was discussed by McMurry in a brief article giving the origin, structure, and some mechanical aspects of the NICEM program.[50]

One of the many manuals issued in individual states for the organization of nonprint media had appeared a year earlier, in 1966, under the imprint of the Michigan Association of School Librarians.[51] Judith Loveys Westhuis and Julia M. DeYoung brought out this publication to assist librarians throughout their state and to promote a coordinated and uniform approach to the cataloging of nonprint media in learning centers and school libraries.

In a 1967 issue of *Library Trends* devoted to nonprint media, William J. Quinly, author of "The Selection, Processing and Storage of Non-Print Materials: Aids, Indexes and Guidelines," reviewed the bibliographic guides currently available and suggested that numerous problems were hindering the full development and utilization of newer educational media.[52] He stated: "These new media and the demand for knowledge will require new concepts of service," concluding that "the future for librarians willing to grow with their profession is bright."

One of the more innovative institutions of higher education, Oral Roberts University, pledged itself to the total media concept in education and learning and an impressive array of facilities and materials were rapidly acquired to support this commitment. A manual of practice and procedures was compiled by Evelyn Clement with accompanying statements by Ruth Peel.[53] Although this comprehensive guide to the organization of nonprint media was constructed for a single institution, it has had considerable influence through the release of public information, articles, and numerous visits to the Oral Roberts University campus by leaders in a variety of professions interested in innovations in instructional technology.

Several new manuals and attempts at standardization were issued in 1968. The tentative draft of the "Manual for Organizing and Administering Audiovisual Media" by the North Carolina State Department of Public Instruction was followed by the culmination of a two-year project in the NEA Department of Audiovisual Instruction (DAVI) Task Force on Computerized Cataloging and Booking of Educational Media. This resulted in the publication of a preliminary list, *Standards for Cataloging, Cod-*

ing, and Scheduling Educational Media. In England, Antony Croghan published *A Faceted Classification for an Essay on the Literature of the Performing Arts.*[54] The latter demonstrated unusual insight into the complexities of organizing information and attempts at its standardization in and beyond this country. The next year, Croghan and Bernard Chibnall filed a research report entitled "A Feasibility Study of A Multi-media Catalogue."[55] The report set forth explicit instructions and specifications to achieve an ideal attainment not yet seriously considered in the United States. Chibnall's conclusion regarding the importance of newer media had been supported earlier by a Survey of the Association for College and Research Libraries Committee on Audio Visual Work reported by Fleming Bennett in "Audio-Visual Services in Colleges and Universities in the United States."[56] A rapidly expanding acceptance of nonprint media in academic libraries was apparent in the responses although there was more intellectual adherence to the concept of media centers rather than their actual existence.

Proposed standards for school media programs were reported at ALA meetings in 1968 although they were not published until the following year.[57] A variety of other guidelines and attempts for the production of standards by audiovisual committees were also reported. The ALA Descriptive Cataloging Committee considered proposals pertaining to a nonprint media chapter in the *Anglo-American Cataloging Rules.*

Up to this time, initial activity in the library profession toward the development of a universal numbering system was limited to monographs and serials. Recommendations for the inclusion of nonprint media as an integral aspect of a universal numbering system was favorably received by those immediately involved.

Early in 1969, there was a discourse on computers, cataloging, and cooperation by the curator of Music and Records at the State University of New York at Buffalo, describing detailed aspects of the institution's conversion of its shelflist "employing IBM Datatext (or ATS) terminals."[58] In the spring of 1969, Richard L. Darling, Montgomery County Public Schools media director and chairman of the ALA Committee for the Use of Audiovisual Materials in Libraries, issued a report on preliminary considerations of his committee for uniform guidelines and invited responses from those in the field of nonprint media.[59] During the ALA Atlantic City Conference an informal agreement was reached among Darling of ALA, William L. Quinly of DAVI, and Jean Riddle Weihs of the Canadian Library Association to request their professional organizations' consideration of the development and publication of joint standards for media services. This activity stemmed from an open meeting in Kansas City sponsored by Darling's committee in an attempt to identify those areas of concern felt by the library profession, the commercial agencies which were attempting to serve them, and the publishers themselves.

Recent Developments

The year 1970 brought forth several long awaited publications in the area of nonprint media. The American Library Association published *Guidelines for Audiovisual Materials and Services for Public Libraries* which set forth definitions, services, materials, personnel, space and equipment, and statistics for improved service.[60] This publication stressed the importance of immediate access to properly organized nonprint media in all formats as essential in our modern society.

The Library of Congress, in response to many requests and with the assistance of several professions, issued *Maps: A MARC Format* and *Films: A MARC Format.*[61] The latter gives specifications for magnetic tapes containing catalog records for motion pictures, filmstrips, and other pictorial media intended for projection. Library of Congress personnel announced that consideration would be given to other nonprint media to be placed in the MARC (Machine-Readable Cataloging) system, e.g. sound recordings.

Equally important was the publication of the preliminary edition of *Non-Book Materials: The Organization of Integrated Collections* by the Canadian Library Association.[62] Provisionally endorsed by ALA, this edition has stimulated considerable activity toward mutual understanding among librarians and audiovisual specialists in Canada, Great Britain, and the United States.

The College of DuPage Instructional Resources Center issued a *Processing Manual for Books and Non-Book Materials* which is comprehensive enough to serve as a useful handbook for other resource centers in schools and academic institutions. This manual, with the text organized around the examples given throughout, serves as a working guide to the processing of all print and nonprint media within an integrated collection. This publication was further explained by College of DuPage Materials Preparation Consultant, Robert A. Veihman.[63]

Antony Croghan, the British librarian thought by many to be the most knowledgeable individual in his country—if not elsewhere too—on the detailed concerns of nonprint media bibliographic control, issued a volume entitled *A Thesaurus-Classification for the Physical Forms of Non-Book Media.*[64] He has also contributed to the understanding and revision of nonprint media aspects of the *Anglo-American Cataloging Rules.* In 1971, he contributed a third volume on this topic, *A Manual on the Construction of an Indexing Language Using Educational Technology as an Example.*[65] He stated that new tools are needed for the active exploitation and dissemination of knowledge in new formats and that "Of all the tools needed by a librarian for these jobs the most fundamental is a language by which to organize and convey the information that is the purpose of the library." Thus Croghan designed this particular manual "to allow the librarian to construct such a tool shaped exactly to the job that it must do." A detailed analysis of educational technology, a synthesis of the subject, detailed notation, an index to the classification, and a thesaurus of verbal concepts are presented.

An unprecedented attempt to bring about a major breakthrough in the bibliographic and physical control of nonprint media for accessibility and preservation was set forth by Senator Howard Baker in the Ninety-first Congress. Then one year later Senator Baker and twenty-nine other colleagues introduced Senate Bill 1169 on March 10, 1971, that was designed "To preserve, for purpose of study and research, nationally televised news and public interest programs."[66] This farsighted bill was relegated to the Senate Committee on Rules and Administration and not acted upon by the Ninety-second Congress.

In August, 1971, the Library of Congress officially announced its intention to "convert the catalog records for motion pictures and filmstrips into machine-readable form beginning in 1972."[67] The library was also considering distribution of the records on magnetic tapes on a subscription basis, similar to the distribution of MARC records for books. This service was actually begun in 1972 utilizing two basic documents: *Films: A MARC Format* and the *Anglo-American Cataloging Rules.* Eight thousand to nine thousand records for films were expected each year, as compared to sixty thousand records for books. In 1972 it was announced that "cards for these new titles will be printed from photo-composed copy produced directly from the tapes by the Card Division's Videocomp."[68] It was also indicated that "sometime in the spring a prototype computer-produced book catalog is planned, and at least the fourth quarterly of Motion Pictures and Filmstrips should be produced in this fashion. By January, 1973, the entire operation should be mechanized."

Individual attempts to establish procedures continue although genuine progress toward a unified approach is evident in professional association activities, publications, and research endeavors. With few exceptions, even those who need to satisfy a specific clientele recognize the value of utilizing the tools and procedures already agreed upon by professional organizations in the United States and beyond.

The initial effort of a Task Force in DAVI to develop standards for the organization of nonprint media was reconsidered by the Cataloging Committee of the renamed Association for Educational Communications and Technology and a revised edition, *Standards for Cataloging Nonprint Materials*, was issued.[69] Because of the close cooperation among personnel involved in the second edition and members of similar committees in the Canadian Library Association and American Library Association, this revised edition has been more widely received and endorsed for use and its demand has required a third edition.

Two USOE Media Institutes were held at the University of Oklahoma: one, in 1968, on the Administration of Audiovisual Programs, and one which began the following August and continued at intervals through April of 1970. The latter involved over one hundred media specialists from three countries and a variety of professions. The proceedings were published as a basic reference and current state-of-the-art volume entitled *Bibliographic Control of Nonprint Media.*[70]

Role of the American Library Association

Authorization for a Committee on Moving Pictures and the Library was voted by ALA Council and Executive Board in 1924, in response to "a presentation by the moving picture industry and contemplating the study of proposals for the printing, cataloging, storage, distribution and display through a library agency of educational films produced commercially."[71] The following year, recommendations were submitted in a report by chairman Clarence E. Sherman:

1. That the public libraries in the larger cities be urged to establish and maintain, in connection with their information service, indexes to the agencies from which moving picture films may be obtained for educational and recreational purposes
2. That an effort be made to induce a selected number of public libraries (chosen with some regard for geographical divi-

sions) to assume the functions of collecting and distributing films for the use of schools, clubs, and other organizations in their respective regional areas

3. That in view of the amount of detail involved in the task of developing and sustaining a consecutive program of co-operation between the public libraries and the moving picture producers, the services of an executive clerk, working at the headquarters of the American Library Association or at the office of the Motion Picture Producers and Distributors of America, Inc., should be secured. It is believed that in the event that the A.L.A. is unable to finance this proposal, the necessary funds can be obtained elsewhere.[72]

Then, in 1927, the committee stated that "No means of adult education has greater possibilities than the film. Educational films are being produced in larger and larger numbers and the public library has a great potential field in the conservation and distribution of these films and in making them widely known."[73] The following year, the committee felt it should enlarge its scope and be charged with "the study of library activities as they relate not only to moving pictures, but to lantern slides, stereopticon reproductions, microscopic equipment, educational exhibits, and museum material, and [be designated] the Committee on Visual Methods."[74] This title recommendation was ironic since audio recording on photographic film became commercially practical that same year. Sound recordings, a rapidly growing part of library collections, was noticeably absent from the committee's list of nonprint media until three years later when authorization for the committee to expand its coverage to other media was voted by Council.

Important work to be undertaken was also suggested by Frank Chase, chairman of the Committee on Moving Pictures and the Library in 1927–28. He advocated the "indexing of films and especially in cataloging the historical, geographical and otherwise educational elements in films originally produced without any direct educational purpose."[75]

Following a two-year period of study, survey, and discussion, an ALA Special Committee on the Bibliographic Control of Audio-Visual Materials issued its report.[76] Responses to the survey questionnaire indicated that motion picture films were collected in 31 academic, 46 public, and 50 school libraries for a total of 115 nonprint media collections, and that there were 176 collections of phonograph records, with 56 in academic institutions, 72 in public libraries, and 48 in school libraries. Although there was some variation in the source of cataloging, most of these collections were organized by library staff members; the sources most commonly utilized were Library of Congress printed cards, the *Educational Film Guide, Educational Filmstrip Guide,* Educational Film Library Association cards, Coronet Film Company cards, Library of Congress descriptive rules, and Music Library Association rules.

The committee's comprehensive survey included questions regarding the essential items on catalog cards, use of classification or location symbols, subject headings, Library of Congress rules as a basis of standardization, and whether there was a need for a manual of procedure. Committee chairwoman Eunice Keen, who had previously issued a manual intended largely for high school libraries, published a list of audiovisual cataloging tools as a supplement to a general list previously printed in the *Journal of Cataloging and Classification.*[77]

Furthermore, her report for the association's Special Committee contained the following recommendations which were endorsed by the ALA Audio-Visual Board:

1. That the chairman of the Committee write a letter to the Library of Congress concerning our findings about the Library of Congress Printed Catalog Cards and expressing a hope that they will be able in the near future to meet these requests
2. That the Committee on Subject Headings study the matter of subject headings for children's recordings
3. That the Executive Board appoint a person or persons to prepare a standardized Manual of Procedure for use in cataloging and processing Audio-Visual Materials
4. That the Committee on Cataloging Policy and Research study the approach of Audio Visual catalog users to this material.[78]

Unfortunately, this coincided with a reorganization of the association which left the proposed audiovisual activities without implementation.

In 1966 the ALA Audiovisual Committee asked that its "Media Research Committee be designated a subcommittee to ensure communication and coordination."[79] It also heard Edward Heiliger's suggestion that the ACRL Audio-Visual Committee, a subcommittee of the ALA Audio-Visual Committee, explore the idea of producing guidelines for audiovisual resources and services in college and university libraries. Mr. Heiliger, Director of Libraries at Florida Atlantic University, Boca Raton, was reporting on the proceedings of the ALA Audio-Visual Committee which had met earlier in the week.

The following year the ACRL Audiovisual Committee reported progress on its guidelines and obtained five hundred dollars to help facilitate the preparation of a draft version, which eventually resulted in *Guidelines for Audiovisual Services in Academic Libraries.*[80] At the same time, a proposal to review nonprint media in *The Booklist* was discussed and interest was also evidenced in a "separate audiovisual evaluation tool and the coverage of nonbook material in *Choice.*"[81] The ALA Audio-Visual Committee received during the same conference a progress report on the Audiovisual Task Force Survey conducted by C. Walter Stone who stressed the survey's primary objective as one of gathering "information and informed opinion from media service personnel regarding new or improved activities and tasks which should be performed by professional associations. . . ."[82]

Also in 1967 the long awaited *Anglo-American Cataloging Rules* appeared with the endorsement and active participation of library associations in Great Britain, Canada, and the United States, as well as the Library of Congress.[83] It was based on previous guides and procedures at the Library of Congress, with agreed upon input from all three professional associations and became known in its two revisions as the "North American Text" and "The British Text."

Many guidelines and attempts for the production of standards by audiovisual committees were reported in 1968, including proposals to the ALA Descriptive Cataloging Committee for a nonprint media chapter in the *Anglo-American Cataloging Rules.*

Furthermore, considerable activity in the library profession was finally demonstrated toward the development of a universal numbering system for library materials. However, the ALA committee established to further this concept in the United States and abroad gave little consideration to nonprint media until members of the USOE Institute on Systems and Standards for the Bibliographic Control of Nonprint Media appeared before it at the annual conference in Detroit. The committee, under the direction of chairman Warren Haus, accepted the position presented that all formats of media should be included in a universal numbering system.

As early as 1968 the Resources and Technical Services Division authorized an ad hoc group to deal with the organization of nonprint media, and its membership actively participated in the development of several proposed manuals. A preliminary edition by three Canadians in 1971 and their first full edition in 1973 were influenced by professional criticism and consultation with members of the committee. The latter publication, a guide to the bibliographic and physical organization of nonprint materials, was reviewed by various units of the association in 1973 for possible endorsement.

The American Library Association published *Guidelines for Audiovisual Materials and Services for Public Libraries* in 1970. Another ALA publication, a compilation of institute proceedings and committee reports, was published in 1972 under the title *Bibliographic Control of Nonprint Media*. This publication represented another effort by the American Library Association to serve a valuable role in the nonprint media area. It demonstrates the interest of academic librarians who were members of the Association of College and Research Libraries' Audiovisual Committee (a unit of ALA) as well as contributors to the publication.

CONTROL OF PARTICULAR AREAS OF NONPRINT MEDIA

Maps

The U.S. Library of Congress map collection, begun shortly after the Civil War, is one of the largest in the world. Library of Congress personnel have, therefore, devoted their expertise to the proper organization of these materials. Even in this early period it was recognized that flat maps, globes, and other forms of maps should be organized and preserved.

W. C. Berwick Sayers' *A Manual of Classification for Librarians and Bibliographers* appeared in 1926 "to explain how classification affects library methods, how it is applied to . . . illustrations . . . and maps. . . ."[84] Numerous cooperative efforts by professional organizations followed, as well as the innovations of individual librarians and other map collectors which led to a wide variety of schemes for map arrangement, storage, and retrieval.

In 1961 Arch C. Gerlach reported that nine years previously the International Geographical Union had established a Commission on the Classification of Geographical Books and Maps in Libraries with one member each from Brazil, France, Germany, Italy, and the United States.[85] This commission was charged "to study classification systems for geographical and cartographical collections with a view toward recommending improvements and possibly even developing an ideal system for those materials." Gerlach noted that the commission was only partially successful, feeling that "the basic difficulty appears to be that librarians have had too little contact with modern geography to recognize works in this field when they see them, and too little understanding of maps to give them the attention they deserve as sources of information." Questioning the value of classification systems already developed for print material, the author said that "a map lies in character between a book and a picture and combines some features of both." Gerlach concluded that alternate schedules of classification for geographical and cartographical works should be created by librarians but he warned that "detailed classification . . . is futile unless library philosophies and procedures can be broadened. . . ."

Canadian Theodore H. Laying published his article "Problems in the Map Room" shortly after Gerlach's article appeared, stressing the importance of maps being placed in proper relationship to each other unless economic considerations require their filing by size and form.[86] Because of this emphasis, Laying felt "the call number of a map is therefore of paramount importance," serving two purposes: first, to locate a map in the filing system and second, to locate the main descriptive entry for that map in the card system. He cautioned by saying "only when he is in control of all the factors of filing, classification, and carding is the map librarian competent to select a set of symbols for map location." Laying then described his own scheme for the organization of maps which employs symbols such as B for a map in a book, M for maps on microfilm, P for maps in portfolio, and C for maps in solander cases.

The organization of map collections in Great Britain was treated by A. M. Ferrar in "The Management of Map Collections and Libraries in University Geography Departments."[87] He stated that "the arrangement of a large collection of maps is essentially a problem of filing" with the first step being classification. Ferrar felt "geography is ill served by the Dewey Decimal System, and none of the other systems in use in large general libraries is any more convenient." He thought that the special classification of the Association of American Geographers "is fairly good," and cited its application with some modifications at Southampton University. Since he felt that there was no ideal letter and decimal system at that time he was pursuing experiments along these lines. In a special issue of *Library Trends*, Lloyd A. Brown addressed the problem of maps, giving an insight into the historical development of map production and collection.[88] Brown proposed that maps be stored in specially designed tiers of thin drawers. An extensive survey of the literature is made by Miss Galneder and Mrs. Koerner in their chapter of this volume that is devoted entirely to the subject of maps.

Pictures

The first picture collection organized for circulation in the United States was opened at the Denver Public Library in 1889.[89] Melvil Dewey suggested in an article on library pictures in 1906 that "Libraries are rapidly accepting the doctrine . . . that what we call books have no exclusive rights in a library."[90] Dewey felt that when the goals of a library can be met better, more quickly, or cheaply by a picture than a book, the picture is entitled to a place on the shelves and in the catalog. He noted that the New York State Library had sixty thousand prints in 1906.

Oklahoma librarian Jane Howe reported the specific methods used for cataloging a photograph collection at the University of Oklahoma Library's Division of Manuscripts, giving detailed examples of cards, subject indexes, and exceptions to the rules for subject headings.[91] Howe detailed a seven-step procedure for the organization of a photograph collection concluding that "flexibility, adaptability and usage are the words for the procedures described above."

Pictures, their copyright, value for public relations, and utilization by specific organizations were the topic of the January, 1965, issue of *Special Libraries.* Two of the articles noted that a vital aspect of this important resource was its organization for quick retrieval. One author, Betty Hale, suggested that collectors "arrange portraits alphabetically, plants and offices geographically, and products and processes by subject."[92] She also felt that if loose documents had already been classified by subject, pictures may be incorporated in the same file to save space.

Scientists continued to display their interest in the bibliographic organization of audio and visual aids as exemplified by Boris W. Kuvshinoff's article in *American Documentation* entitled "A Graphic Graphics Card Catalog and Computer Index."[93] This physicist reviewed the development of his "low-cost library control system for visual aids based on punched cards . . ." whereby miniature pictures are actually printed on the keypunched cards, while identifying information is keypunched and additional information is entered by typewriter.

Slides and Transparencies

In her article "Routine for the Cataloging and Processing of Slides," Adelheid G. Ladewig of the Hamilton College Library reported that slides were classified according to the Dewey Decimal classification system and Cutter numbers added as for book materials.[94] Information provided by the Hamilton College card catalog included the call number, name and dates of artists, title of work, nationality of artist, reproduction in color or black and white, location of original painting, and source and catalog number of the slide. Abbreviations of the Color Slides Cooperative were utilized for location purposes. Lyle F. Perusse, in "Classifying and Cataloging Lantern Slides for the Architecture Library,"[95] described the symbols which were developed for a classification scheme at the University of Minnesota School of Architecture and incorporated by the American Institute of Architects in the *Standard Filing System for Architectural Plates and Articles.*

A major collection of slides in England was described in 1960 by its librarian, P. Havard-Williams.[96] The holdings, begun in 1955, were a working collection of fifteen thousand slides, filed in order of accession, with retrieval by a subject and author catalog. The basic rules established for cataloging these 2″ x 2″ slides were (1) form of entry, (2) rules for filing, and (3) form of heading. The author illustrated these rules, which generally conform to practices utilized for the general university book catalog.

A historical review of slide development in Europe with a consideration of current practice of identifying, processing cataloging, projecting, and copying slides at the European Organization of Nuclear Research was shared by Alfred Gunther in his "Slides in Documentation."[97] This organization (CERN) relies heavily on a variety of sizes of slides. Gunther gave five "standard" sizes and concluded that the 2″ x 2″ slide is rapidly becoming the one standard because it is "less bulky and can be projected with cheaper projectors."

As information specialists became more anxious over the lack of automated control of information, some began to turn their attention to areas previously the exclusive domain of librarians and related bibliographers. One such attempt was that by Morton N. Wasserman who wrote an article entitled "A Computer-Prepared Book Catalog for Engineering Transparencies," claiming that the "initial response to this index has been excellent. This system has simplified searching and saved many man hours locating and obtaining the proper transparencies of our vast data base."[98]

In November, 1967, Brenda White issued a survey on slide collections in the fields of architecture, building, and planning.[99] She stated the aims of her survey were "to establish whether there is any standard practice in the organization of slide collections," and to "formulate recommendations based on such a standard practice." She found that the size and scope of collections varied so widely that general recommendations for application to all seemed impossible. White's report offered a detailed analysis of the methods utilized in a wide range of libraries for the organization and management of slide collections.

Two research grants for the development of slide retrieval systems were in progress simultaneously at opposite ends of the United States with each of the investigators unaware of the other's endeavor. Robert M. Diamond completed his USOE grant report and submitted it in March, 1969, as *The Development of a Retrieval System for 35mm Slides Utilized in Art and Humanities Instruction.*[100] Diamond's scheme was based on assigned content identifiers in computer format, numerical identification numbers, and fixed storage location of the slides in a particular collection. The author's research report recommended a national interdisciplinary system of slide labeling and shelving, a national list of content identifiers, separate identifier lists for specialized collections, field testing of the above, and the support of a series of cooperative projects with resulting publications to accomplish these recommendations.

The second grant for the development of slide control was funded by the Council on Library Resources and given to Wendell W. Simons and Luraine C. Tansey at the University of California, Santa Cruz. In contrast to Diamond, a curriculum audiovisual specialist, the Californians were both librarians. Their preliminary report entitled *A Universal Slide Classification System with Automatic Indexing* was followed by a subsequent and more refined report of the same research, more modestly entitled *A Slide Classification System for the Organization and Automatic Indexing of Interdisciplinary Collections of Slides and Pictures.*[101] Simons and Tansey examined existing classification schemes for books and found them incompatible with the needs of their users, reasoning that

> a picture is more analogous to a sentence or a single word than to a book. It makes a single statement on a single theme; a book can be encyclopedic in its coverage or very narrow. Book classifications provide for the very general, the very specific, and everything between. Classification of slides and pictures can make use of only the most specific.

Although their classification scheme does not differ greatly from those of books, an effort was made to identify terms that are most useful to a pictorial collection. Comprehensive divisions and subdivisions were made for most subject disciplines with detailed numbering for automated sort fields, and an expanded Cutter table was evolved for the letter "S". An authority list for over 400 of the most commonly used artists' names was prepared as a part of the published report.

Betty Jo Irvine, supervisor of the photograph and slide collection in the Fine Arts Library, Indiana University, made a significant contribution with her article "Slide Collections in Art Libraries."[102] Her survey of the literature and her insight into the often unplanned growth of slide collections served as both a warning and assistance to those currently responsible for the organization and administration of library slide collections. She later joined with Wolfgang Freitag of Harvard University in writing the chapter on slides in this volume.

Film and Filmstrips

Although early British films date back as far as 1896 (to a one-minute 60mm film of the return of the president of the French Republic to Paris after a military review), it was not until much later that the preservation and organization of films became a matter of concern. Elton says, "An attempt systematically to store and catalogue film for historical purposes was made in Britain after the 1914–18 war. This material is preserved at the Imperial War Museum."[103]

Later, a monumental task was undertaken by Edgar Dale and others in developing a summary of the literature. *Motion Pictures in Education*, published in 1938, reviewed five classification systems reported in the professional literature.[104] Dale and his associates also reviewed six proposed national plans, including those of Carlos E. Cummings, who put forth "suggestions for a national exchange for lantern slides," and George E. Stone, who proposed a depository for negatives of all kinds—to be filed by a librarian and stored in the proper physical conditions with a psychologist and his department to "keep in touch with the needs of teachers." Two other particularly important chapters given in Dale's volume were a description of the British Film Institute, which appeared to be far ahead of any U.S. effort, and Dale's own chapter entitled "A Discussion Concerning the Proposed American Film Institute."

Film collections became big business and the complex arrangements with film publishers and distributors required increasing sophistication on the part of individual librarians. Lorraine Noble discussed the cooperative efforts of several national agencies in what became known as the American Film Institute.[105] This informal association of agencies and interested individuals had been encouraged by USOE, following a survey prepared in 1934 for the Rome Congress on educational films. The survey and congress had revealed the backward condition of the United States and had suggested that steps be taken to establish a national organization to cope with pressing problems. Thus, two years later, a group of people representing all areas of interest in the organization of films were called together by the American Film Institute, a group of committees serving under the American Council on Education. They established guidelines "for any film institute or organization that might be created to administer the needed service." The cooperating agencies addressed themselves first to the problems of existing films, having on hand approximately fifty thousand copyright film entries since the film copyright program was established in 1912. Miss Noble reported that no one had attempted a classification of these films and that a nationwide search for film owners had been undertaken to find what films of an educational nature were still in circulation. Only films copyrighted after 1926 were considered. An elaborate classification of three thousand films and a listing of another two thousand films was made. She states that for "the first time since educational interest attached itself to films, these subjects have been given Dewey Decimal numbers."

From this collection of films, the H. W. Wilson selected 1175 nontheatrical films to include in the first edition of the *Educational Film Catalog*. The inclusion of Dewey decimal numbers in this publication provided professional cataloging and a specific classification scheme to film libraries for the first time. The remaining four thousand films posed such a monumental task that they remained uncataloged or unclassified.

The agencies comprising an informal national film institute encouraged two other projects. One, carried out by Fannie Dunn, Audio Visual Education Director at Columbia Teachers College, was a listing and classification of more than three hundred articles and books, which were purported to be all the literature on visual instruction. The other project, administered by Cline Koon, of USOE, with financial assistance from the American Council on Education, was a survey to determine the status of visual instruction in public schools and was carried out by a questionnaire mailed to twenty-one thousand superintendents. Some ten thousand replies were received—a 90 percent return from communities of over five thousand population—indicating a "phenomenal interest in the future of visual instruction."[106] Librarians, finding themselves increasingly involved in the field of nonprint media, began to make more clear the distinction between educational and commercial films. In summarizing this distinction, Noble urged librarians not to become alarmed at the size of the celluloid publisher with his two billion dollar industry, the world's best craftsmen—an amazing "distribution network that daily serves 28,000 miles of film to 14,000 theaters."[107]

The U.S. National Archives, established June 19, 1934, by an act of Congress, set up a division of Motion Pictures and Sound Recordings the following year. The first problems to be faced by the fledgling division were those of storage and preservation. In addition to the various manuscript materials envisioned for the archives, there were also maps, sound recordings, photographic records, and motion pictures. In processing motion picture film, archive reviewers analyzed the subject matter of the reel, compiled its source and history, recorded titles, prepared a synopsis of the action, and detailed both the scenic content and sound sequence. An alphabetical card catalog was developed by catalogers who planned for the use of film pictures far into the future by "adapting library bibliographical methods to the special characteristics of motion-picture film." These matters as well as problems of copyright date, actual time of the action recorded, and manufacturers' refusal to disclose their dating codes were specific problems related by Dorothy Arbaugh in the *American Archivist.*[108] She suggested that standards be established to guide what should be photographed in order to assure the preservation of history, the deposit of all government agency films, and the creation of a motion picture film library "comparable to the library for government publications maintained in the office of the Superintendent of Documents." Arbaugh noted that "the Library of Congress has by purchase and by means of the gifts it has received, rounded out a collection that has become a headquarters for research in a national library to be regarded with pride."

The ALA Visual Methods Committee, in June, 1938, heard Mary Rothrock call attention to the annotated bibliographic list "Books About Educational Films Selected From the Educational Film Catalog" which was available for free distribution from the H. W. Wilson Company. She raised a number of questions relating to the use of educational films. Miss Rothrock was followed by H. W. Wilson who gave a stirring speech on the "Talking Film

Book," in which he spoke of the need for and anticipated the development of talking film books for the blind, urging librarians to welcome them as an integral part of their library collection.[109] Wilson was concerned that

> perhaps the present-day book librarian does not care to bother with the problems of storing, cataloging, and preserving talking film books, but is that librarian not setting the stage for a situation that might be unpleasant in the future when the talking picture book becomes an active competitor of the printed book? Why should not the printed book librarian be the librarian of books in all forms?

Frank K. Walter of the University of Minnesota Library then took an entirely different position, stating that his institution was "one in which the visual instruction activities . . . are combined in a separate division so efficient and cooperative that independent service on the part of the university library seems quite undesirable."[110] This separation, or fragmentation of nonprint media became a widespread practice on academic campuses. Walter concluded with the remark that "the one thing that seems certain is that the change has already begun [picture taking the place of the text in the library] and that no librarian can reasonably overlook it."

Motion pictures continued to receive journal space in 1938, evidenced by John Abbott's article describing the cataloging and filing of motion picture films at the Museum of Modern Art Film Library in New York City.[111] This library was established by a Rockefeller Foundation Grant and private gifts in June, 1935, for the preservation of meritorious films, their distribution, their study by those interested in film as living art, and the history and development of film. The library files the list of its collection under title in alphabetical order on specially designed 4″ x 6″ printed cards. A "progressive numerical method identifying the films for storage purposes is used by which each film, as it is added to our collection and filed in the vault, is given a can number which is then inscribed on the appropriate card in the master file so that a cross reference between the title of the subject and the physical location of the film in the vault is complete." This is similar to the somewhat more elaborate identification system currently in use by the Library of Congress.

Following the showing of films at the 1939 ALA Visual Methods Committee meeting—by this time a well established practice—

Boyd B. Rakestraw, University of California Extension Division assistant director, concluded that "we have to get together and forge new tools—tools made for doing a job which has never arisen before, a job which cannot be solved in any of the old ways."[112] Mary Rothrock summarized the committee's increased concern "that while the educational films movement offers a future challenge to public libraries, it is already pressing insistently upon school and to some extent also upon college libraries, as a present administrative problem."[113]

A grant of $5,500 from the Rockefeller Foundation was announced in 1939 to fund a Joint Committee on Educational Films, representing the American Film Center, the American Library Association, the Association of School Librarians, and the Motion Picture Project of the American Council on Education. Its purpose was to "encourage library experimentation in the handling of educational films, to cooperate with such libraries and to facilitate the exchange of information between them, to devise uniform methods for recording experiences and to encourage their use, and to report from time to time on the experiments."[114]

Gerald D. McDonald of the New York Public Library secured a seven-month leave to survey literature and visit film libraries and film distribution centers before submitting his report to ALA for publication in the fall of 1941. McDonald concluded that "thus far librarians have done virtually nothing in the handling of films and very little even in providing information which would further their use."[115] In response to this report, the Joint Committee made six recommendations where experimentation, demonstration, or development were especially needed:[116]

1. The possible uses of adult films in adult education need to be explored much more fully.
2. A primary need is the development of facilities to train librarians for film service.
3. Experimentation is needed with other patterns of film service in various types of libraries and communities.
4. The medium for the prompt and systematic listing of films as currently produced and withdrawn from circulation is indispensable to reasonably satisfactory film service in libraries.
5. Study, research and experimentation on various problems of preserving educational film as historical records is of immediate importance.

6. Some attack needs to be made on the immediate problem of getting 16mm projectors into libraries.

A descriptive encyclopedia, *Selected Educational Motion Pictures,* was prepared in 1942 for the Committee on Motion Pictures in Education of the American Council on Education to facilitate the effective utilization of films in the curriculum of American schools and colleges.[117] Five hundred 16mm films were reviewed by fifty-five hundred teachers and twelve thousand students for consideration of their inclusion in the encyclopedia, with each entry receiving an appraisal and description of the contents. Age group level and sources of evaluation were also given for each entry. Particularly valuable aspects of the volume were two lists, "Subject Classification of Films" and "Index of Film Contents," which offered assistance to those developing their own subject headings and indices of films.

In July, 1945, John G. Bradley of the United States National Archives wrote an article entitled "Cataloging and Indexing Motion Picture Film," emphasizing the development of a carefully planned catalog.[118] The following year, Patricia O. Blair stressed the concept that librarians are guardians of all forms of information regardless of format, and urged them to accept the fruits of modern science and invention.[119] She set forth the needs for proper physical facilities and procedures for handling films. Blair also stated that "another much more complex, more scholarly problem to which film librarians are turning their attention is that of cataloging film." She found the Dewey Decimal Classification system workable at the Cleveland Library Film Bureau, which had a "printed book-form catalog which contains annotations; printed twice yearly, it may be taken home by our borrowers." She also announced that "the H. W. Wilson Company has launched a project of printing catalog cards, just as it prints sets of book cards; this service is of enormous help to us all." Blair reported that since no standard subject heading list was available, some film librarians were adapting the index of the *New York Times.*

During the year following the conclusion of World War II several activities were reported in issues of the *ALA Bulletin*: Hoyt Galvin's development of a manual on nonprint media, two meetings sponsored by ALA devoted to audiovisual equipment, and The Library of Congress Motion Picture Division's plans to take the lead in distributing government films.[120] Also, a proposal for the position of film specialist at ALA headquarters was published, as was the suggested financing of an advisory service to libraries on a national scale.

This same year Alice Pattee stressed the achievement of co-operation between her ALA Resources and Technical Services Division and the Library of Congress, especially concerning the *Proposed Rules for Cataloging Motion Pictures and Filmstrips* and the *Rules for the Descriptive Cataloging of Phonorecords.* At the same division business meeting Evelyn Hensel presented a report of the code for cataloging music prepared by the joint committee of the Music Library Association and her committee.[121] Also issued in 1951 was a report entitled *Classification of Slide Films and Motion Pictures,* the product of a Carnegie Endowment for International Peace under the direction of H. R. Wei.

In a four-page issue of the *EFLA Service Supplement* it was reported how cataloging of films was done at the Ferguson Library in Stanford, Connecticut; how the Dewey Decimal system was utilized with colored cards for slides, filmstrips, and maps at the University of Oklahoma; how bibliographic entries were handled for a published catalog of the film library at the University of New Hampshire; and how the alphabetical, subject matter, and grade level classification order of listings were used in the audio-visual catalog in the New Albany, Indiana, school system.[122]

During the same year a conference was called by Eastman Kodak Company Consultant John B. Flory and held in Rochester, New York, on September 29 and 30, 1951.[123] The First International Film Cataloging Conference was convened under the auspices of the Film Council of America and the proceedings edited by John Flory and Norman B. Moore, Head, Reynolds Audio-Visual Division, Rochester Public Library. The success of this conference and personal dedication of Library of Congress personnel Richard Angell and others led to a second conference. Fifty-two specialists from the field of film production, film evaluation, and film cataloging met in 1953 at the Conference on International Standard for Film Cataloging.[124] This meeting of film specialists and librarians was convened at the Library of Congress upon the request of UNESCO with its objective being ". . . to make recommendations toward the development of internationally acceptable standards for cataloging descriptions, appraisals, and availability of educational films and filmstrips." Agreement was reached on the following principles:

1. That it is practicable to establish international standards for cataloging (description, appraisal, availability) of films and filmstrips.
2. That the system of cataloging should be based upon a three-card system (one card for the descriptive entry, the second

for an evaluation, and the third for availability data), with provision for recording such additional data as may be practicable, including, if necessary, a microcard.

3. That the rules for descriptive cataloging used in the Library of Congress and in the British Film Institute should form the basis for the descriptive catalog entries, and that the resolution of any differences should be made between these institutions, UNESCO to be kept informed of any completed or actual changes.
4. That the status of appraisal and evaluation is such that an internationally acceptable manual is needed to establish the desired standards, and that a suggested draft shall be prepared to accompany the report of the Conference.
5. That a new form for availability entries, and methods for determining such entries as are recommended by one of the Conferences work groups, should be studied by UNESCO with a view to its inclusion in the standard three-card system.

By 1956, leaders in the media cataloging field were turning their attention to international aspects of the problem. The preliminary aspects of an international system for cataloging films and filmstrips were proposed in the *UNESCO Library Bulletin.*[125] Based on rules already developed in the United States, Canada, and the United Kingdom, the proposal also anticipated a need for national card production and information centers. Two documents cited as particularly important to the UNESCO proposal were (1) *The International Standard System for the Cataloguing of Educational, Scientific and Cultural Films and Filmstrips* and (2) *A Manual for Evaluators of Films and Filmstrips,* for guidance in those countries which have not previously engaged in evaluation activities. The latter was prepared for UNESCO by the Educational Film Library Association of New York.

Bernard Chibnall of Great Britain, in an article entitled "The National Film Library and Its Cataloging Rules," described the library which had grown to a size of six thousand films dating from 1895. The National Film Library, established in 1935, "has always followed principles and practices appropriate to a National Archive and, in addition to overcoming the difficulties of storing a highly inflammable and unstable material, has attempted to catalogue its holdings as fully as possible." Chibnall discussed the third edition of the national library's "Rules for Use in the Cataloguing Department," concluding that "in the future the importance of the film as a source of information is bound to grow and good catalogues will be the foundation upon which this expansion can take place." Further attention to nonprint media was given by English librarian Robert L. Collison in *The Treatment of Special Materials in Libraries*, published in 1957.[126]

David Grenfell, chief cataloger of the National Film Archive, in his article "Standardization in Film Cataloguing," addressed himself to the central aspects of film cataloging that should be standardized for the assistance of both librarian and user.[127] He included a "List of Selected Terms, Possibly Synonymous, Requiring Definitions and Possible Abbreviations" as well as a "Definition of Selected Terms." Grenfell's 1959 discourse was followed by G. Crowther's article on "The Cataloguing and Classification of Cine Film at the Royal Aircraft Establishment."[128] With a need to organize analytical, research, and record films for the establishment's instrumentation department, several unique problems had to be faced. Film stock of various shots without the usual bibliographic recordings had to be organized for immediate retrieval. After considerable travel and study by a professional librarian, "it was decided to use the Universal Decimal Classification, a name already in use in the R.A.E. main library." Crowther reported that "despite some difficulties in the beginning it appears to have been a sound choice and works well in practice." Retrieval was assured through the utilization of nine indexes maintained on 3″ x 5″ catalog cards: aircraft, missile, departmental, author, numerical, title, subject, aircraft by individual name, and edge number indices.

Englishman David C. Fanning wrote that "the National Film Archive has published its own rules and these have been adopted by most of the film libraries in England and the film archives abroad."[129] He delineated the main points of agreement and differences among these rules and those of other cataloging codes. The National Film Archive maintained six card indexes "to provide several approaches to the main entries: subject, biography, form, treatment, title, and production credits." Fanning reported that

> Rules for use in other types of film libraries, such as Rayant Pictures, the B.B.C., Associated-Rediffusion, and other film companies, are being drawn up by a sub-committee of the Film Librarians Group of Aslib. The Committee hopes to publish its work in the near future. Meanwhile, the rules of the Archive remain the most useful published code for film archives.

Although the organization of nonprint media has attracted only the marginal interest of audiovisual specialists, in December, 1961, computerized access to film libraries was discussed in *Audio-visual Instruction.* Robert A. Cox set forth the advantages of an automated data system with details of procedures and expenses experienced at the Educational Film Library at Syracuse University. Shortly thereafter, in 1962, Ellinor Archer and Shirley Gawaith discussed the cataloging of the materials in the Victorian State Film Centre in their article entitled "Cataloging a Film Library" in the *Australian Library Journal.*[130] The article was devoted to film storage, main entry and descriptive cataloging, and the centre's subject index. The coauthors cited the Library of Congress, British, and UNESCO authorities for the development of their state film center, and concluded that "the problems of film cataloging are only just now emerging with any clarity."

In March, 1963, Bernard Chibnall, the editor of *British National Film Catalogue,* wrote "The British National Film Catalogue and Its Contribution to Information Work."[131] He found the present state of film information to be "nothing short of chaotic," but felt that his national catalogue, with proper support and professional interest could "benefit the industry and the user [and] in the long run help this remarkable medium to contribute fully to our society today." The catalog is a cooperative venture relying on strong support of seven English association councils and societies.

The selection, evaluation, cataloging, and processing of filmstrips is treated by Carl T. Cox in a late 1963 issue of *Wilson Library Bulletin.*[132] Cox first asked "what is a filmstrip" and proceeded to give the specific physical aspects of this particular format. He then discussed selection aids, evaluation techniques, and cataloging procedures with ten rules for the development of filmstrip cataloging based primarily on the authoritative guides of the Library of Congress. Suggestions for containers and circulation cards were also given.

As the cost of organizing collections of information continued to rise, L. R. Lindeman wrote "A Unique Venture in Joint Audio-visual Materials Cataloguing," where he suggested plans by audio-visual directors of educational film libraries in the Rocky Mountain states for cooperative cataloging of films be related.[133] This was one aspect of their concern for the reduction of expenditures in identifying, booking, and lending films throughout the region. Detailed cost of film listings by the Mountain Plains Film Library Association were referred to and some figures given. Lindeman felt that "over-all reactions have been excellent, the cost has been reduced, distribution areas have been expanded and income increased."

Experienced film librarian Betty Stoops reported on a presentation by librarian Leila Doyle of Gary, Indiana, before the DAVI convention in 1964, at which Doyle presented her concerns for organization and her suggestions for cataloging instructional materials.[134] The speaker recommended a color code, Dewey Decimal numbers, Gaylord storage boxes for recordings, a separate accession record book for picture sets, and a card catalog where all bibliographic records for materials would be interfiled. Betty Stoops published another article concerning films, "Film Titles and Credits—Are They Adequate?"[135] As implied in her title, she did not find them sufficient and presented twelve points on this subject during the 1965 DAVI national convention in Milwaukee. She stated, "conversations with film producers and distributors have convinced me that most of them would cooperate in providing adequate information on their materials if film users and film library people could agree on what they need."

Educational Film Library Association Administrative Director Emily Jones presented the background and philosophy of film library service in an article tracing the origin and development of film library service in the United States, emphasizing published guides, and reviewing media for its selection and utilization.[136] Jones declared that

> we must divorce librarianship from the idea that film service is not a legitimate library function. Film librarians are convinced of this and must work to make the idea generally accepted by all librarians. . . . the important thing is to provide the opportunity for the public to acquire, to analyze, to understand and to use quality films. Where this is our standard, we need not concern ourselves with the relative value of the role of film librarian.

Robert Steele turned his communication expertise to the organization of film literature in the United States and Canada when he published *The Cataloging and Classification of Cinema Literature* in 1967.[137] Steele considered classification principles and problems, presenting the specific schemes found in the Academy of Motion Picture Arts and Sciences, Canadian Film Institute Library and Information Service, Museum of Modern Art, and the Library of Congress. A less extensive treatment was given to some colleges and university special film collections.

A reorganization of the National Medical Center in Atlanta, Georgia, was announced with three operational branches: production; acquisition, distribution and reference; and education systems and development. The center's collection in 1968 included over one hundred thousand still pictures and one million feet of unedited motion picture sequences with its nine hundred different film titles accounting for over ninety-two thousand loans during this one fiscal year. The center publishes a catalog entitled *Film Reference Guide for Medical and Allied Sciences* to provide access to its resources and services.[138]

The indexing and cataloging of 8mm film received attention from Fred and Mildred Winston who coauthored an article in *Instructor* magazine.[139] Although developed for formal school environments, this scheme set forth specific characteristics of the medium and proposed methods for indexing and cataloging this increasingly popular film size.

As television continued to gain prominence among both the general public and educators, those responsible for handling it became conscious of the lack of a system for its organization and retrieval. Masaaki Ogi, of the Japan Broadcasting Corporation, published an article "Pattern-Matching Technique Applied to Indexing and Retrieving Films for Television Use," stating that "this system, together with the 'Image and information retrieval by computer' now under research and the 'Fully automatic processing and service' expected to be implemented in the future, is to comprise the total mechanization system of film library."[140] The author reviewed the documentation of films in the TV Film Library of NHK Nippon Hoso Kyokai (Japan Broadcasting Corporation) and presented the application of visual index cards already in use and which have "greatly improved the efficiency of our retrieval process." Other aspects under consideration by this library are the KWIC (Key Word in Context) or KWOC (Key Word Out of Context) systems, direct machine retrieval, or a combined system of a computer and a microfilm reader. Ogi reported "The Radiotelevisione Italiana (RAI) is already utilizing KWIC system for its film library."

Sound Recordings

The first phonodisc collection outside the Library of Congress was founded at the St. Paul Public Library in 1914.[141] However, phonodiscs were not circulated to the public until nine years later, when the Springfield, Massachusetts, Public Library began its service. During the intervening period, numerous articles began to appear in the professional literature reiterating the position taken earlier by Melvil Dewey.

Edah Burnett reported in 1926 on the organization and care of Victrola phonograph records in the St. Paul Public Library, where the staff found it easiest to classify by record number.[142] This made a very simple classification arrangement with the call number written in the upper right-hand corner of the envelopes, which were then filed numerically. When the recordings themselves were circulated the envelopes were left in their filing cabinets, which were specially designed in collaboration with the Library Bureau. Records were given full cataloging with cards for the composer, title, artist, subject, and number. The numerical file of Victrola record numbers served as a shelf list.

The Springfield, Massachusetts, library developed a catalog for their rapidly expanding record collection in the early 1930s. Reflecting holdings of two thousand records, it contained "cards for composer, title, artist, instrument, kind of music, and other helpful entries." Individual records were filed under a label number which was also used for checkout purposes. The problem of record damage was the first worry of the library when they began circulating this media. It is one of the library's anecdotes that "the first record was broken by the chief librarian himself, who promptly established a precedent by paying for his mishap."[143]

A more detailed phonograph record catalog was developed during this same period by Ralph Ellsworth, then librarian at Adams State Teachers College, Alamosa, Colorado.[144] The *A.L.A. Cataloging Rules* were used for the card format, while an accession scheme was established for shelving and circulating the college library's sound recordings.

The Music Library Association, established "to promote the development of music libraries and encourage the study of the organization and administration of music libraries and music in libraries" decided to make a study of filing and cataloging of phonograph records.[145] The committee established for this purpose sent a form letter to libraries throughout the country requesting information concerning practices in use. A questionnaire containing sample catalog cards was circulated later. Conclusions drawn from this study gave considerable impetus and direction to the organization of phonograph records in public libraries. It was recommended that records be filed vertically in heavy envelopes as they were in shops, that cabinets be constructed for this specific purpose, and that records be filed by accession number. It was noted that many libraries filed their recordings by composer, musical form, or company number. The committee agreed records of different sizes should be filed separately and that all should be arranged where only library personnel would handle them.

It was also recommended that the same cataloging rules used for music books be utilized for other forms of music. The main entry was to be made under the composer with the following additional entries if desired: (1) title, (2) artist, (3) form, (4) subject or medium. The Carnegie Music Set card, which included the following, was recommended:

1. Composer
2. Title
3. Number of sides
4. Issuing company
5. Number
6. Size
7. Artist
8. Reverse side
9. Same side if two pieces occupy one face
10. Reference to score, if work is in library's collection
11. For vocal music, author of the text and original language, as well as language in which record is sung
12. Listing of the movements of a larger work
13. Reproduction of the opening theme (if possible)
14. Date of the recording (if possible)
15. Date of issue
16. Matrix number (for identification when record is released in different countries).

The latter seven were recognized as desirable information, but not essential should space prevent their being included. The Music Library Association's special committee also urged the development of a list of standardized abbreviations in the field of music, which could be utilized in the organization of phonograph records.

Philip Miller, of the New York Public Library music division, reported "on correspondence with the recording companies concerning the possibility of issuing a printed card for each new release, such as the Library of Congress supplies for new books."[146] This solution to the standardization of information and the expense of individual library cataloging and classifying was recognized. The following rules were devised for the form of the printed card and could also be applied to typed cards:

1. Main entry will be made on the same principles as apply to scores
2. Standard title will be made or blank line left, as for scores
3. Label-title will be cut down to the specific name, including list of the movements, if given in the title; title will be given in paragraph form
4. Publisher's number will be given in same paragraph, in place of imprint; if the publisher's number does not include the publisher's name, the name will be given before the number
5. The date of issue of the record will follow three spaces after the publisher's number (year only); if the date of recording varies from that of issue, both will be given; the date of recording indicated by "rec.," will follow the date of issue and will be enclosed in brackets, round if the information is on the record, otherwise square
6. Beginning a new line, and in 8-point type, will be given the number of sides and the size, in inches, of the record; three spaces will be left between the items
7. The matrix number, if any, will be placed three spaces after the size
8. The first note will state if the record is Acoustic; No note necessary if electric
9. The second note will indicate the artist or organization represented
10. Contents will be given, if necessary, for selections from operas, etc.
11. Other notes will be given as needed
12. If other works are recorded on the same side, a list of them will be given, indicated by a, b, c, etc., preceded by SAME SIDE
13. Contents of the reverse side will be indicated in the same manner, preceded by REVERSE.

Funds for nonprint material in academic libraries usually came from sources other than the regular budgets. Antioch College students initiated a record collection with senior class pledges. The new materials were so popular that the new service had to be expanded. Even though the college had only 125 albums, Guy R. Lyle had reported in 1934 that there was a need for them to be organized.[147] He therefore had instituted a classified arrangement according to record or album number until this scheme was discarded in favor of an alphabetical arrangement by composer under large subject groupings. Record albums were treated in basically the same way as the book collection, but the small size of the former did not seem to justify detailed organization.

Agnes Green Rhodes, in reorganizing the Union College Library record collection, concluded that one of the first questions to be settled in classification was that of distinguishing between different works by the same composer.[148] All albums were to be arranged by the composer's name and different works distinguished by letter according to the time of acquisition. The library favored conventional cataloging utilized for book materials.

In organizing his nonmusical phonograph record collection following World War II, Charles E. Stow found the Carnegie Corporation scheme, already being utilized for musical recordings, impossible to adopt for nonmusical recordings, although conformity with some of the rules seemed wise.[149] Stow developed a set of rules that were "for the most part adaptations of rules developed in larger libraries and for musical recordings."

Inez Haskell noted that the first libraries to start record collections were forced to improvise systems of their own, which led to a great variety of methods drawn to individual needs.[150] The Music Library Association committee had studied this situation and issued its *Code For Cataloging Phonograph Records* in 1942.[151] Haskell found that "this Code has been widely studied but rarely adopted entirely, either because of the previous use of some other system or because it was felt it did not adequately fill the needs of the individual library." She presented procedures for organizing musical and nonmusical recordings utilized in various libraries to "help us to understand some of the problems involved, and illustrate the various ways of solving them."

In the summer of 1946, Helen Maywhort issued the plan for phonorecord cataloging at the Sullivan Memorial Library of Temple University.[152] Accession numbers were to be used for each record album to allow a fixed location. This call number would be located through the use of a main catalog and shelf list, and patrons would browse only through the alphabetically arranged catalog. Records were to be stored vertically, with labels on the album cover and on each disc. Maywhort reported that the main entry would usually be the composer and would be established by consulting the Library of Congress *Catalog of Printed Cards.* The conventional title was used as recommended by the Music Library Association's preliminary version of the *Code for Cataloging Music.*

The Library of Congress, in 1952, began cataloging musical recordings and some comedy on a nonretrospective and selective basis, but their initial efforts were limited to 33 rpm recordings with virtually no 78 rpm records cataloged; one exception was early recorded works of Shakespeare. The same year Richard Angell and David Haykin of the Library of Congress were conferring with the ALA Audio-Visual Board on the matter of subject headings utilized for motion picture and filmstrip cards.[153] By the fall of 1952 the AV Board had established a Subcommittee on *Booklist Film Reviews*, a Motion Picture Review Committee, a Subcommittee on Library of Congress Film Cards, and a Television Committee. Furthermore, the Library of Congress issued its preliminary edition of *Rules for Descriptive Cataloging: Motion Pictures and Filmstrips.*

The Code for Cataloging Music and Phonorecords, prepared by a joint ALA-MLA committee, was issued by ALA in 1958. It contained procedures based on the previous practice and experience of numerous librarians throughout the profession and was a welcome sight indeed to those with rapidly expanding collections of recorded sound. The published code encouraged articles such as "Phonorecord Cataloging—Methods and Policies."[154] Written by Beryl McPherson, a public library cataloger, and Carolyn Berneking, cataloger at the University of Kansas, the article contained hints for simplified cataloging procedures and the preparation of records for storage and retrieval. Recognizing the recent appearance of audio tapes, which they purposely omitted, the authors stated that "the circulation of tapes involves too many problems for libraries." They referred to Edward Tatnall Canby's address to the 1958 New Jersey Library Association convention at Asbury Park in which he reasoned that tapes "are much more expensive than LP's and contain in essence the same recordings. . . ."

Still another example of techniques for handling phonograph records was discussed by Sister M. Edmund Lincoln, who cautioned against such simplified arrangements as trade symbols and manufacturer's numbers.[155] For St. Catherine's College, she preferred a method of arrangement by form and medium of performance, using a symbol combined with a Cutter number to provide alphabetical arrangement while allowing for continued expansion of the coding system. She advocated the use of catalog cards and such established bibliographic guides as recommended by the Music Library Association's *Code for Cataloging Phonograph*

Records. Sister Lincoln reported at MLA's annual meeting in 1955 that the association voted to proceed with the publication of the *Code for Cataloging Music,* which was substantially the same code as that used at the Library of Congress.

A survey of fact and opinion concerning record collections, sponsored by the *Library Journal* and reported by Chester K. Davis was based on approximately 260 replies from 500 libraries surveyed.[156] The libraries were selected because they had established record collections relatively early. The University of Wisconsin Library began its collection in 1915, and although a few others were established in the subsequent two decades, most were begun during the 1940s and 1950s. The advent of the plastic long-playing (LP) record encouraged libraries to purchase and circulate records at an unprecedented rate. The collections surveyed ranged in size from one hundred to fifteen thousand discs with most libraries reporting between one hundred and one thousand discs. Two cataloging and processing approaches were found in an equal number of libraries. The first approach utilized either accession numbers or the manufacturer's serial numbers as the complete call number, with full cataloging and closed stacks. The second method was found to involve a classification system such as Dewey, Library of Congress, or a specifically devised symbol schedule, developed to bring recordings together in a subject relationship, in part for the convenience of browsing by both the public and staff.

The "Classification of Four Track Tapes" was the subject of a brief article by Allen Cohen, with examples, describing a numbered classification system with up to five lines of numbers for detailed classification needs. Donald L. Foster, cataloger at the University of Illinois, published a forty-page issue of that university's *Occasional Papers* (1962), illustrating representative types of notes used by the Library of Congress for cataloging music and phonorecords between 1959 and 1961.[157] Foster cautioned librarians to use discretion and restraint in following "a good rule of thumb: when in doubt as to the value of a note, one should not use it."

A guide for record librarians in Great Britain appeared in 1963 under the sponsorship of the International Association of Music Librarians. Edited by Henry F. J. Currall, the publication was entitled *Phonograph Record Libraries: Their Organization and Practice.*[158] A second edition of this invaluable collection of writings was issued in 1970.

In April, 1965, C. B. Hagen wrote "A Proposed Information Retrieval System for Sound Recordings," an ambitious undertaking begun at Mount St. Mary's College in Los Angeles by a sound engineer and librarian.[159] Hagen saw the project as one of "preserving on magnetic tape important lectures, speeches, TV and radio documentaries, important newscasts, drama and theater productions, live broadcasts of local concerts and recitals, broadcasts of international music festivals, phonograph records no longer available, and other material that cannot be normally obtained on commercial recordings." The college was also acquiring commercial recordings both on records and on tape. Hagen shared his system for organization with observations on specific aspects of classification and cataloging procedures through which he could retain a maximum amount of useful data for a minimum of expense, time, and labor.

Sherman Anderson, phonorecord cataloger at the Detroit Public Library, wrote "Cataloging the Contents of Certain Recordings," stating that the selection of subject entries only for the content of the records should be questioned and more value be placed on personalities presented.[160] Because recordings were accessioned and not classified at the Detroit Public Library, it was felt subject entries had to be given careful consideration. Specific examples to support Anderson's thesis were provided with recommendations that apply to both musical and spoken recordings.

Two publications on recordings were issued by English librarians in 1966, when Brian Redfern published *Organizing Music in Libraries*, and Hilary Hammond published an article entitled "A Punched Card Gramophone Record Catalogue at Luton Central Library."[161] Hammond stated that "members have direct access to the records, which are kept in accession number order." The library also issued a printed catalog, produced by Multilith from VariTyped plates, resulting in a four-year period in twenty-five hundred records and four thousand entries in the catalog, a quantity which led to the use of punched cards, a line printer, and photo reduced printouts on lithography plates. Annual additions could be produced quite simply and "the catalog information made more easily accessible for printing out sectional lists."

A comprehensive scheme for the organization of sound recordings (disc, reel, cartridge, and cassette) was published in 1969.[162] Roger B. McFarland and Caroline Saheb-Ettaba's work on "the alpha-numeric system for classification of recordings" was issued in response to two questions: "Do recordings need to be classified, and is a separate classification scheme necessary for recordings?" Their company's continued encounters with librarians and audiovisual specialists throughout the United States, who often expressed their need for a manual to organize their sound recordings, encouraged Saheb-Ettaba and McFarland to publish this volume.

CONCLUSION

The control of nonprint media has received the attention of many professional organizations. As noted earlier, the American Library Association, as well as the Music Library Association, the Special Library Association, the Educational Film Library Association, and the Association for Educational Communication and Technology have been instrumental in bringing some concentration of attention to the problems of nonprint media for nearly fifty years.

Noteworthy contributions are also being offered by commercial organizations, which are assuming the responsibility for the complexities of bibliographic control, a professional concern traditionally reserved to librarians. This trend is viewed as a mixed blessing by many librarians since it leads to a variety of formats, schemes, and procedures which are then utilized by libraries. A notable exception to this is the recent work of the Baker and Taylor Company. Through the leadership of company officer James Haughey, a group of professional librarians and audiovisual specialists from the United States and Canada were supported to meet and recommend standard procedures basic to the organization of nonprint media. These recommendations by professional leaders and authors represent a current attempt to standardize procedures, bibliographic elements, symbols, and terminology. The results given in full in the following appendix are specific recommendations for use in all manuals, guides, and rules utilized to organize nonprint media.

Individual attempts to establish procedures continue although genuine progress toward a unified approach is evident in professional association activities, publications, and research endeavors. With few exceptions, even those who need to satisfy a specific clientele recognize the value of utilizing the tools and procedures already agreed upon by professional organizations in the United States and beyond.

APPENDIX: NONPRINT MEDIA GUIDELINES

A task force of librarians and audiovisual specialists assembled on November 10, 1972, to resolve the differences among several guidelines currently available for the cataloging of nonprint materials, and to establish a media code suitable for both manual and automated systems. Two formal meetings of the task force were made possible by funds from the Baker and Taylor Company. However, the resulting recommendations of this task force are not tailored to the activities or procedures of any single library or processing center. Rather, they are—in the judgment of the composite task force membership—recommendations for the basic procedures, terminology, and codes essential to the organization of all nonprint media. While the task force questions the feasibility or desirability of complete standardization of all aspects of bibliographic control, they do strongly recommend the widespread adoption of the basic elements given in this report.

Members of the task force were chosen by the chairman who selected, in conjunction with consultants, those persons from all types of library and information science service centers who have shown leadership, demonstrated a special expertise, placed their ideas before their peers in writing, and agreed to serve in this capacity. Their work on the task force was without remuneration. Each person was chosen for his own extensive experience in the practice, administration, and utilization of nonprint media; different geographic regions and sizes of institutions were represented. All are leaders in their professional organizations and most have published writings in the field. Although some members of the task force have differing views on some aspects of these guidelines, they all agree that these are the few basic guidelines for which universal acceptance is urgently needed.

Pearce S. Grove, Chairman
Task Force
Library Director
Eastern New Mexico University
Portales, New Mexico

Evelyn G. Clement, Chairman
Department of Library Science
Memphis State University
Memphis, Tennessee

Katharine Clugston, Former Head
Audiovisual Section
Descriptive Cataloging Division
The Library of Congress
Washington, D.C.

Ruth Ann Davies, Coordinator
School Library Services
North Hills School District
Pittsburgh, Pennsylvania

Mazie Lassiter
Liaison Librarian
Department of Educational Media
Montgomery County Public Schools
Rockville, Maryland

James Limbacher
Audiovisual Librarian
Dearborn Public Library
Dearborn, Michigan

Glenn McMurry, Chief
Information Branch
National Audiovisual Center
Washington, D.C.

William J. Quinly
Assoc. Professor
College of Education
Florida State University
Tallahassee, Florida

Vivian Schrader, Acting Head
Audiovisual Section
Descriptive Cataloging Division
The Library of Congress
Washington, D.C.

Alma Tillin
Technical Services Media
Specialist
Library Center
Berkeley Unified School District
Berkeley, California

1. Bibliographic Records

Bibliographic information for both print and nonprint media should always be made compatible, and wherever possible, integrated into one card catalog, book catalog, automated listing or microform record. Data should allow for a single or divided (two or more units) catalog of bibliographic information.

2. Cataloging

The basic principles of cataloging as set forth in the *Anglo-American Cataloging Rules* are the adopted standard. The rules for main and added entries in Parts I and II are applicable to nonprint materials. The essential elements of information and their usual sequence are, if appropriate: author, title, medium designation, edition, producer-distributor, sponsor, date, physical description series, educational level, note, content description, and tracings. Additional information may be given in the body of the card or in notes as prescribed in the *Anglo-American Cataloging Rules*. All data should be compatible for manual and automated systems. Two or more interdependent media are cataloged by the dominant media, with the less significant media listed in the physical description or in a note, e.g., a filmstrip and a tape recording which explain the pictures of the filmstrip are cataloged as a filmstrip; a tape recording and a filmstrip which illustrate the sound visually are cataloged as an audiorecording.

A package of two or more media, all significant and related but not necessarily interdependent, is cataloged as a kit. Bibliographic information for kits should be sufficient to enable each part to be treated as an analytic entry, or as a separate integral unit with its own main entry.

3. Classification

A classification scheme best suited to the full integration of the subject content of print and nonprint media is recommended. The Library of Congress and Dewey Decimal Classification (unabridged and abridged) schemes have proven useful for the organization of both. All formats of media should be classified by the same scheme. Bibliographical records should be fully integrated although the physical units of materials may be segregated into separate areas due to special requirements for shelving, storage, humidity control, and equipment. If segregated collections of specific media are maintained a simple sequential order for storage may be preferred. This is useful for archive collections, collections that are closed to the public, and very small collections. It should, however, be remembered that small collections increase in size and closed collections may become open for browsing purposes.

4. Subject Headings

   It is recommended that the same list of subject headings be used for all formats of media. If either the Library of Congress or the Sears list is favored for one medium it should be used for the others. This is particularly important to the integration of bibliographic records.

5. Media Designations

   Media designations are used to distinguish one type of physical format from another in both the bibliographic and classification data. They should always be given in full (spelled out) unless it is absolutely necessary to use code symbols. Media designations are either general designations for basic formats or specific designations for the more exact identification of media formats.

   a. General physical form designation in the bibliographic record

      The general media designation, in singular form, is always given in parentheses or brackets following the full title. Its purpose is to notify the user briefly and immediately of the general type of material listed. Users interested in the type of material designated will be prepared to read further for more detail while those not interested in this general type of material may pass on to the next listing.

      The use of general designators may also prevent the proliferation of media designations, a hazard associated with the use of specific designators. In either case the use of a standard list of terms and codes is recommended. It is anticipated that the general designations listed in these recommendations will be hospitable to future media.

   b. Specific physical form designation in the bibliographic record

      The specific media designation, if used, is given in the physical description or in a note. Its purpose is to refine further a specific function of the primary media and to indicate the type of equipment required to use the material. If needed, information concerning the specific type or make of playback equipment required to use the material described is given in a note.

6. Media Codes (symbols)

   a. Media designations in the classification data

      Media designations that accompany the classification number are placed above it and become part of the call number. However, should media be stored in separate areas, specific media designations in conjunction with the call number *may be* needed for location purposes. The degree of specificity is determined by the media distinctions needed for location, shelving, and filing. In highly integrated collections general media designations are usually sufficient.

      In manual systems the media designation, spelled out in full and without abbreviation whenever possible, may be needed in the call number for ease of recognition. Codes are desired under some circumstances for brevity. A list of recommended designations and codes are included. They should be followed for either a manual or an automated record system.

b. Automated systems

Automated procedures usually require the codification of data. It is recommended that codes for media designation in automated records be the same as those of media designations in manual systems. These designations include both the general designations and the specific designations for the physical forms of media. The same designations should be used, if needed, in other pertinent records such as acquisitions, circulation, and inventory.

c. Color codes

Color codes are not recommended for the designation of specific forms of media. This practice is discouraged for both manual and automated systems and is particularly impractical in automated systems.

MEDIA DESIGNATIONS AND CODES

The following terms and codes are recommended as standard for general and specific media designations and their use exactly as given below is encouraged.

General Designation	Specific Designation	Code
I. AUDIORECORDING		AA
	a. Audiobox	AB
	b. Audiocard	AS
	c. Audiocartridge	AR
	d. Audiocassette	AC
	e. Audiocylinder	AY
	f. Audiodisc	AD
	g. Audioroll	AO
	h. Audiotape	AT
	i. Audiowire	AW
II. CHART		CA
	a. Chart	CH
	b. Flip chart	CF
	c. Graph	CG
	d. Flannel board	CL
	e. Wall chart	CW
	f. Relief chart	CR
III. DATA FILE		DA
	a. Digital cassette	DC
	b. Digital disc	DD
	c. Digital tape	DT
	d. Punched card	DB
	e. Punched paper tape	DP
IV. DIORAMA		OA
	a. Diorama	OD

General Designation	Specific Designation	Code
V. FILMSTRIP		FA
	a. Filmslip	FL
	b. Filmstrip	FS
VI. FLASH CARD		HA
	a. Flash card	HC
VII. GAME		GA
	a. Game	GM
	b. Puzzle	GP
VIII. GLOBE		QA
	a. Globe	QG
IX. KIT		KA
	a. Exhibit	KE
	b. Kit	KT
X. MAP		LA
	a. Relief map	LR
	b. Wall map	LW
	c. Map	LM
XI. MICROFORM		NA
	a. Aperture card	NC
	b. Microcard	ND
	c. Microchip	NP
	d. Microfiche	NH
	e. Microfilm	NF
	f. Microjacket	NJ
	g. Micro-opaque	NO
	h. Microprint	NT
	i. Microstrip	NS
	j. Ultrafiche	NU
XII. MODEL		EA
	a. Figure	EF
	b. Mock up	EM
	c. Puppet	EP
	d. Sculpture	ES
XIII. MOTION PICTURE		MA
	a. Kinescope	MK
	b. Motion picture cartridge	MR
	c. Motion picture cassette	MC
	d. Motion picture loop	ML
	e. Motion picture	MP
XIV. PICTURE		PA
	a. Art original	PO
	b. Art print (reproduction)	PR
	c. Photograph	PP
	d. Picture	PI

General Designation	Specific Designation	Code
	e. Post card	PC
	f. Poster	PT
	g. Study print	PS
XV. REALIA		RA
	a. Artifact	RF
	b. Specimen	RS
XVI. SLIDE		SA
	a. Film slide	SL
	b. Glass slide	SG
	c. Microscope slide	SM
	d. Stereoscope slide	SS
	e. Audio slide	SO
XVII. TRANSPARENCY		TA
	a. Transparency	TR
XVIII. VIDEORECORDING		VA
	a. Electronic video	VE
	b. Laser disc	VB
	c. Videocartridge	VR
	d. Videocassette	VC
	e. Videocube	VQ
	f. Videodisc	VD
	g. Videotape	VT

BASIC REFERENCES NEEDED FOR THE ORGANIZATION OF NONPRINT MEDIA

These volumes are recommended for use in the cataloging and processing of nonprint media. Although the authors of these publications are not in complete agreement the publications nevertheless form a basic reference collection of guides and information tools. The guidelines given above are only a few basic ones which should be considered supplemental to the books listed here.

Association for Educational Communications and Technology. Information Science Committee. *Standards for Cataloging Nonprint Materials.* 3rd ed. Washington, D.C.: The Association, 1972. (William J. Quinly, Committee Chairman and Editor.)

Anglo-American Cataloging Rules. North American Text. Chicago: American Library Assn., 1967. (Revision in progress for chapters 6, 7, and 12.)

Dewey, Melvil. *Dewey Decimal Classification and Relative Index.* 18th ed. Lake Placid Club, New York: Forest Press, 1971.

———. *Abridged Dewey Decimal Classification and Relative Index.* 10th ed. Lake Placid Club, New York: Forest Press, 1971.

Grove, Pearce S., ed. *Nonprint Media in Academic Libraries.* Chicago: American Library Assn., 1974.

Hicks, Warren B., and Tillin, Alma M. *Developing Multi-Media Libraries.* New York: Bowker, 1970.

Non-book Materials Cataloguing Rules. Integrated code of practice and draft revision of the *Anglo-American Cataloguing Rules–British Text Part III.* Working Paper No. 11. Prepared by the Library Association (England), Media Cataloguing Rules Committee. Huddersfield, Great Britain: National Council for Educational Technology and the Library Association, 1973.

U.S. Library of Congress. Subject Cataloging Division. *Classification.* (Parts of this multi-volume set were published and are revised at different times.)

U. S. Library of Congress. Subject Cataloging Division. *Subject Headings Used in the Dictionary Catalogs of the Library of Congress.* 7th ed. Washington, D. C.: The Library, 1966.

Weihs, Jean Riddle, Lewis, Shirley, and Macdonald, Janet. *Nonbook Materials: The Organization of Integrated Collections.* 1st ed. Ottawa: Canadian Library Assn., 1973.

Westby, Barbara M., ed. *Sears List of Subject Headings.* 10th ed. New York: Wilson, 1972.

Selection and Acquisition

Robert N. Broadus

Robert N. Broadus is Professor of Library Science, Northern Illinois University, DeKalb, Illinois.

A great deal has been written about the selection of audiovisual material by teachers for use in classrooms; considerable attention has been given the task of choosing media for learning resource centers in elementary and secondary schools; but little advice has been offered for the selection of these intellectual, inspirational, and entertaining forms of information by academic librarians. Those facts and theories used by the teacher, as he or she chooses materials for achieving some specific goal in the classroom, have some relationship to the building of a library collection as a whole. The differences are also significant.

RESPONSIBILITY

In planning a collection for the college or university library, one of the first questions to be settled is the role to be played by the classroom faculty in the selection process. Their contribution may vary with the difference in intended use of the materials. If it is assumed that motion picture films, for instance, will be shown before assembled classes only, and not viewed by students as individuals, then the faculty should have primary authority for their selection. If, however, the items are to be integrated with the library's book and periodical resources, so that students may use them according to individual interests as well as class assignments, then the librarian must take primary responsibility for their selection, as is done in the case of printed materials.

Lane has documented the growth in the influence of the librarian, as opposed to that of the teaching and research faculty, in building collections.[1] This movement away from faculty dominated selection is a phenomenon of the twentieth century academic library. Felix Reichmann, in a recent survey of research libraries, found evidence confirming the assumption that faculty participation in selection is declining.[2] It makes sense that the librarian, skilled in evaluating materials, should, as Pringle suggests, take the leadership in collecting audiovisual and similar materials.[3] The librarian alone is in a position to see the collection as a whole and also comprehend the vast array of items available for acquisition. Few persons limited to a particular subject field can have such a comprehensive view.

Perhaps it goes without saying that choices should be made with the advice (and probably consent) of the classroom faculty. The librarian, and those on the staff to whom authority for selection is delegated seek guidance wherever it can be found—whether in periodicals, books, computer data banks, or from knowledgeable persons. Those faculty who are interested enough to make thoughtful suggestions for the library collection are to be treasured and cultivated. They are more likely to use the materials and to recommend them to their students. The librarian should, therefore, encourage faculty members to offer suggestions by making catalogs and other aids available, routing announcements to instructors, and providing opportunities for them to preview possible purchases.[4] Teamwork is required, although the librarian must make the final decisions.

The fact that the librarian takes primary responsibility for building the collection does not necessarily preclude the allotment of some portion of funds to departments of instruction, provided these allocations are kept fluid. It should be made clear to all faculty that this money is not being given to the departments; it still belongs to the library or, rather, to the institution as a whole. Departmental allotments thus can be treated as an administrative convenience to facilitate a spread in expenditure so that no units of instruction are slighted. If a significant portion of the budget is divided among departments, there is an advantage in placing all forms of material in these allotments. Not only does this procedure provide a fairer distribution, it will also stimulate the departments, their faculties, and perhaps their students to become more aware of and concerned with nonprint media.

If a department then advises buying several color motion pictures, the point can be made that such a purchase may reduce the number of books, periodicals, and other materials which may be obtained in the field. It is very important, though, that a film or other expensive item useful to more than one department, not be rejected because a single department is not willing to have the entire price taken from its own allocated fund.

THE FIELD FROM WHICH TO COLLECT

When the librarian, with his or her staff, assumes responsibility for the collection of nonprint along with the usual library materials, it becomes necessary for certain broad assumptions to be made as to which ones will be best for the particular library. The librarian is then forced to come to terms with the stubborn question of what constitutes the specific library. Strangely enough, there is no satisfactory answer, for definitions of the library are woefully inadequate. Is it a service organization? If so, what is the precise nature and limit of that service? Is it a collection? If so, what specific kinds of material does it collect?

So far the answers to these questions are not entirely rational. The academic library does not collect and distribute things such as animals (as some public libraries do proudly), nor does it collect vials of odors from which the clientele may identify chemical compositions (as at least one special library does). How, then, shall the limits of a library's resources be described? Some people, trying to define policy, say that the library collects the materials of communication, but this province also is too broad. Ogden and Richards, in their *Meaning of Meaning,* say that all experience is either "enjoyed or interpreted . . . or both," and that very little experience fails to be interpreted in some way.[5] And everyone knows that the campus will have many materials of communication—materials which are to be "interpreted" but which are not under the jurisdiction of the library.

In the present state of the art it should be admitted that each director of an academic library has to decide how large an empire to build, bearing in mind that conquered territory sometimes has to be defended.[6] It is important, though, that each college or university work out a policy which contains a clear statement of what resources are to be the responsibility of the librarian.

Once the general boundaries are established in terms of the kinds or forms of materials to be gathered, the objectives of the institution should be taken into consideration, and the collections built accordingly. These objectives are not always well defined, but differ slightly from one institution to another. Although it may seem that they are chosen more for appearance than for purposes of practical guidance, they must be an integral part of the selector's thought process. As Robert Haywood suggests, the librarian by rights should get together with deans and academic departments, establishing the goals each part of the institution intends to pursue and setting up priorities for courses and library needs.[7] Then yearly changes in faculty will be less likely to disrupt the building of the collection. Resources which support the curriculum are of first importance. However, there is both precedent and reason for obtaining so-called recreational materials for they too can have significant value.

As a general proposition, the library should collect those items which convey the most important information and the knowledge most worth having—materials which stimulate thought on the gravest problems of life, which build acceptable attitudes, which develop desirable skills, which entertain constructively. Within this framework, the utilitarian philosophy of the best (most useful, most valuable) materials obtainable for the money would seem most sensible. Its application is not simple. Those responsible for decisions do not know what materials are going to be published and have to make judgments, based largely on the production of previous years. They are aware of some gaps to be filled, but do not know how long certain items now available will remain so. At the end of the year, is it possible to know how much has been spent for each type of media, such as books, periodicals, transparencies, maps, filmstrips, photograph records, motion pictures, tapes, cassettes, and slides? Twyford's estimate that the number of new films, filmstrips, tapes, recordings, models, and graphic materials produced each year totals about five thousand is undoubtedly low.[8] In 1967, the National Information Center for Educational Media (NICEM) surveyed seven forms of materials (16mm motion pictures, 35mm filmstrips, 8mm motion cartridges, overhead transparencies, video tapes, phonodiscs, and audio tapes) and concluded that their annual production totaled thirty thousand.[9] The number of obtainable nonprint items surely approaches that for books, periodicals, and pamphlets published in the English language. To purchase all print and nonprint materials (of the types commonly collected by academic institutions) offered each year in English would require something over $1 million. This statement should not, of course, be interpreted to mean that older items or those in foreign languages should be neglected.

RELATIVE VALUES OF DIFFERENT MEDIA

If the selection process is to be intelligent, that is something other than random, haphazard, and opportunist, the librarian must have some overall assumptions about the relative values of different media. If a color motion picture film is purchased, it means some thirty books or twenty filmstrips must be rejected. Even free materials are an expense, for time and money are required to obtain each item and then to catalog, store, service, and discard. With a budget of $100,000, less than one-tenth of the relevant, current, English language materials can be obtained. Assumptions as to value have to be made in spite of the fact that no one has enough information to make decisions with a great degree of assurance.

Nonprint media are highly diversified. Their capabilities and psychological implications vary widely. Some are appropriate for groups, others for individuals. Some convey messages through the eye, others through the ear, and many utilize both. There are materials for presenting specific concrete facts, others for creating moods or emotional tones. How shall one judge these types? C. J. Duncan of the University of Newcastle-upon-Tyne, has said that the real dilemma in the use of audiovisual materials in higher education is the interaction between cost and appositeness.[10] The simpler, cheaper aids tend to be more specific for a selected audience. Those which are more expensive to produce are usually planned to appeal to larger audiences (in order that costs may be recovered) and unfortunately their messages are often too diluted or blunted for specific classwork. With reference to art education, William H. Allen has a chart showing the relationships of particular kinds of instructional media to learning objectives, estimating the relative effectiveness (high, medium, low) of nine forms or combinations, vis-à-vis given purposes.[11] More analyses of this kind are needed, but in the meantime, some general considerations involved in getting the most useful materials for the cost will be discussed.

Durability of the Physical Item

Ordinarily the longest-lasting form is preferable to the fragile. Books normally are damaged very little by reading, while films in clumsy hands are particularly vulnerable. Recordings, may be scratched, but have no pages to be torn out. The durability of each form may be increased by improved technology; e.g., phonorecords are less subject to breakage than they were only a few years ago.

Durability of Information

Some fields of thought change rapidly. Facts on such subjects as political boundaries, manufacturing processes, dress fashions, and hair styles are quickly outdated while other information remains stable over a long period of time. The atom, the tree, and the hyena have about the same nature in 1971 as they had a few thousand years ago. There is, however, another dimension to the problem of change. The object studied may remain stable, while information about it increases rapidly: the moon presumably has changed little for millenia but informational materials describing it are constantly becoming outdated.

The general rule is that for rapidly changing subjects the less expensive media is to be preferred for purchase while the more expensive item may be rented. Thus replacement can be made as required. For concepts that change slowly, expensive items are favored for purchase.

A similar problem is pointed out by Frank Johnson of the University of Leeds.[12] He feels that professors in higher education are close enough to the frontiers of knowledge that they tend to present in their lectures a distinctively individual view. While the substance taught in a history course in one high school may be quite similar to the content of the same course taught in another school, at the university level each professor is more likely to prefer his own interpretation. Hence, a film which is useful for modern history in one college, may not satisfy the faculty responsible for the same course in another institution.

Effectiveness in Communication

It is extremely difficult to get reliable information on the relative effectiveness of communicative media. Numerous experiments in classrooms have proven disappointingly little with regard to the relative effectiveness of various presentation formats.[13] Individual differences among users are important but difficult to measure without isolated factors that reveal reliable data from which to base generalizations. One student seems to get more from a book, another from a film. Motion pictures obviously are better for objects which need to be shown in motion, especially scientific subjects, while they may be less effective for other topics. Though it would seem that a medium presenting its information through two sensory channels, e.g., eye and ear, would be more instructive than a medium using only one such channel, recent studies seem to demonstrate this assumption is not necessarily true.

People are taught how to read, but spend far less time learning to look at pictures. If we were instructed more thoroughly in extracting information from pictorial matter, nonprint media would undoubtedly be more useful. To some, films have the advantage of novelty, but as the novelty wears off, effectiveness may be reduced. In television, color seems to show little if any learning advantage, at least for some subjects, over black and white, though it may bring more pleasure and satisfaction to the user.[14] This conclusion does not necessarily imply that it is valid for libraries to save money by obtaining other formats in black and white rather than color. Indeed, a great deal is yet to be learned about these matters, requiring the librarian to refine his views as more results of research studies become available.[15]

Convenience of Use

Other things being equal, a format which is fast and easy to use should be preferred to one which is inconvenient. Mere portability is a factor. A book ranks high in this respect, since it is easy to carry about, and may be used for relatively long periods of time, several hours on the average. Since 1948, the use of phonorecords outside the library has become more convenient due to long playing discs. A student is willing to carry a bulky package home to get more music or spoken time. Tape cartridges add to this advantage. Video recorders and players appear to have a promising future as equipment for them is standardized.

The requirement of a projector or other machine reduces for most people the satisfaction with which materials can be used. Pocket and lap-size viewers for microforms now in research stages may well increase the relative value of these materials. Since few people today have microform readers in their homes, use is largely confined to libraries and even that is still none too satisfactory. Easier loading projectors improve the desirability of films. Also, 8mm film cartridges have some advantage over conventional films, in that they provide easy access to a small subject without the viewer having to endure a long reel in order to reach a specific point of interest. Forsdale says that the 8mm is to the 16mm as the freely circulated book is to the manuscript that was chained to the monastery table.[16]

Cost Factors

On the basis of financial considerations one may judge that a book or two on a subject represents a better buy than a filmstrip, since the book can be used longer and more conveniently. However, the filmstrip may present matter not found in any book or may offer it in a more effective fashion thus justifying its purchase. After the three or four leading books on a subject have been obtained, the law of diminishing returns (owing to repetition of matter from title to title) may indicate that a filmstrip is the next wise purchase. Obviously, also, there are stimuli which a printed item simply cannot convey.

The task is complicated by the fact that seldom is there a simple question of book or periodical versus film or recording for a given topic. Masses of material overlap one another rendering it difficult, if not impossible, to make exactly the right selection in each case. One should recognize that mistakes will be made, and that even if correct choices were wisely made each time, others might not recognize and appreciate the fact. Nonetheless, the librarian would like to make intelligent choices for the maximum benefit of the library program.

BUILDING A COLLECTION

Once a collection is established, the process of further building is often one of considering each item available and making one of three decisions about it: (1) to select and acquire it at once, (2) to reject it, or (3) to reserve judgment and file notes for later consideration. Each decision should be based on factors such as those previously discussed, and on such questions as:

1. Is the content of the item useful, important? Are extraneous or distracting elements filtered out?

2. Does the item present the facts? Is it accurate and up-to-date? Is it truthful? These are not easy questions to answer for an informational item, in printed or nonprint format. Even if the librarian is expert, there will always be some doubt. The most reasonable course is to obtain a consensus of competent opinion, and to act on that. Some items thought to be untrue may be obtained anyway, for historical use or as examples of unusual points of view.

3. Is the item's arrangement satisfactory? At higher levels of study a logical order may be best; but for some purposes a progression from known to unknown, or from simple to difficult, may be preferable. If there is a summary or review, is it handled well?

4. Is the subject one which is well presented by the particular medium used? Does the specific format teach this subject better

than is possible with other media? If the purpose is to preserve or store information (rather than to teach), is the medium selected for this purpose the most effective and practical?

5. Is an item appropriate for college level? This criterion is particularly difficult to apply. The claim made for some films is that they may be used in kindergarten through college. This may be but it is rather uncommon. However, a slide of a tarantula may be fascinating to a small child and educationally valuable to a graduate student. Even a reproduction of "Whistler's Mother" may be appropriate for young and old. Pictures without accompanying words can appeal to a wide range of levels, as can phonorecords, especially those containing certain kinds of music. It is the use of words which usually limits an item to specific age levels. Even here, there are exceptions such as Walt Disney films, which appeal to children as well as their grandparents. Moreover, a children's book on a technical subject may be read with profit by an adult. As a general rule, though, printed materials are likely to have a smaller range of use level than visual items. Sound films and tapes of personal interviews tend to be restrictive, while purely pictorial or other nonverbal materials have an advantage in this regard.

6. Regarding films, is commercialism held to an acceptable level, not distracting from the central theme and informational content?

7. Finally, is the technical quality acceptable? Is it artistic? Are physical size, format, and color satisfactory? Is the workmanship of high quality? Are background music, narration, and other presentation devices of particular items handled well?

SOURCES OF INFORMATION

Unfortunately the bibliographies, indexes, review journals, and other guides to nonprint materials are not organized in such a way as to facilitate selection and acquisition by college and university libraries. Quinly remarks on the ironic fact that selection tools are available in inverse ratio to the cost of the form of material.[17] Many guides are set up in terms of school libraries. The typical arrangement is by kind of medium, rather than by subject. Thus the academic librarian finds it difficult to locate materials, especially if interested primarily in a subject approach. Hicks and Tillin note that reviewers tend to view materials as aids to instruction rather than as items for individual use.[18] Fortunately, conditions are improving.

Publications which list, review, and evaluate nonprint materials may be thought of in five categories, though not all fit in a single category: (1) commercial and educational catalogs; (2) guides which are devoted to materials in one or more media; (3) periodicals which are chiefly concerned with the nonprint approach, regardless of subject; (4) guides or bibliographies devoted to a subject and/or its materials; and (5) periodicals published primarily for a subject field, but with reviews or other notes pertaining to nonprint media. For each of these types, some representative publications are noted.

Catalogs

The colorful and elaborate catalogs of producers and distributors who offer nonprint items are a delight to peruse. Some of them are huge but, as is true in the book industry, there are many small producers who issue only a few items a year. All these catalogs, when filed by subject or other convenient plan, make a good repository of information. Also, the catalogs listing materials held by such universities as Minnesota, Indiana, Illinois, and Florida State afford suggestions for purchase, in somewhat the same way as catalogs of Lamont and other undergraduate libraries have been used for the selection of books.

Media-centered Guides

Two important general surveys in this area are: *Guides to Newer Educational Media*, by Margaret I. Rufsvold and Carolyn Guss (3rd ed.; Chicago: American Library Assn., 1971, 116p.), which describes lists of those materials requiring special equipment or physical facilities for presentation, and *Audiovisual Market Place: A Multimedia Guide* (New York: Bowker, annually), whose sections headed "Reference" and "Serials and Review Services" are helpful in selection.

For a direct listing of individual items, the publications of the National Information Center for Educational Media (NICEM) at the University of Southern California are of fundamental importance. A number of guides to specific media have been announced.

The Educational Film Library Association publishes the *8mm Film Directory, 1969–70*, compiled and edited by Grace Ann Kone (produced and distributed by Comprehensive Service Corporation, New York, 532p.); *Film Evaluation Guide, 1946–64* (New York: 1965, 528p.) with its supplement for 1964–67 in 144 pages, and other works in addition to the reviews on EFLA cards.

Feature Films on 8mm and 16mm, edited by James L. Limbacher (3rd ed.; New York: Bowker, 1971, 169p.) is updated regularly in the periodical *Sightlines*.

A rather ambitious project, *Learning Directory, 1970–71* (New York: Westinghouse Learning Corporation, 1970, 7 vols.) lists by subject over two hundred thousand items, including printed materials, with an indication of level (including "college or higher") for many of them. No judgment of quality is given. This tool parallels, approximately, the *Subject Guide to Books in Print*.

Useful in the United States is a publication of the British and Scientific Film Association, *The British National Film Catalogue*, which originated in 1963, and which is issued quarterly with annual updating. It lists and annotates films as they become available in Great Britain. Included is a subject section arranged by the Universal Decimal Classification.

Two publications by the U.S. Library of Congress have some relevance here: *Motion Pictures and Filmstrips* (quarterly) and *Music and Phonorecords* (semiannually). The subject indexes, based on L. C. subject headings, are a help in collection building; the alphabetical sections in identification of titles.

The U.S. Office of Education *U.S. Government Films for Public Educational Use—1963* (Washington: Govt. Print. Off., 1964, 532p.) is still useful, covering many subjects, as does *U.S. Government Films: A Catalog of Motion Pictures and Filmstrips for Sale by the National Audiovisual Center* (Washington: General Services Administration, National Archives Publication 70–3, 1969, 165p., and its supplement, 140p.). The guides to free materials issued by the Educators Progress Service, Randolph, Wisconsin, have some use for higher education, though the items listed are not always available at the exact time preferred.

There is no shortage of bibliographies representing sound recordings. To cite one specialized example for music, James Coover and Richard Colvig have compiled *Medieval and Renaissance Music on Long-Playing Records* (Detroit: Information Service, Inc., 1964; Detroit Studies in Music Bibliography, no.6, 122p.). Note also the discographies each devoted to a single composer.

An excellent guide to nonmusical recordings is *Spoken Records* by Helen Roach (3rd ed.; Metuchen, N.J.: Scarecrow, 1970, 288p.), which includes documentaries, lectures, interviews, speeches, readings by authors, readings by other than authors, and plays. The descriptions are in bibliographic essay form with an introduction on the evaluation of these recordings. The National Education Association, et al., *National Audio Tape Catalog* (Washington: The Association, 1967, 114p.) offers a subject arrangement plus Library of Congress classification number for each entry.

Periodicals Devoted to Nonprint Materials

Though most of these media-promotion journals are geared to secondary school and lower, they are worth checking for college collections. *Film Library Quarterly* is essential for its articles and longer reviews of films. *Sightlines*, published by the Educational Film Library Association, is notable for its "Film Review Digest," "Film Review Index," and its subject approach to new films and filmstrips. See also the annotated list, "Films for Now," compiled by Abigail Bishop (4:9–10, Jan.-Feb. 1971). *Multi-Media Reviews Index*, 1970– (Ann Arbor, Mich.: Pierian Press, 1971, annually) is updated by a regular column in *Audiovisual Instruction. Film Review Index* lists reviews of all film formats. *Landers Film Reviews*, issued ten times a year, is very good for critical evaluations of 16mm films. Among the other periodicals in this group worthy of inspection are: *Business Screen*; *Educational Media*; *Film News*; *Educational Screen and Audiovisual Guide* (with an annual "Blue Book" issue devoted to materials, arranged by subject); *Media and Methods*, with its annual *Educator's Purchasing Guide*; and the *AV Forum*, in cassette tape form.

For evaluation of phonograph records, *High Fidelity* (and its annual *Records in Review: a Cumulation of Evaluative Notes*), *Tape Recording*, *American Record Guide*, *The Gramophone* (British), *Stereo Review*, and *Records and Recording* are outstanding. The *Harrison Tape Guide* (*8-track/cassettes/Open Reels/Quadraphonic 8-track and Reels*) is issued every other month, and *Billboard* has an annual Buyer's Guide number on music, records, and tape. *The Schwann Record and Tape Guide* is indispenable. *Recorded Sound* (British) includes interesting lists of musical and nonmusical recordings, such as the sounds of nature.

Subject-centered Bibliographies

It may be surprising that serious bibliographies devoted to particular topics practically never include nonprint items, but this is true even for some subjects in which films and recordings are of major importance. However, there is a fair number of guides to films (and sometimes other materials) on specific subjects. The publication divisions of the National Education Association offer considerable help in the selection of materials used in teaching such subjects as art, music, and business (e.g., *Films on Art*, published in 1965 by the National Art Education Commission, 60p.). The National Education Association also produces many nonprint, as well as printed, items on its own. Other national associations often are good sources for specialized lists.

For a few other examples of subject bibliographies, there are: Harry A. Johnson, ed. and comp., *Multi-Media Materials for Afro-American Studies* (New York: Bowker, 1971, 353p.); Pennsylvania State University's Psychological Cinema Project, *Films in the Behavioral Sciences 1967, 1968, 1969* (University Park, Pa.: 1969– , 104p.); and American Medical Association, *Medical and Surgical Motion Pictures* (Chicago: The Association, 1966, 485p.).

Subject-centered Periodicals

It is surprising to compare the large number of journals carrying book reviews with the small number featuring reviews of nonprint materials. An exception is the magazines published by teachers of particular disciplines. They often include individual bibliographies of items in several media, and many of them also carry regular (or irregular) columns which review these materials. Again, the problem is that they are not generally directed at college level, but this group is worth perusal by the selector: *American Biology Teacher, Business Education World, English Journal, Journal of Biological Education* (British), *Journal of Geography, Mathematics Teacher, Social Education, Social Studies, Speech Teacher, School Shop,* and *Science Teacher.*

Some references to the periodicals in librarianship are needed. Especially helpful are notes about resources in *Learning Today* (formerly *The Library-College Journal*). *Booklist* includes 8mm film loops, 16mm films, filmstrips, and recordings. A new Bowker publication, *Previews: News and Reviews of Non-Print Media,* appears highly important for academic as well as other types of libraries. An example of an occasional list is Helen R. Wheeler's "Films for the Community College Library," *Wilson Library Bulletin* 42:411–14 (Dec. 1967). *Bookmark* and *Library World* (British) are of help also. Of particular interest is: Bethany Ochal, "Selected Microforms on Legal Subjects," *Law Library Journal* 63:311–46 (Aug. 1970), which gives cassettes for continuing legal education, 16mm films on law and related disciplines, and a selection of sound recordings on legal topics. *Saturday Review* should also be noted for the attention it has given to recordings and films.

Some other subject periodicals which review nonprint media with a degree of regularity are: *Contemporary Psychology* (with an occasional section on "Instructional Media"), *American Anthropologist, Association Management, Theatre World, Royal Society of Health Journal* (British), and *Science News.*

The numerous and frequent lengthy reviews of music recordings are appropriately handled in the "Index to Record Reviews," compiled and edited by Kurz Meyers for *Notes*, the quarterly journal of the Music Library Association. In addition to the well known general music periodicals which give opinions on recordings (e.g., *Musical Quarterly*), there are several specialized journals, such as *Ethnomusicology* and *Journal of the International Folk Music Council. Journal of American Folklore, Africa Report,* and *Journal of Child Psychotherapy* (British) are examples of periodicals which, though outside the field of music proper, nevertheless review music recordings.

These then are types of bibliographic coverage for nonprint materials, along with some of the representative titles available at the time of this writing. This bibliographic survey may be of assistance in keeping abreast of the continuing publications which offer help in the selection of these forms. Undoubtedly, if academic libraries take more responsibility for collecting works of this kind, there will be more lists compiled to meet the need. The Commission on Instructional Technology has recommended that a National Institute of Instructional Technology be established and that one of its duties be the provision of information about materials in all subject fields.[19] In the meantime, we use the tools we have, and are grateful that their quality is improving.

Standards

Evelyn G. Clement

Evelyn G. Clement is Chairman, Department of Library Science, Memphis State University, Memphis, Tennessee.

The practice of cooperating to establish standards for library service has been prevalent among librarians since the first sessions of the American Library Association in 1876, when the Committee on Cooperation turned its attention to the development of a standard method for designating the various sizes of books. Standardization was one of Melvil Dewey's favorite causes and he frequently admonished his colleagues to adopt standard library equipment and practice in order to achieve maximum economy in the administration of libraries. Despite the acceptance early in this century of lantern slides, pictures, stereographs, phonograph records, and music rolls as library materials, none of the commonly accepted practices or standards related to audiovisual service, material, or equipment until C. C. Certain included these in his report adopted by the American Library Association in 1918.[1] The Certain standards enumerated some nontraditional materials and equipment to be included in a high school library.

Standards may actually operate in several ways to achieve different objectives. They can be defined as acknowledged measures of comparison—objects that under specified conditions define, represent, or record the magnitude of units or specify the level of requirement, excellence, or attainment. A standard is established by authority, custom, or general consent as a model or example, or as a rule for the measure of that which is to be compared. *Quantitative standards* specify a numerical value to be achieved, which may represent a minimum level, a norm, or an ideal, and which may be expressed either in absolute numbers or as a ratio or formula. *Qualitative standards,* while they may include the expression of a quantitative level to be achieved, are generally concerned with the specification of the characteristics, attributes, or properties of the thing to be measured. While quantitative standards are primarily concerned with size, weight, extent, and frequency, qualitative standards deal with levels of value, excellence, or achievement.

Librarians have tended to develop and accept qualitative rather than quantitative standards largely because, while it may be highly satisfying and comfortable to establish that every library of type A serving N population should have X books and Y other materials, it has, in fact, been nearly impossible to identify such absolutes. While various size collections and volumes per capita have been suggested for colleges and universities, no universally accepted quantitative standards do, in fact, exist. Further recognition of the individual nature of libraries and their services coupled with an increasing necessity for cost effectiveness has led to a recent trend toward performance standards. In performance standards, the required results are specified while the manner of implementation remains general, thus allowing flexibility for experimentation with the method of execution and development of alternatives while maintaining high levels of performance.

Apparently, no one standard or one type of standard will adequately serve all components of librarianship, nor even that part of the field which is the subject of this paper—audiovisual services in academic libraries. There probably should not be comprehensive standards for audiovisual librarianship, but rather the achievement of unanimity among the components which comprise the whole, with cooperation to ensure compatibility.

STANDARDS FOR SERVICE

There are presently no widely accepted or official standards which are primarily concerned with audiovisual services in academic libraries. However, several documents do deal with these problems and there are projects in progress which should provide assistance with these services in the future.

Mendel Sherman and Gene Faris developed standards for non-library based media programs which were adopted by the Department of Audiovisual Instruction (DAVI) and by the Association of Chief State School Audio-Visual Officers (ACSSAVO) in 1965.[2] Expanded from tentative guidelines developed by the DAVI Committee on Professional Standards, these standards set quantitative requirements at a basic and an advanced level for materials, equipment, personnel, and budget. W. R. Fulton, with the assistance of the DAVI Consultant Service Committee, obtained a grant to develop a self-evaluation instrument which included criteria for physical facilities, budget, and staff.[3] Both of these documents have serious limitations for use by the academic librarian, however. First, the service described is physically and administratively separate from the library. Second, as quantitative standards, they have become quite out of date. Third, these standards were not developed by consensus of a broad concerned audience, but were propounded by a relatively small group. The Program Standards Committee of the Association for Educational Communications and Technology (AECT) has recently established four task forces to work on the creation of new standards and the revision of existing standards for media programs. These task forces, which include one for two-year institutions and another for colleges and universities, are apparently making amends for earlier deficiencies in standards development by working with representatives of the American Association of School Libraries (AASL), the Association of College and Research Libraries (ACRL), and the American Association of Junior Colleges (AAJC), and by repeated calls for recommendations from the profession.

Also of little assistance to the academic librarian are the recent guidelines developed by the Audiovisual Committee of the Public Library Association.[4] Since these guidelines were adopted to serve as a yardstick for public libraries and library systems, most of the recommendations are quantitative. These are formulas for determining adequate materials, personnel, space, and equipment to serve a given population. The guidelines do not include criteria for selection or evaluation of materials nor do they provide recommended procedures for technical processing. They also fail to stress the integration of nonprint with print collections in public libraries.

In the 1959 "Standards for College Libraries," the ACRL Committee on Standards recognized audiovisual materials as an integral part of modern instruction and proposed that their libraries should be concerned with them, taking the initiative to provide the materials and service if no other agency was currently doing so.[5] Going one step further, they recommended that the same high standards be used for the selection of nonprint material as for the print collection. A working draft of "Guidelines for College Libraries" asserts the role of the college library as an essential device for the systematic collection of all forms of information.[6] Nonprint materials required for general reference by the academic community should be represented in the library collection and should be organized to promote their full utilization by the provision of efficient and effective access. Both the earlier standards and the proposed guidelines avoid quantitative or organizational specifications while endorsing the principle of the integrated collection.

The "ALA Standards for Junior College Libraries" also affirm the importance of nonprint media in the learning process and recommend their collection by the library unless another campus agency is administering them effectively.[7] Whether or not audiovisual materials are housed and administered by the library, they should be indexed in the library catalog. The AAJC-ACRL-AECT committee, which developed new guidelines for two-year college learning resource centers, found that the accelerated evolution of libraries away from the traditional print orientation made it advisable to incorporate the concept of the integration of print and nonprint into a single administrative unit to provide adequate resources for academic endeavor on junior and community college campuses.[8] Therefore, in these guidelines, the term learning resources includes library, audiovisual, and telecommunications and thereby negates the necessity of separate guides for audiovisual materials. Like those for college libraries, these standards make no quantitative recommendations; rather they indicate a desired level of performance.

Standards for academic library service may be further directed toward the integration of print and nonprint resources by the increasing acceptance and implementation of the *Standards for School Media Programs* at the elementary and secondary school level.[9] Service expectations of those students whose experience has included the full range of media use throughout their school years will encourage certain change in the academic library. Although these *Standards* are not yet fully implemented in all schools in all states, and although they have, in fact, caused considerable controversy and dissent, their strength lies in their development by a joint committee of the American Library Association and the Department of Audiovisual Instruction with an advisory board representing twenty-eight professional associations.

The ACRL Audio Visual Committee prepared basic guidelines for academic libraries assuming the administration of an audiovisual program.[10] These guidelines serve to introduce the academic librarian to his responsibilities in the provision of audiovisual services. They contain no quantitative standards and do not serve as an accrediting instrument.

CATALOGING STANDARDS

All of the library standards or guidelines (these terms are being used almost interchangeably today) discussed thus far have espoused or affirmed the philosophy of library-based audiovisual service, but none have made explicit the method or technique to be employed in the provision of this service. Nevertheless, several tentative standards have been proposed for the cataloging of nonprint media, coming from both the audiovisual and the library professions.

A task force on Computerized Cataloging and Booking of Educational Media was formed within the Department of Audiovisual Instruction in 1966, in response to the felt need for new methods of storing and retrieving information about media, including more efficient booking and scheduling. One group was assigned the responsibility for developing cataloging standards and another was to devise coding standards for computerized cataloging. The resulting *Standards for Cataloging, Coding, and Scheduling Educational Media* was published in 1968, with the expectation that through audience response and discussion there might be further refinement leading to the development of a national standard.[11] Since the two groups worked independently in their development of standards for cataloging and for coding, there are some inconsistencies in media designations, maturity range indicators, and in the physical description of materials. Although the document received wide distribution, it was actually used in very few situations, and the anticipated response and discussion simply did not occur.

Perhaps one factor in the failure of the DAVI standards to become accepted was the publication of the *Anglo-American Cataloging Rules*, which included, in part 3, rules for the cataloging of nonbook materials.[12] Apparently, many librarians preferred to adopt these library-developed guidelines which proposed compatible book and nonbook cataloging rather than experimenting with the standards proposed by the audiovisual specialists. It soon became evident, however, that part 3 of the *Cataloging Rules* was not completely satisfactory and yet another tentative proposal was developed.

Non-Book Materials: the Organization of Integrated Collections was written by three Canadian catalogers who found DAVI standards and the *Anglo-American Cataloging Rules* difficult to apply.[13] They wisely developed rules compatible with parts 1 and 2 of the *Cataloging Rules,* then tested and revised them. The Canadians worked with the Technical Services Committee of their school library association but also consulted with many groups in the United States and Canada who were interested and concerned. These included representatives of the Library of Congress, the Association for Educational Communications and Technology, and the American Library Association. Although this Canadian manual was called a preliminary work, embodying provisional ideas, it was nevertheless based on considerable experience, discussion and research. It was written specifically for school libraries, but the principles can be applied to any library organization in which books and other media are housed together and are listed in a single unified file of holdings.

The Association for Educational Communications and Technology produced a revised edition of its cataloging standards while seeking but not waiting for endorsements from interested organizations at the national level.[14] They did consult with members of the American Library Association, the Canadian Library Association, the National Audio-Visual Association (NAVA), and the Library of Congress, and made a genuine effort toward cooperation among librarians, media specialists, and commercial producers in the development of these rules. Endorsement by library organizations in both North American countries, however, leans toward the principles proposed in the Canadian publication, and it appears that consensus may be reached in the near future, settling on rules which embody the best of these tentative proposals.

BIBLIOGRAPHIC CONTROL

As an outgrowth of early efforts by the University of Southern California to produce and maintain a catalog of its own collection, the National Information Center for Educational Media (NICEM) has made several landmark contributions to the bibliographic control of nonprint resources.[15] Through the production of its own catalog and more than 350 catalogs for schools and colleges, the center established guidelines for computerized cataloging and compiled a massive data bank. Beginning with the *Index to 16mm*

Educational Films in 1967, McGraw-Hill and, more recently, Bowker, have published indexes reflecting the data bank holdings by type of media.

Perhaps the most important contribution in terms of standards development, however, is the standard report form which the National Information Center developed in cooperation with the Library of Congress. Use of this form by media producers has led to uniform reporting of cataloging data both to the National Information Center and to the Library of Congress. The Educational Media Producers Council (EMPC) has recently initiated a campaign, urging its members to use the National Information Center form in reporting their productions to the Library of Congress, which will then provide printed catalog cards.

The staff of the Copyright Office first began to draft rules for the cataloging of motion picture films in 1946, very wisely asking the advice and opinions of film librarians and other potential users before beginning the distribution of printed cards in late 1951.[16] Although the Library of Congress catalogs material and produces cards primarily for its own integrated catalog, it has also recognized its responsibility to provide these services to libraries whose collections differ markedly. This national library, in scope if not in name, has led in the development of cataloging rules for films and filmstrips, phonorecords, maps and atlases, and globes, and provides printed cards for these materials. For those materials not physically collected by the Library of Congress, cataloging is done from data supplied by the producer. The rules for films and filmstrips are presently being expanded to include sets of slides and sets of transparencies because librarians have indicated that they require these rules.

When the staff of the Machine-Readable Cataloging (MARC) project began to develop a format for monographs, they recognized the importance of providing flexibility so that the MARC format might serve as a standardized communications format for a wide variety of bibliographic data.[17] That the basic structure is hospitable to all types of bibliographic information has been demonstrated by the development of *Films: A MARC Format*.[18] The Library of Congress plans to use the machine-readable records for film material to produce their printed book catalogs for motion pictures and filmstrips; to produce printed cards; and possibly to expand the MARC distribution service to cover film material. Another dimension of the flexibility of the MARC format is found in its applicability and acceptance across international boundaries. With minor modification, it has been adopted in Great

Britain (UK/MARC) and has become an international standard. With the international acceptance of the MARC format and the possible extension of the International Standard Book Numbering system to include nonprint media, it may be expected that an efficient, fast, and accurate exchange of information about media will be possible.

The Standard Book Numbering system began in Great Britain in 1967 for the use of the book trade.[19] Rather than establish a separate but basically similar system, U.S. publishers chose to adopt the British system. The central agency for this in the United States is provided by a collaboration among the American Book Publishers Council, the American Educational Publishers Institute, the American National Standards Institute Z39 Committee, the Library of Congress, and the R. R. Bowker Company. The function of the agency is to supervise the system whereby unique identifying numbers are assigned to each unique item produced. The numbers may be used in a manual system, but are particularly suited to machine manipulation.

Libraries in the United States have also begun to make use of the numbers in their local control systems. The Standard Book Numbering system has been established, through the International Standardization Organization (ISO) TC46 committee, as an International Standard Book Numbering system with only slight modification. Germany, Holland, Denmark, and Sweden are also implementing the system.

Book publishers who also provide books on tape or microform may assign an International Standard Book Number, since these are considered separate editions of their books. For those publishers who also produce nonprint materials, a block of numbers may be assigned for internal order fulfillment purposes, but these may not be labelled as International Standard Book Numbers. Several publishers have selected to utilize such a block, with one omitting the check digit, another using the full number, and two others using only a portion of the full number. The advantages of using a unique identifier for the acquisition, control, and retrieval of nonprint media are many and obvious. Increased accuracy in a field where the principal "handle" for retrieval has been a title, which is often similar to many other titles, would alone be worth the effort to implement a standard numbering system.

STANDARDS FOR EQUIPMENT

The Educational Media Council, whose members are fourteen national nonprofit organizations, has long recognized the complex problem of standards for educational equipment and material. Jointly with the Bureau of Libraries and Educational Technology of the United States Office of Education, the council sponsored, late in 1971, a two-day seminar which was attended by some seventy education and industry representatives. The published report of this seminar is "in part a detailed statement of the problems it addresses and in part the product of a concerted and concentrated attempt . . . to recommend viable solutions for those problems."[20] Through its unique membership composition and its recognized concern for the development and promulgation of standards, the council could appropriately establish a coordinating mechanism which might initiate, facilitate, and expedite standards development by those agencies or organizations most directly concerned while avoiding costly and wasteful duplication of effort.

Another area of standards development which is important to libraries, but little known to many librarians, is the work of the American National Standards Institute (ANSI). Organized in 1918 as the American Engineering Standards Committee, the institute is a nonprofit, nongovernmental federation of more than 160 technical, professional, and trade organizations and more than one thousand companies. It does not develop standards; the member bodies do this. The institute provides the organizational mechanism by which voluntary national standards may be systematically developed and approved, with assurance that all parties with a substantial interest are afforded the opportunity to participate. In most other countries, there is a single governmental unit responsible for standards, but voluntary standardization is a well established tradition in the United States. Although there has been some recent insistence of mandatory federal standards, this can be most effectively avoided by the utilization of the system which the American National Standards Institute provides.

International standards are the result of recommendations developed by the technical committees of the International Organization for Standardization, the International Electrotechnical Commission, and the Pan American Standards Commission. The American National Standards Institute is the only representative of U.S. industry to these nontreaty organizations, with its strength dependent on effective delegations representing a consensus of all interested and affected parties.

The publications *News About ANSI*, *News About Z39*, and *Standards Action* are distributed by the institute at no cost in order to increase and encourage public surveillance and comment on standards. *Standards Action* lists the title and description of each standard on which action is proposed, with the name and address of the organization from which copy may be obtained.

While a majority of the standards developed within ANSI committees are industrial and technical, a number of these have at least an indirect bearing on academic audiovisual library services. The work of several of these committees should be of direct interest to librarians, audiovisual specialists, and other information scientists on academic campuses.

The work of the C83 Committee—Components for Electronic Equipment—includes standards for many of the physical specifications of magnetic tape recording. Committee C98 is concerned with video magnetic recording, and C104 with closed circuit television cameras. The photography (PH) section works with characteristics and specifications for photography and motion pictures, including consideration of photographic film, sensitometry, apparatus, and processing. Specifications for a wide range of details which assure the user that when a 16mm film is threaded into a projector, everything will fit—including sprocket holes, take-up reels, picture image, and even the sound track—are provided by PH22–Motion Pictures. Some work on sound level measurement and on loudspeakers and microphones has been done by S—Acoustics, Vibration, Mechanical Shock, and Sound Recording. Computers and information processing are the concern of X3. In most of these areas, it might be expected that the academic librarian would be interested, or perhaps even grateful, but probably would not participate directly in the development of standards.

Committee Z39—Standardization in the Field of Library Work, Documentation and Related Publishing Practices—is chaired by Jerrold Orne, University of North Carolina. The scope of Z39 includes standards for concepts, definitions, terminology, letters and signs, practices and methods in the fields of library work, in the preparation and utilization of documents, and in those aspects of publishing that affect library methods and use. This committee, sponsored by the Council of National Library Associations and supported by grants from the Council on Library Resources and the National Science Foundation, has more than forty member organizations. Of the approximately twenty committees presently constituted, only the work of Z39.4—Bibliographic References—has the slightest bearing on academic audiovisual librarianship. Its proposed standard for citation included a section on audiovisual materials, but because of many unresolved problems which would delay the possible acceptance of the standard, this section was dropped from the most recent proposal.

Committee Z39 is the logical place for library audiovisual standards development. Standard terminology, statistical measurement and reporting, citations, catalog entry, and many others have been identified as critical needs. Interested, knowledgeable, diligent workers are required who will identify the needs, locate and secure sponsors and financial assistance, then devote the time and energy required to develop acceptable national standards within the framework of the American National Standards Institute. Orne has spoken directly to this matter in his article "Standards in Library Technology."[21] While noting recent significant advances in standards work through the institute and the International Standardization Organization, he also pointed to a number of specific areas where considerable work is needed. Among these

> The many varied fields of the media specialist have not been touched, mainly for lack of resources, both fiscal and human. Despite the occasional association or industrial guidelines, there are virtually no national standards for most of their materials or methods. There lies a vast program of work, which should be led by the specialists . . . and finally subjected to the national consensus and approval system of . . . ANSI.

Sponsored by the National Association of Photographic Manufacturers, the Association for Educational Communications and Technology, and the National Audio-Visual Association, Committee PH7 Audiovisual Materials and Equipment was recently established to develop standards for audiovisual materials and equipment. While it may be expected that there will be some overlap with other PH committees, the general orientation of PH7 is directed toward the user rather than the manufacturer. One of its first considerations, for instance, is the labeling of filmstrips. Raymond Wyman, University of Massachusetts, who is chairman of the AECT Committee on Technical Standards, is also chairman of PH7.

Many of the technical standards developed by ANSI committees pertain to the production of microforms, but, as voluntary standards, they have yet to become fully adopted by producers. Libraries must continue to examine incoming micropublications for photographic quality and physical condition.[22] *The Evaluations of Micropublications* was published by the Library Technology Program to serve as a handbook for the library/consumer and as "required reading for all micropublishers . . . a first step toward the establishment of industry-wide standards."[23] The handbook, which is concerned with the evaluation of all aspects of micropublications except the literary or subject content, contains an extensive and useful bibliography which includes a list of pertinent ANSI standards. The Rare Book Libraries' Conference on Facsimiles, in response to concern over the rapid growth of reprint publishing, has approved for circulation a list of editorial standards for both microfilm and hard copy facsimiles.[24]

The Library Technology Program (LTP) of the American Library Association recently tested eight cassette recorders in order to determine if the premium price of heavy duty equipment was justified and to identify specific data by which cassette tape recorders could be selected for library use.[25] It is expected that a further outcome of this project will be the postulation and writing of performance standards for this equipment. Other test programs are being planned from which performance standards may be derived. A most welcome sign of cooperative effort is seen in the 1970 agreement between the Library Technology Program and the Association for Educational Communications and Technology to jointly sponsor and finance the drafting of performance standards for audiovisual equipment.

STANDARDS FOR INFORMATION SYSTEMS

Because of the increasing interaction between computer and communication systems, there is a growing awareness of the need for consistent practice. Since standards for telecommunications technology and for information processing have evolved completely separate from each other, there have been significant differences which may be resolved in the future only by establishing a formal review of standards and coordination of procedures among those concerned.[26]

The *Federal Information Processing Standards Index* includes an annotated list of publications on federal information processing standards, a cross index of international, national, and federal standards, and brief descriptions of information processing standards activities.[27]

> The movement during the last decade or so for the creation of a national library and information system has brought into sharp focus the need for a central technical authority with responsibilities for the development of standards and techniques

> applicable broadly to library and information work. For lack of such an authority, we have seen the mushrooming growth of national-system proposals . . . and a variety of schemes for collecting, organizing, and communicating bibliographic and other literature-derived information. . . . Without some degree of standardization or provision for conversion, data files and programs developed at one installation are unlikely to be usable at another. . . .[28]

The committees of the American National Standards Institute provide one avenue for achieving the necessary standards. Another is the acceleration of the development of certain techniques in large and influential libraries, letting the resultant products provide de facto standards. Both methods may be necessary. "Not enough of our colleagues are aware of their individual need to share in this work, to give their wisdom and strength to it, to assure the swiftest application and the most effective utilization of new technology which only new standards can make possible."[29]

Sound Recordings

Gerald Gibson

Gerald Gibson is a music cataloger at the Library of Congress, Washington, D.C.

The technology to produce sound recordings (cylinder, disc, tape, and wire recordings) was first known in 1877. Furthermore, two men, working in separate parts of the world, simultaneously developed the theories that made this technology possible.

Charles Cros, a French poet-scientist-inventor, wrote a paper on April 18, 1877, describing his ideas for a process of recording and reproducing sound.[1] Possibly due to his lack of funds, Cros was unable to build a working model or acquire a patent on his concept of mechanical sound reproduction. Attempting to protect some possible future rights, he deposited a copy of his paper with the Académie des Sciences in Paris on April 30, 1877. Cros' ideas were made known in the publication *La Semaine du Clergé* on October 10, 1877, where his proposed machine was called the "phonograph."[2]

Thomas Edison, the American inventor, submitted an application for a patent on his "phonograph" (also Edison's name for the invention) on December 24, 1877. This patent, on a machine developed and completed between August and December, 1877, or between December 4 and 6, 1877 depending upon the source accepted, was granted on February 19, 1878.[3] As is obvious from the overlapping and vagueness of dates, along with the question of Edison's accessibility to the October issue of *La Semaine de*

Clergé, there is a continuing discussion of the actual inventor of the phonograph.*

The ideas governing the work of Cros and of Edison were very similar, with two notable differences: Cros specified the use of a disc while Edison used a cylinder; and Cros specified lamp-blacked glass and a photoengraving process while Edison used tinfoil.

Edison's machine was an instant success, with the Edison Speaking Machine Company being established in January, 1878, a month before Edison's patent was granted. However, the immediate success of the invention was shortlived for the apparatus had little use except as a novelty item. It required a practiced technician to record and to play back the results with anything approaching success; recording time was only slightly over a minute; and the tinfoil cylinders seldom lasted more than ten plays. Thus, as its initial novelty ended, the phonograph disappeared for a time.

Approximately ten years later the phonograph reappeared to stay. The first major improvement on it was patented in June, 1885, by Chichester A. Bell and Charles Tainter and consisted, among other things, of the use of wax in place of tinfoil for the recording surface of the cylinder. The second major advancement was the successful use of the lateral-cut disc made in 1887 by Emil Berliner. Finally, in 1899, Vladimir Poulsen developed the means to record on magnetic wire and tape. Thus, the basic methods to record sound as it is known today and the major elements of the modern recording industry were established. A more complete sequence of the events from 1877 to the advent of high-fidelity has been documented in Roland Gerlatt's *The Fabulous Phonograph: from tinfoil to high fidelity,* cited earlier.

The development of sound recording collections in libraries is not nearly so clear or so easily traced. Edison predicted in a June, 1878, issue of *North American Review* that the phonograph would benefit mankind in ten ways, among them: " . . . educational purposes: such as preserving the explanations made by a teacher so that the pupil can refer to them at any moment, . . . the teaching

*To complicate matters, some sources give varying dates of completion and/or patenting of Edison's invention. For example, the *Oxford English Dictionary* in its article on "phonograph" states " . . . phonograph . . . in 1877 (patented 30 July) . . . " but later states in the same article " . . . specific U.S. patent 24 Dec. [1877]." Neither date agrees with information available from the patent office.

of elocution, [and] phonographic books" for the blind. Also, editors of *Scientific American* had written, shortly after Edison's visit to their offices in December, 1877, that " . . . the voices of such singers as Parepa and Titiens [sic!] will not die with them, but will remain as long as the metal in which they may be embodied will last." In 1914, over forty years after the invention of the phonograph, a library journal, *The Public Librarian,* finally advocated the acceptance of the record in libraries.[4]

COLLECTIONS

One of the first collections to which the public had access was in the Salon du Phonographe, owned by the Pathé brothers and by no means a library. It was located on the Boulevard des Italiens in Paris and was opened in the mid-1890s. For the price of a few centimes, the public entered into an elegant salon, made their selection, and waited for the cylinder to be played for them on listening tubes. These tubes, a forerunner of present day headphones, were connected to a lower level work room where the recordings were stored and played by clerks. In many ways this procedure calls to mind the listening arrangements of some major collections of today.

The first officially recognized collection was established in Vienna in 1899. It was the Phonogramm-Archiv of the Akademie der Wissenschaft, organized by a physiologist, Sigmund von Exner.[5] The main reasons for the collection were to record and survey the languages and dialects of Europe, to record the music of primitive races for comparative study, and to record the voices of famous persons.[6]

The first known library collections were in the United States. Eric Cooper cites the first recordings in a library through a gift of vocal and operatic recordings " . . . to a university library before the First World War."[7] The first documented library collection known to the writer appeared in 1913 in the Public Library of St. Paul, Minnesota, the gift of a public spirited citizen. The collection numbered ninety-three recordings in 1915.[8] These two collections were limited in their use: the first to members of the university teaching staff, and the second to the use of the local school systems and civic clubs.

The August, 1915, issue of *Library Journal* was devoted entirely to music collections in public libraries in the United States. This issue cites five libraries which had sound recordings in their collections and gives a brief description of each. It also carried an article by R. R. Bowker entitled "Music Selection for Public Libraries" which included a section on sound recordings.[9]

The documentation of sound recording collections in academic libraries seems not to have taken place until they were well established. The first specific reference to academic library sound collections came 13 years after the August, 1915, *Library Journal* first mentioned public library sound collections. The 1928 issue of *Pierre Key's International Music Year Book* listed fifty-three academic institutions whose libraries had music collections, of which only twelve were cited as holding sound recordings:[10] Idaho State Normal School Library, 150 records; Grinnell College School of Music Library, 50 records; University of Kansas Library, 500 records; Bowdoin College Library, 300 records; Smith College Library, 300 records; Mount Holyoke College Library, 150 records; Wellesley College Library, 78 records; Minnesota State Normal School Library, 125 records; University of North Dakota, 300 records; Oberlin College Library, 150 records; State University of Oklahoma Library, 300 records; and University of South Dakota, 350 records. Some of the colleges and universities listed as having music collections but without recordings are Yale University School of Music, Oberlin Conservatory, Northwestern University School of Music, University of Illinois, Columbia University, Vassar College, and the Eastman School of Music. Information available from the schools in question indicates that the statements in the Key's *Year Book* concerning recording holdings appear to have been accurate.

Changes were slowly taking place. For example, Sibley Music Library of the Eastman School of Music, University of Rochester, did not have recordings at the date in question, but did have recordings long before their first accession book for recordings (late 1940s) indicates—possibly as early as 1930. The explanation given for this is that recordings were considered ephemera and as such were likely to be disposed of; therefore, the librarian was reluctant to make their presence official by accessioning or cataloging them. In addition to the "unofficial" presence of recordings in the library, many departments and classrooms at the Eastman School of Music held recordings for their own use. Similar situations appear to have existed at other schools.

Thus, it may be concluded that prior to 1928 there were few academic libraries in the United States which had official collections of musical recordings; and, since the majority of recordings are and have been of music, it seems to follow that there were virtually no nonmusic collections for this period. Possibly it was for this reason that the Carnegie Corporation of New York authorized in 1927 the preparation and distribution of "College Music Sets" for use in music study in liberal arts colleges. These sets included music scores, books on music, and music recordings. The first catalog of the "College Music Sets" was published in 1933, with further catalogs continuing until 1943.[11] The sets were distributed to 371 universities and liberal arts colleges, with each set being considered an entity within itself.[12]

From the information furnished by the major collections of today, only one, the University of Syracuse, dates its recordings collection from the "College Music Sets" as furnished by the Carnegie Corporation. None of the remaining major academic collections appear to date their holdings from this period. The majority of such collections—archival, references, and circulation—seem to have their official origins in the period immediately before or after the advent of long playing records in 1948, with an additional ten years elapsing before the collections were considered of enough importance to have special housing considerations in the construction of library buildings. William Greckel, investigating selected recordings collections in twelve colleges and universities, stated in 1969: ". . . no building over 10 years of age had included in its original plans any provision . . . for a recordings library."[13] If the twelve collections studied by Greckel and the dates furnished for official founding of collections which follow have any relationship to the events taking place elsewhere in the country, academic sound collections as serious and viable sources of information did not exist prior to the end of World War II.

Among the major collections officially established since 1945 are: Stanford University Archive of Recorded Sound, 1958; the Historical Sound Recordings Program of Yale University, 1961; the Archives of New Orleans Jazz at Tulane University, 1958; the Syracuse University Audio Archives, 1964 (this does not take into consideration the "College Music Sets" of the Carnegie Corporation, since no date of their receipt is established); and the library collection of the Eastman School of Music, Sibley Music Library, late 1940s.

Undoubtedly, there were recordings in colleges and universities and probably within a vast number of the libraries of these institutions before the advent of the long-playing record, but they were usually short-lived and appear to have been considered, in the majority of cases, to have had little lasting value and little official existence.

As seems to have been the case with many other nonbook materials, these "classroom collections" came into the library by the back door and were deposited there because the particular department could no longer process or circulate them, or because the teacher who had used them was no longer in the employment of the school. Frequently unrequested and unwanted, they came to the library and were adopted. Possibly this accounts to some extent for the lack of prepared defenses for the existence of academic library recordings as observed by Mr. Greckel.[14]

However, once these collections became a formal part of the library they began a period of rapid growth. To build a large collection of anything, regardless of its format, in twenty to twenty-five years is notable for any library; and yet it is not uncommon for the major academic sound collections across the country to number their holdings in the tens if not hundreds of thousands. Not all major collections are significant in view of their size. A number are considered major holdings because of comparative size of subject content and not total count. Subject areas of these collections cover the entire scope of sound producing sources: from music in all its form and characters to animal noises; from public speaking to dramatic readings; from sex research to political history; and from public speaking to the sounds of space.

A few of the major academic collections of today are:

Yale University's Historical Sound Recordings Program and its Music School Library collection—approximately 70,000 recordings in the fields of musical performances by composers, musical theater, dramatic recitations, literary readings, and classical music

Tulane University's Archive of New Orleans Jazz—approximately 17,000 recordings in the field of New Orleans Jazz

Stanford University's Archive of Recorded Sound and the Music Library Collections—approximately 115,000 recordings in the fields of classical music on 78 rpm discs, popular music on 78 rpm discs, folk music from many countries, spoken materials on a wide range of subjects by famous speakers, and classical music on long-playing records LP

Syracuse University's Audio Archives, its music library collection, and a circulating collection of spoken word and music materials—approximately 210,000 recordings in all fields with emphasis in Edison disc records

Indiana University's Archive of Traditional Music, the School of Music Library recordings, and the Institute of Sex Research mately 20,000 recordings with emphasis on documentary speech can music, spoken materials, Afro-American and African music, ethnic music in general, and sex research

Michigan State University's National Voice Archive—approximately 20,000 recordings with emphasis on documentary speech. The Laura Boulton Collection of Traditional and Liturgical Music at Columbia University—approximately 10,600 recordings and 60,000 feet of film, with worldwide emphasis and special stress on ethnology

The Eastman School of Music's Department of Recording Services and Sibley Music Library—approximately 65,000 recordings in all areas of music with emphasis in the fields of American classical music, western classical music, and instantaneous recordings of school concerts and recitals since 1934.

These examples of sound recording collections within the academic communities of the United States do not necessarily include all collections within a particular library or institutional system. Archival, circulating, and reference collections are included as they frequently fall within the jurisdiction of the library and, if not a formal part of the library, furnish the types of material and information which is expected from a library source today.*

ACCESSIBILITY

Many collections cited make their materials available on a very generous basis. Circulating collections may be borrowed from a period of overnight to two weeks with fines and circulation restrictions similar to collections in other formats within the library system. Reference collections are for use within the library, unless needed in a class by faculty or lecturing students, and are fre-

*For information concerning specific holdings, copying services, and user restrictions for these and other sound collections, see: *A Preliminary Directory of Sound Recordings Collections in the United States and Canada*, prepared by the Association for Recorded Sound Collections, 1967, and available from the New York Public Library at Lincoln Center; *A Directory of Ethnomusicological Sound Recording Collections in the United States and Canada*, available from the Society for Ethnomusicology, School of Music, at the University of Michigan, Ann Arbor; and The International Folk Music Council's "International Directory of Folk Music Record Archives" in volume 2 of *Recorded Sound*. All three directories carry information on private, public, and academic sources.

quently available to the entire academic community and/or non-institution persons. Archival and research collections have the same types of restrictions one would expect to find in any collection of rare or difficult to obtain materials: use is permitted when the listener has properly identified himself and his area of study. A letter of introduction is always in order if the user is unknown and will have numerous or extensive requests. Appointments are frequently required for work within most archival collections and in some reference collections, due to the limitations of space and equipment.

Playback equipment available for academic sound collections covers the entire range of commercial, custom-made, and amateur machines. Headphones are used, as a general rule, in order to conserve space and to reduce the noise pollution to other library patrons, but speaker auditions can generally be arranged. Most people responsible for collections state that stereo playback equipment is available, if the collection requires it. Disc and tape playbacks are available in most instances with some collections offering only open reel tape listening and others beginning to collect tape recordings in casette and cartridge containers. Articles for the evaluation of recording and playback equipment on a continuing basis may be found in periodicals, e.g., *American Record Guide, Audio, Consumers Bulletin, Consumer Reports, Gramophone, Hi Fi/Stereo Review, High Fidelity, Saturday Review,* and the *New York Times.* A clear and concise explanation of the basic aspects of sound equipment, with illustrations, can be found in the Music Library Association's *Manual of Music Librarianship* on pages 76–98.

Tape reproduction of a library's recordings is generally not allowed because of the numerous legal and ethical questions involved. If the listener feels he must have a copy of a given recording, written permission from the manufacturer and/or performer(s) and/or holder of rights to copyrighted works performed may be required for commercial recordings, and from the performer(s) and/or depositor for instantaneous recordings. The impact of copyright coverage of sound recordings (effective February, 1972) and its influence on library collections remains to be considered by lawyers, legal consultants, and library administrators. The legal question of dubbing of commercial recordings prior to the February, 1972, law is skillfully set forth by M. William Krasilovsky.[15] A brief discussion of the new law may be found in *Music Educators Journal,* February, 1972, on pages 69–71.

STAFFING

The majority of the collections in the United States do not have full-time staff members devoted to their operation, unless they are within the archive realm. Even archival collections must frequently share such personnel as director, catalogers, and sound engineers with other sections of the academic community. If the individual responsible for the collection is not assigned full time to his recording collection duties, the most frequently added position is that of music library director. If the director is serving in that capacity full time, he is most frequently head of a division of the music library or some other departmental library with subject emphasis, rather than a separate branch of the academic library system. Once again the exception to this is the archival collection. It will usually be a separate department designed to serve all subject areas of the university or college community. In either a full- or part-time position, the head of the sound collection most frequently has a strong background in music—a B.M. or B.A. in music, with an M.M. or M.A. in music history or musicology—and an M.S.L.S. from an accredited library school. It is becoming more and more frequent that one will also have a Ph.D. in some area of music research, most often musicology. The obvious question that arises is why should music be such an important part of the qualifications for the head of a sound collection. The answer is related to an earlier statement: the majority of recordings available are musical in nature, which obviously requires a musical background. If the collection has a subject emphasis other than music, then most certainly the value of musical knowledge is replaced by that of the subject area emphasized.

In all but the rarest cases, the cataloger for the sound collection is either the director "under another hat" or a music cataloger with multiple duties. In either case, the education of the cataloger is similar to that of the director, with additional emphasis in the area of advanced cataloging. Most successful catalogs are based upon the *Anglo-American Cataloging Rules*, the American Library Association/Music Library Association/Library of Congress rules for cataloging music and phonorecords, or combinations and derivations of them. In any case, few librarians accept all rules from either or both sources. The most frequently ignored or altered rule (rule 5) is that of limiting the number of composer/author–title added/analytic entries.[16] In a survey taken in the late 1960s by the Phonorecords Analytics Committee of the Music Library Association, the vast majority of record libraries replying stated that they did not comply with the rule in question and that they did attempt, as funds permitted, to make composer/author–title entries for each selection on a recording. The majority of those who were complying with rule 5 were doing so because of cataloging policies of their various institutions and not because of agreement with the rule.

CATALOGING

The average sound collection catalog consists of cards from a number of sources. The major source is the Card Division of the Library of Congress. The National Union Catalog has included records since 1953 in a separate set of volumes entitled *Music and Phonorecords*.[17] Unfortunately, there are several problems when relying upon this source for card copy. The first is that the Library of Congress has not received all records available in the United States, since the majority of their acquisitions come from copyright deposits, and recordings were not covered by federal copyright law until February, 1972. Virtually all recordings for which LC cards were available prior to 1972 had been given to them by the manufacturer.

The second problem in relation to LC card copy is that the congressional library does not make the composer/author–title analytics desired by many libraries due to the current cataloging rules and practices used for cataloging sound recordings. This is especially lamentable when one realizes that current rules call for a cutoff of composer/author–title added entries at or about three (similar to aforementioned rule 5) and that the average long-playing disc has at least seven titles. This problem has been repeatedly discussed at local and national Music Library Association meetings. A survey carried out by members of the association determined that most libraries do want additional entries but cannot afford to make them available. Numerous solutions have been offered, among them: (1) a wait-and-see attitude towards the LC Machine-Readable Catalog (MARC) and what it might offer, even though it appears that it may require several years to properly program for music and related subjects;[18] (2) shared cataloging, although thus far only one library, Oberlin Conservatory Library, Oberlin, Ohio, is known to make its cataloging available on a cost basis, and (3) an independent commercial venture called "Cards for Records," now offering several hundred card sets.[19] (Information is available from: "Cards for Records"; 310 West 86th Street; New York, New York.) Of the three solutions offered above, the last two are intended as supplements to LC card stock and not as a replacement for it.

The second major source for recording catalog copy is original cataloging by each library. This is at best a slow and expensive method and, since few libraries have the tools, qualified catalogers, or funds to search and establish the uniform titles and main entries necessary for a successful music/record catalog, it frequently produces almost unusable results. Original cataloging of records is greatly complicated by the haphazard manner in which many recording companies identify the performed selections. It is not unknown for a selection to be both improperly identified on the record jacket and absent from the disc. Reissues are seldom marked as such and are frequently cited as new recordings, creating a problem similar to a new printing being listed as a new edition. The practice of virtually all record companies not to give any information concerning date or place of recording or, prior to 1972 copyright coverage, release date, further complicates the attempts to catalog one's own recordings.

It is difficult to have complete composer/author–title analytics for the sound collection. The catalog which carries other information, such as complete performer entries, 78 rpm matrix numbers, recording or release dates, liner note annotators, translators of texts and notes, timings of works, previously issued copies of this same recorded performance, or a break down of record manufacturer numerical codes is not only a rarity but the dream of many record collection administrators and their users. Geoffrey Cuming's article, "Problems of Record Cataloging," covered the topic extremely well.[20]

Information available about the nonclassical music and nonmusic collections indicates that there are virtually no accepted standards in degree or type of cataloging being practiced. What is workable in one collection is inadequate in another. It is true that the Library of Congress is making card copy available in all fields of commercial recording which are furnished to them by record manufacturers; but this reaches few of the needs in the fields of ethnomusicology, speech, drama, language, or popular music. The information on LC cards in these subject areas is considered less satisfactory than that for classical or art music because the vast majority in the former contain selections numbering far beyond that permitted for added and analytic entries. Furthermore, it is needless to say that neither the Library of Congress nor the various cooperative or commercial cataloging ventures can furnish cataloging for instantaneous recordings.

CLASSIFICATION

The classification of sound recordings is, if possible, in even more doubt than cataloging. Gordon Stevenson covered the problem very well in his article "Classification Chaos."[21] At that time (1963), questionnaire responses received from 392 libraries with record collections indicated several classification/shelving systems, but only 37 libraries were knowingly using systems established elsewhere. Information available today seems to imply a continuation of this policy. Numerous classification systems are in use with a slightly higher percentage of collections utilizing the commercially assigned manufacturer name and number or accession number for shelving purposes. The collections of an archival or research nature tend to prefer manufacturer name and number shelving because it gives added access to their collections in addition to their own catalogs. If an arbitrary number or location device, such as a class or accession number, can be bypassed, then commercial and discographical listings can be utilized. The large and medium size collections of a reference and circulating nature appear to prefer accession-number shelving due to its conservation of space and its ease of application. The smaller collections, and those of all sizes that wish to encourage browsing, favor class numbers. Classification systems are frequently based upon a modified Dewey or LC class system, with some preference shown toward the system that is in general use throughout the library system. Special classification schemes for the sound collection are used from time to time, but it appears to be generally held that a system with some carryover from the rest of the library is desired. Numerous articles have been written both pro and con on classification, shelving by accession number, and by manufacturer name and number: P. T. Barkey, "Phonorecord Filing Systems"; G. A. Marco and W. M. Roziewski, "Shelving Plans for LP Records"; J. Coover, "Computers, Cataloging and Co-operation"; and Gordon Stevenson's "Classification Chaos," mentioned above.[22] Parts of the following two books, mentioned earlier, also deal with classification: E. T. Bryant, *Music Librarianship: A Practical Guide* and The International Association of Music Libraries' *Gramophone Record Libraries*.[23]

SELECTION

Selection and acquisition of commercial recordings is a problem of great concern and second only to cataloging and classification in magnitude. The difficulties of determining what has been recorded, what is currently available, and where and at what price it can be obtained consume much of most collection directors' time. To the uninitiated it is a simple task. All one needs to do is obtain a current *Schwann Catalog*, make a decision, and give the order to the local dealer.[24] Realistically, it is hardly as simple as that. At present there are three *Schwann Catalogs*: the standard monthly catalog; the biannual *Schwann* supplement that has all monophonic recordings in it, as well as imported, noncurrent pop records, spoken, etc.; and the occasional *Schwann Artist Issue* which indexes the long-playing records then available by performer. The librarian must know which, if any, of these has the information wanted and needed.

There are many labels generally available in the United States which are not included in the *Schwann Catalogs*—labels that contain materials the larger companies feel are not financially feasible for them to release, but which many educational institutions feel are a necessary part of their collections. Also, there are other labels that have limited and/or regional distribution which *Schwann* does not include, once again excluding materials frequently desired by academic libraries. Nor do *Schwann's* catalogs include the many foreign labels, some imported into this country in limited quantities, which contain materials of genuine value to the United States' institutions of higher education. Unfortunately, current catalogs take no notice of the previous twenty-four years of long-playing recordings deleted from current catalogs, the seventy-plus years of 78 rpm discs recordings, or the countless university press recordings that continue to appear. How then do the major collections locate recordings and their sources? It is a consensus of opinion that no firm bibliographic control of sound recordings exists, necessitating an on-the-job apprenticeship approach, whereby one proceeds to add a few labels, catalogs, and addresses as one becomes more familiar with this special format of information.

Bibliographic aids particularly important for the selection of recordings are: the *Schwann catalogs* mentioned above; the *One-Spot publications*; *Bielefelder Katalog*; *the Diapason*; *Gramaphone Classical Record Catalog*; *The World's Encyclopedia of Recorded Music* and its supplements; the Library of Congress *Music and Phonorecords Catalog*;[25] and the numerous speciality discographies in the fields of composers, performers and specific subjects, such as James Coover's and Richard Colvig's *Medieval and Renaissance Music on Long-Playing Records*, Victor Girard's *Vertical Cut Cylinders and Discs*, and Allen Koenigsberg's *Edison Cylinder Records, 1899–1912.*[26]

In addition to these and other commercial catalogs, the majority of record companies issue catalogs generally available upon request, as do importers of foreign labels. Some label catalogs, such as *Musical Heritage*, and importers, such as Peters International, are far more than conveniences; for if the labels in question are not included in previously mentioned standard sources, and many are not, the latter two catalogs must be obtained to know what is available, the price, and where it can be obtained. It is generally accepted that if a label is not in *Schwann*'s monthly catalog, record shops will probably not have it nor know where it might be obtained. Additional information on catalogs, lists, and sources are given here in the appendixes bibliography.

After determining what is or what was available, the person in charge of selection must decide which version will best suit the needs of a specific clientele and established collection. There are often two or more recorded versions of each recording the average library will want to acquire. Many records are purchased on the basis of reviews from such periodicals as *American Record Guide, High Fidelity, Library Journal*, and the *New York Times*. Access to these and other reviews is greatly enhanced by Kurtz Myers' and Richard S. Hill's book, *Record Ratings*, an index to numerous record reviewing sources.[27] It is kept up to date by Mr. Myers' regular column in the Music Library Association's journal, *Notes*. A second edition of *Record Ratings* is currently in preparation.

Replies to questions concerning dealers, jobbers, services desired, and order procedures were in general so vague and inconclusive that statements can hardly be made with anything approaching authority. Appendixes 1 and 2 furnish information available to the author concerning record companies and dealers/jobbers. Mary Pearson furnishes some additional information on the subject in her book *Recordings in the Public Library*, although some materials included have proven to be outdated.[28] Of special note in Pearson's book are the names and addresses of record companies and dealers in all subject areas, including music, diction, literature, grammar, dictation, ethnic, drama, children's materials, and foreign language.

PRESERVATION AND STORAGE

Preservation and storage seem to produce the greatest amount of agreement in principle and some of the widest divergence in practice. Almost everyone with whom these were discussed agreed with and supported the conclusions of Pickett and Lemcoe as presented in *Preservation and Storage of Sound Recordings.*[29] Yet, there were no collection spokesmen who would state that they followed completely the authors' recommendations for shelving and storage. The most commonly ignored points were the Pickett and Lemcoe recommendations concerning (1) the storage of tape recordings and the dangers to them of magnetic fields and metal shelving, and (2) their recommendations for shelving and housing acetate discs to protect them from infection by fungus.[30]

Certainly, the past century has brought vast movement and progress in the technology of producing sound recordings—not only in methods of cataloging, classification, or preservation, but also in accessibility and quality. Indeed, at this writing, there seem to be limitless opportunities for future exploration in the media of recorded sound.

APPENDIX 1: RECORD COMPANIES

A list of addresses for record companies that do not appear in the U.S. section of the *International Billboard Buyer's Guide:* Music, Records, Tapes (12th annual ed., New York: Billboard Publications, 1971–72).

Accompanists Unlimited, Inc.
P. O. Box 5109
Grosse Point Branch, Mich. 48236

A. C. McClurg and Co.
2121 Landmeier Rd.
Elk Grove, Ill. 60007

Africambaince
B. P. 138
Doula, Cameroon

African Music Society
P. O. Box 138
Roodepoort Nr. Johannesburg, Union of South Africa

AMA *see* International Library of African Music

American Indian Center
411 N. LaSalle
Chicago, Ill. 60607

American Indian Sound Chief
713 N. W. 33rd St.
Oklahoma City, Okla. 73100

American Sound Chief
216 W. Kentucky St.
Anadarko, Okla. 73005

Andre Emmerich Gallery
18 E. 77th St.
New York, N. Y. 10021

A.R.E.A. (Les Applications et Realisations electriques et acoustiques
16, rue La Fantaine
16e Paris, France

Ars Nova/Ars Antiqua
606 Raleigh Pl., SE
Washington, D.C. 20043

Arteco
42, rue de Paradis
10e Paris, France

Arturo Toscanini Society
Box 1265
Dumas, Tex. 79029

Biblia *see* Record and Tape Sales (appendix 2)

Boekhandel Pegasus
Hoogstraat 143
Rotterdam, The Netherlands 77401

Book Records, Inc.
222 E. 46th St.
New York, N. Y. 10017

Boston Music Co.
116 Boyston St.
Boston, Mass. 02116

Boston Records
see Boston Music Co.

Budget Sound
222 W. Orange Grove Ave.
Burbank, Cal. 91502

Calig *see* Record and Tape Sales (appendix 2)

Calypso Records
Port of Spain
Trinidad

Cameo *see* Cameo-Parkway

Cameo-Parkway
309 S. Broad St.
Philadelphia, Pa. 19107

Cannabia-Sativa
12 Penny Ln.
Needles, Cal. 92363

Cantemos Records
P. O. Box 492
Taos, N. M. 87571

Canyon Records
Arizona Recording Productions
6050 N. 3rd St.
Phoenix, Ariz. 85012

Capri *see* Polydor (appendix 2)

Celebrity Records
68–34 Fleet St.
Forrest Hills, L. I., N. Y. 11375

Collosseum Records
Oakwood Rd.
Norwalk, Conn. 06856

Commodore Records, Inc.
136 E. 42nd St.
New York, N. Y. 10001

Cabot *see* HRS Record Co.

Concert Hall Record Club, Ltd.
Concert Hall House
St. Ann's Crescent
London SW 18, England

Concert Series
see Washington Univ. Records

Cornell Univ. Records
Cornell Univ.
Ithaca, N. Y. 14850

Cornet Recording Co.
375 Broad St.
Columbus, O. 43215

Cuca Label
R.L.P. Record Co.
Baraboo, Wis. 53913

Cycnus *see* Societé Phonographique Philips

Donemus A/V *see* C. F. Peters Corp. (appendix 2)

Dorian Records
1815 N. Kenmore Ave.
Hollywood, Cal. 90028

Droll Yankees, Inc.
Providence, R. I. 02906

East African Records, Ltd.
P. O. Box 587
Nairobi, Kenya

East-West Recordings
see East-West Press

East-West Press
East-West Center
Honolulu, Hawaii 96813

Elektra Stratford Record Corp.
361 Bleeker St.
New York, N. Y. 10014

E. M. S. Publishing Co.
905 Gaffield Pl.
Evanston, Ill. 60201

EMS Records
see E.M.S. Publishing Co.

Enchante Records
Gary, Ind. 46401

English Folk Dance and Folk Song Society
Cecil Sharp House
2 Regent Park Rd.
London NW1, England

Ethnographic Museum
VIII Koenyvea Kalman-Korueut 40
Budapest, Hungary

Euphonic Records
357 Leighton Dr.
Ventura, Cal. 93001

Eurodisc *see* Record and Tape Sales (appendix 2)

Fairmount *see* Cameo-Parkway

Festival Foundation, Inc.
119 W. 57th St.
New York, N. Y. 10019

Ficker Records
Old Greenwich, Conn. 06870

Fidulafon *see* Record and Tape Sales (appendix 2)

Folk Promotions
1549 Lee St.
Charleston, W. Va. 25301

Gate Five Records
see Source Records

Golden Crest
220 Broadway
Huntington Station, L. I., N. Y. 11746

Gospel Recordings, Inc.
124 Witmer St.
Los Angeles, Cal. 90026

Greek Sacred and Secular Music Society, Inc.
1324 S. Normandie Ave.
Los Angeles, Cal. 90006

Henry Mielke Co.
242 W. 86th St.
New York, N. Y. 10028

Herwin Records
P. O. Box 306
Glen Cove, N. Y. 11542

The HRS Record Co.
Ottenheimer Publishers, Inc.
1330 Reistertown Rd.
Baltimore, Md. 21208

IFAN *see* Institut Français d'Afrique Noire

Indian Chant Records
Box 63
Flagstaff, Ariz. 86001

Indian House
Box 472
Taos, N. M. 87571

Institut Français d'Afrique Noire
Dakar, Senegal

Institute of Ethnomusicology
Univ. of California
Los Angeles, Cal. 90024

Instituto Nacional de Cultras y Bellas Artes
Apartado 6238
Caracas, Venezuela

International Library of African Music
P. O. Box 138
Roodepoort, Transvaal,
South Africa

International Record Collectors Club
P. O. Box 1811
Bridgeport, Conn. 06601

Kokusai Bunka Shinkoki
Osaka Shosen Bldg.
2 Kyobolshi 1-chome
Chouku, Tokyo, Japan

The Library of Congress
Recorded Sound Section
Music Division
Washington, D. C. 20540

Link Records
Box 7
Salisbury, Rhodesia

Mambo Press
Box 779
Gwelo, Rhodesia

Markay Enterprises
42 Maplewood Ave.
Maplewood, N. J. 07040

Marlboro Recording Society
1430 Spruce St.
Philadelphia, Pa. 19102

Minnesota Historical Society
Central Ave. at Cedar St.
St. Paul, Minn. 55101

MK Records *see* Victor Kamlin Book Store (appendix 2)

Monogram Records, Inc.
1650 Broadway
New York, N. Y. 10001

The Museum for the History of Music
Slottsbacken 6
Stockholm C, Sweden

Musica Viva
Bayerische Rundfunk
Munich 2
Rundfunkplatz, W. Germany

Music in America *see* Society for the Preservation of the American Musical Heritage

Music Research, Inc.
2023 N. Woodstock St.
Arlington 7, Va. 22210

Musurgia Records
P. O. Box 242
Jackson Heights
New York, N. Y. 10072

Now Records *see* Society for the Preservation of the American Musical Heritage

OASI Records
1236 60th St.
Brooklyn, N. Y. 11219

Oberlin College Records
Oberlin Conservatory of Music
Oberlin, O. 44074

Ottenheimer Publishing, Inc. *see* The HRS Record Co.

Paul Lazare
Muhlendamm 41
Hamburg 22, W. Germany

Peabody Museum
Harvard Univ.
Cambridge, Mass. 02139

Penn State Music Series *see* Penn State Univ. Pr.

Penn State Univ. Pr.
University Park, Pa. 16802

Pleiades Records *see* Southern Illinois Univ. Pr.

Qualiton Records, Ltd.
39–29 58th St.
Woodside, N. Y. 11377

Record Album
254 W. 81st St.
New York, N. Y. 10024

Resonances
6, rue de l'Oratoire
Paris 1e, France

Ricordi *see* Arteco

Rikkskonserter
Sturegatan 22
Stockholm 0, Sweden

Rivoli/Tikva
1650 Broadway
New York, N. Y. 10019

R.L.P. Record Co.
Baraboo, Wis. 53913

Rococo Records *see* Ross Court and Co. (appendix 2)

Sa Gomes Studio
Port of Spain
Trinidad

Seghers
12, rue Cavallotti
Paris 18e, France

Societé Phonographique Philips
6, rue Jenner
Paris 13e, France

The Society for the Preservation of the American Musical Heritage
P. O. Box 4244
Grand Central Station
New York, N. Y. 10017

Society of Participating Artists
404 Broadway
Saratoga Springs, N. Y. 12866

Source Records
330 University Ave.
Davis, Cal. 93616

Southern Illinois Univ. Pr.
Carbondale, Ill. 62901

Soviet Long Playing Records
V/O "Mezhduanrodnaya Kniga"
Moscow G-200, USSR
see also Victor Kamlin Book Store (appendix 2)

Swiss Composers League
Communaute de travail
11 bis, Ave. du Graumont
Lousanne, Suisse

T'Aidonia A. H. Records
269 W. 27th St.
New York, N. Y. 10001

Testament Records
123 N. Swall Dr.
Los Angeles, Cal. 90048

Tetragrammaton
359 N. Canon Dr.
Beverly Hills, Cal. 90201

Tikva *see* Rivoli/Tikva

Time
101 W. 57th St.
New York, N. Y. 10019

Toshiba *see* Kikka Trading Co. (appendix 2) and Peters International (appendix 2)

Tou-Sea/Bell
1776 Broadway
New York, N. Y. 10018

Tradition Records, Inc.
80 W. 11th St.
New York, N. Y. 10003

Veritas Records
1340 Connecticut Ave. NW.
Washington, D. C. 20036
(25% off list to libraries)

Violoncello Society, Inc.
119 W. 57th St.
New York, N. Y.

Virtuso
222 E. 135th Pl.
Chicago, Ill. 60627

Visaphon
78 Freiburg 1 Br.
Merzhauser Str. 110
Postfach 1160, W. Germany

Washington Univ. Records
Washington Univ. Dept. of Music
6500 Forsyth
St. Louis, Mo. 63130

Wattle Records
254 Little Collins St.
Victoria, Australia

Wergo Schallplatten GmbH
Weihergarten
Mainz, W. Germany

Western Michigan Univ. Aural Pr.
Kalamazoo, Mich. 49001

APPENDIX 2: RECORD DEALERS

This selected list of dealers in the United States, Canada, Europe, and Japan does not constitute a recommendation for their services or discounts, nor does the absence of a particular dealer constitute a negative recommendation. The information furnished by dealers concerning discounts, services, and specific comments was given in the spring of 1969 and unless otherwise noted, applies only to libraries. Services offered may change.

A and A Books and Records
351 Yonge St.
Toronto, Canada
Discount: 30%, imports excepted
Specials: classical, spoken, all other catagories; sheet music. More information on request.

Abbey Records
All Saint's Passage
Cambridge, England

Aktiebolaget Waidele
P. O. Box 240
S–401 24 Goteborg 1, Sweden
Discount: 10%; "fair amount," 15%. Records delivered promptly on receipt of payment
Specials: classical music, Scandinavian folk and spoken. "We run a specialized service for libraries in this country and would like to expand it to other countries."

AMA Distributors
22 E. 17th St.
New York, N.Y. 10003

Applause Productions, Inc.
85 Longview Rd.
Port Washington, N.Y. 11050
Discount: 15% on 6 or more records
Specials: spoken word, poetry, literature, other forms. Catalogs on request.

Artist Direct
Blue Mounds, Wis. 53517
Discount: 25% off list to libraries
Specials: never before recorded works of J. S. Bach, Liszt, Busoni.

Bärenreiter & Neuwerk
3500 Kassel-Wilhelmshone
Heinrich-Schültz-Allee 35,
W. Germany
Discount: not mentioned
Specials: speech, classified folk, European labels. Special labels: Barenreiterp Musicahon, Cantate, Valois, Muza, Qualiton, UNESCO.
Catalogs with special record offers on request.

Bremen House, Inc.
218 E. 86th St.
New York, N.Y. 10028
Discount: 20% on orders of 25 or more placed at one time
Specials: records and cassettes imported from Austria, Germany, Switzerland.

Cambridge Music Shop
All Saint's Passage
Cambridge, England
Discount: most British labels free of purchase tax; orders over value of 20 (?) are post and packing free, sent within 7 days
Specials: classical records only: specials in choral and early keyboard music, specialists labels, continental recordings, some spoken word. complete Abbey catalog; continental labels not in stock take 6–8 weeks to

obtain. Will furnish materials information on above, and include name on mailing lists for records and sheet music.

C. F. Peters, Corp.
373 Park Ave. S.
New York, N.Y. 10016

Chesterfield Music Shops, Inc.
12 Warren St.
New York, N.Y. 10007
Discount: varies with yearly volume, no conditions regarding size of each order; special rates/ sales catalogs list thousands of specific records, name brands, at special net prices equal to as much as 80% off
Specials: supplying just about all the records that a library wants; 100% mail order, records are fresh.

Collectors' Corner
63 Monmouth St.
London WC 2, England
Discount: net list price, free of British purchase tax; orders over $50 post/shipment free
Specials: classical repertoire, good coverage of vocal and historical issues; large range of European imports. Can usually advise on availability of most obscure operatic matters. Carry certain stocks of 78rpm of historical interest, vocal and spoken word records, and instrumental items of special interest (composer as performer, etc.).

Country Sales
311 E. 37th St.
New York, N.Y. 10016

Discount Records, Inc.
800 White Plains Rd.
Scarsdale, N.Y. 10583

Discurio
9 Shepher St.
London W1, England

Diskothek
4400 Münster/Westfalen
Schliessfach 1064, W. Germany

Disques Ades
141, rue Lafayette
Paris 9e, France
Discount: special 35%
Specials: contemporary music, theatre, poetry, literature, books and records for children

Domaine du Disque
320, Galerie de la Toison d'Or
Bruxelles 5e, Belgium

Educational Audio Visual, Inc.
Pleasantville, N.Y. 10570
Discount: not mentioned
Specials: producers of AV materials for schools in the fields of music, literature, social studies and foreign language. Material is mainly record/filmstrip corresponding sets. Also produce records and tapes independently.

Educational Record Sales
157 Chambers St.
New York, N.Y. 10007

E. Ploix-Musique
48, rue St. Placide
Paris 6e, France

The French Book Guild
595 Madison Ave.
New York, N.Y. 10022
Discount: not mentioned
Specials: encyclopedia Sonore, French records in all fields, poetry, theater, history, song catalogs.

Goldsmith's Music Shops, Inc.
401 W. 42nd St.
New York, N.Y. 10036

Discount: as listed in catalogs
Specials: foreign language, music, and spoken materials. Catalogs on request.

Sam Goody, Inc.
46-35 54th Rd.
Maspeth, N.Y. 11378

Gramola
Winter and Co.
Wien I, Graben 16, Austria
Discount: not mentioned. classical music, operas, chamber music; 78rpms. "We have the largest program music on classics in Austria."

Hi-Fi Record Review and Tape Service
Dept. S.D.
New York, N.Y. 10016
"Will search for hard to find records/tapes. Need title/ manufacturer name-number. . . ."

Hofmeister
Bielefeld
Oberstr. 15, W. Germany

Houghton Mifflin Co.
53 W. 43rd St.
New York, N.Y. 10036 (for address in your area, see company representative)
Discount: 1–4 records, 25%; 5–24, records, 33⅓%; 25 records, 40%
Specials: Caedmon catalogs and other information.

Jerocho Centre di Disque Chretien
31, boul. Latour-Mauborg
Paris 7e, France

Kikka Trading Co., Inc.
7–9 Asagaya Minami 1-chome
Suginami-ku
Tokyo 166, Japan
Discount: 40% on domestic label (retail price)
Specials: traditional Japanese music, contemporary, folk, pop. Labels include: Denon, King, Crown, Toshiba Nivico, Polydor, Teichiku, Minorupon. Delivery time, 2 weeks after payment.

King Karol Records
Mail Order Dept.
P. O. Box 629
Times Square Station
New York, N.Y. 10036
Discount: \$1.98 for \$1.55; \$2.50 for \$1.85; \$2.98 for \$2.20; \$3.98 for \$2.75; \$4.98 for \$3.35; \$5.98 for \$4.15; \$6.98 for \$4.65; tapes, 25% off list. More information on request.
Specials: all orders in U.S., A.P.O., and F.P.O. orders free of mailing and handling charges.

Lido-Musique S.A.
78, Ave. des Champs-Elysees
Paris 8e, France
Discount: 10%
Specials: "We are the most important store in Europe, only records; . . . all French records"

Lyric Sales, Inc.
P. O. Box 20307
Los Angeles, Cal. 90006
Discount: 30% to all libraries on all labels *except* Telefunken, L'oiseau-lyre, Argo; all other labels listed in catalogs (Lyric Sales, Inc.) and sold at prices listed therein
Specials: large selection of imports from 71 countries, including many emerging African nations. Usually ship orders within 1 week of order; pay postage on orders over \$50. Catalogs.

Peters International, Inc.
600 8th Ave.
New York, N.Y. 10001

Point Park College Recording Series
Wood Street and Blvd. of the Allies
Pittsburgh, Pa. 15222
Discount: not mentioned
Specials: American wind symphony orchestras commissioned contemporary works for wind orchestras; available with scores thru American Wind Symphony Orchestra Editions of the C. F. Peters Corp.

Polydor S. A.
Export Dept.
2, rue Cavallotti
Paris 13e, France
Discount: not mentioned
Specials: classical, jazz, pop records; children's records with books; literary records

Qualiton Records, Ltd.
39–29 58th St.
Woodside, N.Y. 11377
Discount: list price
Specials: special library price of $4.78; in case of 10 or more copies of a record, an additional discount of 10%.

Record Album
254 W. 81st St.
New York, N.Y. 10024

Record and Tape Sales
821 Broadway
New York, N.Y. 10003

The Record Hunter
507 5th Ave.
New York, N.Y. 10017

Ross Court and Co.
3244 Yonge St.
Toronto 23, Ontario, Canada

Sam the Record Man (mail order)
347 Yonge St.
Toronto, Ontario, Canada
Discount: 30%
Specials: all types of music

Smolian Sound
310 W. 86th St.
New York, N.Y. 10024

Valiant Instructional Materials
237 Washington Ave.
Hackensack, N.J. 07601

Victor Kamlin Book Store.
1410 Columbia Rd. NW
Washington, D.C. 20009

Zalo Productions
P. O. Box 913
Bloomington, Ind. 47401
Discount: 10% on volume only (entire series)
Specials: flute recitals, solo records series, and interpretation series which includes guides on technical discussions of performance.

Slides

Wolfgang M. Freitag
Betty Jo Irvine

Wolfgang M. Freitag is Librarian, Fine Arts Library, Fogg Art Museum, Harvard University. Betty Jo Irvine is Fine Arts Librarian, Indiana University.

The earliest noted academic slide libraries in the United States date from the 1880s and include those at Bryn Mawr College, Cornell University, Dartmouth College, Princeton University, the University of Illinois, and the University of Michigan. It was not until 1884, however, that George Eastman patented the roll film system; consequently, collections begun prior to this time depended upon the "lantern slide" which is a 3¼″ x 4″ slide with glass used as the medium upon which the image is printed. Lantern slides dating from the seventeenth century were originally hand-painted, with many of the older ones being works of art in their own right. The glass lantern slide is still a part of many collections in the United States that were established before 1940.

In the 1930s color dye processes were perfected by Leopold D. Mannes and Leopold Godowsky, Jr. in collaboration with the Kodak Research Laboratory.[1] The result of this work was the introduction of the three-color Kodachrome film process, the perfection of which led to a wide acceptance of 35mm or 2″ x 2″ slides. During the eighty years from 1880 to 1960, only the 1940s and 1950s witnessed a significant rise in the initial establishment of slide collections. The period after 1960 should also reveal a large number of beginning collections which will have matured enough for documentation by 1980. This increase is very likely due to the added benefit of the color slide and the fact that it is far less expensive to produce than the standard lantern slide. Consequently, it was financially more feasible for colleges, museums, and universities to begin their collections after World War II. These trends might also be indicative of the steady rise of art historical studies as more than a mere adjunct to the liberal arts curriculum in the United States.

The use of slides is a fundamental and integral part of every fine arts and art history curriculum in colleges, universities, art schools, and colleges of architecture. Most art museums also have slide collections which are heavily used by the curatorial staff for lectures or by nearby academic institutions whose own collections are inadequate. For example, the Art Institute of Chicago and the Metropolitan Museum of Art in New York City have slide loan procedures (fees are charged on either an institutional or individual basis) for institutions within their area. The study of fine arts, however, is multidisciplinary and includes research in history, literature, philosophy, religion, and the sciences. There are over five thousand art, history, and science museums in the United States; eight hundred college and university art departments; and thousands of colleges and universities which include the arts in their humanities programs. The vast majority of institutions which focus on educational programs for the general public or for students make use of slides.

Slide libraries, like other audiovisual collections such as collections of architectural drawings, photographs, and maps, were often begun outside the library setting by individuals who had been gathering materials in a haphazard manner. A box of 35mm or 2″ x 2″ slides sitting on someone's desk has been expanded to a collection of over seventy-five thousand slides before the users recognized and considered the problems engendered by the lack of standardized organization and management principles such as those applied to "book libraries." Even the process of building a quality collection of color and black and white slides often suffered from the pressing demand for vast quantities of slides for research and teaching purposes. Like print materials in university or research libraries, slide collections are rarely weeded because the older material often provides definitive visual data for destroyed works of art including architectural structures, or for book illustrations (many slides are copied directly from book plates) which are no longer available. Consequently, it is not surprising that there are slide libraries of several hundred thousand slides in some of the major American museums and universities.

There are hundreds of smaller collections being established or nearing the ranks of major slide libraries as they expand to large proportions.

Unlike the costly acquisitions necessary in building book collections, slide libraries can double or triple within a few years with a relatively small expenditure per slide. It is not uncommon to find a collection to which ten thousand slides are being added annually. What is often neglected, however, is the cost involved in efficiently organizing and maintaining these visual resources. The low costs of making and allowing initial space for their storage has all too frequently reinforced careless organization. By the time a collection reaches one hundred thousand slides, the expense involved in reorganizing, classifying, recataloging, relabeling, and acquiring adequate storage and retrieval facilities for slides, in addition to hiring a qualified staff, is often beyond the reach of both school and museum. Guidelines are needed during the mushrooming phase itself so that the slide collection can be developed within the framework of standardized and systematized library procedures—either those specifically designed for a slide library or those adapted from book library techniques.

The rapid expansion of materials during the 1960s demanded formal notice of the complex nature of visual resources and of the necessity to establish valid criteria for their effective utilization and development. These criteria need to be formally stated and made available to individuals in art, audiovisual, library, and all other instructional media fields.

MAJOR ACADEMIC SLIDE LIBRARIES

The major academic slide libraries in the United States are located primarily on the East Coast and in the Midwest, with the average size ranging between fifty thousand to sixty thousand slides, and a "major" collection being defined as one having one hundred thousand or more slides. These figures are based upon the data gathered in preparation to write a manual for slide libraries and are discussed summarily in Irvine's *College and Research Libraries* article.[2] Slide libraries with one hundred thousand slides are located at Bryn Mawr College, the University of Cincinnati, and the University of Minnesota, with the largest academic collection being that at Columbia University, which contains approximately 285,000 slides. Other collections falling within the range of a major collection include Cornell University, Harvard University, Indiana University, the Institute of Fine Arts of New York University, Oberlin College, Princeton University, the

University of California at Los Angeles, the University of Chicago, the University of Illinois at Chicago Circle, the University of Michigan, the University of Pennsylvania, the University of Wisconsin, and Yale University.

Only three major slide collections were established after 1940, with the latest initiated in 1953 at the University of California at Los Angeles. As a consequence of their early origins, many of these slide libraries still have lantern slides. Yale University not only has a sizable collection of lantern slides but is also engaged in having them made at their audiovisual center on campus. Although most of the slide libraries which were started before 1935 still use lantern slides, only a small percentage produce or purchase them at the present time.

The majority of the slide libraries located in U. S. institutions of higher education were initiated and supervised by faculty members. As collections expanded, they became too cumbersome for the faculty to administer on a part-time basis, thus necessitating the employment of full-time staff personnel, most frequently on a clerical level, to assume the maintenance of the collection. Fortunately, there were occasions when a professional staff member was hired to precede faculty supervision of the collection. With only two exceptions, the major academic collections are staffed at the present time with one to four full-time professionals possessing either a master's degree in art history or library science. More than half of the major collections have a full-time staff of two or more individuals. Current research indicates that the staffing of slide libraries with professionals having graduate training is the most desirable staffing arrangement. Clerical skills are not adequate to handle the classification, cataloging, and retrieval problems created by a collection of thousands of discrete bits of visual information.

BIBLIOGRAPHIC SURVEY

Slide libraries, like other audiovisual resource collections, have suffered from general neglect until recently. The only major publication to date on slide libraries is *A Universal Slide Classification System for the Organization and Automatic Indexing of Interdisciplinary Collections of Slides and Pictures* by Wendell Simons and Luraine Tansey.[3] Other than this report and the recent paper by Betty Jo Irvine, there exists little substantive literature of value. A comprehensive bibliography of relevant literature, based on an extensive search of periodical indexing services from 1876 to 1970 yielded only twenty-four articles (they are given in the general bibliography). Most of them are either too narrowly involved with a single topic, subject, or discipline or are too general in scope. The lack of published literature dealing with specific problems of slide collections coupled with the communications gap on a formal level among slide librarians and curators has hindered the development of information gathering techniques and standards. Correspondence, trips to other collections, and trial and error practices are helpful but not satisfactory methods for resolving academic library problems.

As a logical consequence of the development of the three-color process in the 1930s, accompanied by the widespread emergence of slide libraries in the 1940s, noteworthy papers began to appear sporadically in the periodical literature. At that time, the controversy between the merits of color 35mm slides and black and white lantern slides are argued by two art historians in the *College Art Journal.*[4] Although over twenty years old, these articles are relevant today because many slide librarians and curators are still faced with buying, producing, using, and dispensing lantern slides. The film discussed in these two papers was Kadachrome, which is still the color film most commonly used for academic slide collections today.

The 35mm color slide was established by the 1950s as an important and necessary part of a slide library. Several articles discussed the relative ease of building a 35 mm slide library placing special emphasis on the economy factor of these slides.[5] Another area of concern at this time was the classification, filing, and general retrieval problems associated with slide collections.[6] The finest general overview of the problems encountered in handling photograph and slide collections was written in 1959 by Phyllis Reinhardt who was then the Art Librarian at Yale University.[7] She discussed the general characteristics of these collections, the importance of developing a quality collection, cataloging and classification, methods used at Yale, and staff training. Hers was one of the first papers to stress the critical need for a properly trained professional to supervise these collections.

In the sixties, major emphasis was placed on classification and cataloguing problems. Slide libraries came of age, reached a new level of prominence, and even entered the computer era. During this period, the previously mentioned universal slide and picture classification system was devised by Simons and Tansey at the University of California at Santa Cruz. A preliminary edition was issued in 1969, with the final edition of their work being published in 1970. While this project was being developed on the West coast, two individuals on the East coast were also making contributions to research in this area. Boris Kuvshinoff of Johns Hopkins University and Elizabeth Lewis of the United States Military Academy libraries discussed two methods of establishing a visual aid card catalog that could be used manually and for machine indexing.[8]

Unfortunately, other than the Santa Cruz system, there are no other formally published classification systems. It is possible, however, to utilize the services of the Bibliographic Systems Center at Case Western Reserve University where a special collection of classification systems and subject heading lists in almost every field are administered. This collection has been machine indexed so that requests are processed by subject with the requester receiving machine-printed catalog clips for each entry on a subject. One selects the items desired and returns the relevant clips to the Center where personnel then use these clips as the charge record for material mailed to the requester.

In addition to the Santa Cruz classification system published in 1970, two more classification systems are due to be published soon. For over three years, Priscilla Farah of the Metropolitan Museum of Art has been working to refine the Metropolitan's classification system so that it can be made available to the art history and library fields. Also, Dimitri Tselos of the University of Minnesota, who had previously written the paper cited above on the classification system he devised, is planning to publish his scheme.

The most recent publication to appear, an article by Betty Jo Irvine, mentioned above, provides the first statistical analysis of slide libraries in academic collections in the United States, including information on types of classification systems, card catalogs utilized, slide production and expansion policies, and staffing conditions.

USE AND ORGANIZATION

It must not be overlooked that most electronic data management and learning devices rest upon the reduction of a living reality to a closed logical system and upon the reduction of the user to a mere link in a closed circuit of ideas. It appears that the book is the only medium of information which does not have that element of coercion characteristic of teaching machines and computers. Information stored in book form requires no apparatus for its use and is presented to the individual without encroaching upon his freedom; he is invited to partake of it, to react and interact, but is under no obligation to do so. The print medium will therefore, we feel, always be of paramount importance as a medium of intellectual liberation. The role of slides in the book oriented college library will remain an ancillary one as long as pictures merely *illustrate* historical or scientific facts. Art slides have an entirely different function as research tools when reproductions of works of art are studied in lieu of the originals.

In most universities and colleges, the principal use of slide collections has traditionally been and still is by faculty members who need visual images to illustrate lectures. Many of these institutions maintain separate departmental collections of slides in the art department, the geography department, the history department, or scientific departments. Recently there has been interest in extending the use of slides to students who must otherwise laboriously hunt for reproductions in books to verify the fleeting impression of a work of art they have seen for only a few moments in class. The primary impact of works of art is visual, which means that the objects must be before the eye of the student for considerable periods of time. But the visual impression can hardly be carried around for any length of time for the visual memory is shorter than the intellectual memory.

Some of the factors precipitating this interest in making slide collections available to individual students are the reduction of cost and time spent in making slides, technological advances in such audiovisual equipment as carousel projectors and zoom lenses, and the increased enrollments in studio and art history departments which necessitate new approaches to student use of audiovisual materials. This trend also stems from a realization that not only is it a waste of students' time to have them comb books for reproductions, but that it actually serves to mutilate materials which become irreplaceable soon after they are published.

The type of program developed for student use of slides depends upon the kind of teaching and testing methods employed in the individual institution. If classes are of a period-survey nature in which picture identification examinations are given, a program which repeats slides shown in lectures would seem most appropriate. Slides would probably be assembled around a specific course topic arranged in small cartridges. One classroom, two carousel or tray projectors, and a part-time staff would represent minimum space, equipment, and manpower requirements to initiate a program of slide study shows throughout the day. The objective would be to have class observed slides on view for extended periods of time to be available to students for review purposes. A schedule of class programs to be given could be posted and, in this manner, provide students the opportunity to observe and study images seen in lectures in lieu of having them draw memory pictures in their notebooks.

A modification of the preceding arrangement would allow interested students to request, at given times during the day, slides from a particular class rerun for individual or group review and study. Thus, students interested in viewing a particular group of slides could request study sessions on a more flexible basis. If examinations are scheduled, the instructors might ask that particular slides be projected for review purposes at a specified time. Or, for smaller classes with less emphasis on memorization of a particular sequence of slides, shows could be set up by the instructor to cover not only the material shown in class, but also supplementary materials, such as works by the same artist or on the same historical events. This latter approach would extend the program as a teaching device and could serve as preparation and inspiration for later reading in the library.

A valid objection to the preceding arrangements could be the tendency for them to become mere memory sessions: A student could thoughtlessly memorize images without gaining an understanding of the study of art or of history as an intellectually and aesthetically integrated and interrelated discipline and not merely a "study in pictures." Needless to say, this objection may never be raised if the system is consistent with the teaching methods used. For beginning undergraduates, their initial exposure to a field might be properly served by visually orientated study sessions. However, it seems appropriate to train people to see visual phenomena before they can be expected to discuss them and to think about them intelligently. In some institutions faculty members have actually experimented by giving classes without words accompanying the slide presentation.

In any library situation, service to the individual should be the supreme consideration, of course, and service to groups is only considered for practical reasons here. The locus of an individual's viewing is often a graphic image around which a whole cluster of associations can dance. The process of free association, which begins as one looks at pictures, often leads to the creative act. This process is unlikely to occur within the group experience. Perhaps, in an ideal system, each student would have direct access to a device operating on the basic principles of a computer. The IBM 1500 is a small computer which can "feed" up to thirty terminals in a variety of ways for programmed instruction and random display of text or images. With this system, the student can create his own private learning environment. Using an on-line control panel or console, he is able to request for individual viewing particular images in connection with lectures he has just seen or material he has just studied. There are in existence other mechanical carrels which can directly store about one thousand slides that have been prearranged in meaningful sequences, but with an IBM 1500 it is also possible to dial into a larger visual data bank —for example, to one maintained away from campus at headquarters of a regional instructional television system.

The direct dial access system is a form of inquiry which is especially relevant if the library uses an encyclopedic system of classification, such as the universal slide classification developed by Simons and Tansey at the University of California under a grant from the Council of Library Resources. While slide classification systems have generally been applied to a single field with art and architecture having received the most attention, the Santa Cruz library scheme represents a first attempt to create a classification useful not only to art but also general history, geography, literature, the classics, foreign languages, the sciences, and the social sciences. As a memory bank (catalog) is built according to the principles of the universal slide classification, of which the sections on art and history have been completed, a student could select any topic that had been in the curriculum and request specific visual information about it. Not only would this student have access to the visual images in the system but also to written data in the catalog, in the form of machine printouts.

In addition to the research completed at Santa Cruz, Robert M. Diamond of the College of Fredonia (State University of New York) has developed a retrieval system for 35mm slides used in the arts and humanities under a grant from the Bureau of Research, Office of Education, U. S. Department of Health, Education, and Welfare.[9] Unlike the Santa Cruz scheme, which puts the emphasis on input classification, this system is primarily concerned with the full exploitation of the retrieval potential inherent in a visual image. Diamond has developed a system of identifiers by which the user can retrieve an item using standard methods such as artist or period; and his scheme also includes the date of the subject in addition to the date of the painting or object, the types of buildings depicted, battle sites illustrated, and other content approaches to the image. The scheme is directed toward both the general and the specialized user so that subject expertise is not a prerequisite for retrieval. At the present time, most collections are arranged for the subject specialist who can locate a specific item because he knows beforehand the period during which certain types of work were created, the country or origin of the artists working in a particular style, and the artist who executed a given work of art. In Diamond's final report, he shows the application of the system to the art, history, and literature of the seventeenth century. The system has been developed in its later stages to be used in conjunction with the Santa Cruz classification system.

It is unlikely that very many institutions of higher education in this country will, at this time, have the staff and the equipment necessary for elaborate programs involving the use of electronic carrels with computer-steered access systems, no matter how committed their teaching staffs are, at least in theory, to instructional technology. The individually operated carousel slide projector that uses programs of slides assembled in a cartridge and developed around a single subject or artist has already been mentioned. Although cheaper than electronic carrels, this equipment may not be affordable everywhere. One way of extending the slide library facilities to individual students would be to produce negatives at the time slides are made. Students could use the negatives to have either contact prints made or enlargements in any size they wish. Thus, each student could build his personal photo archive based upon the holdings of the institutional slide collection. Contact prints made from slides can be useful in a number of ways, e.g. they can be mounted on the catalog cards. This is not only a time saving device for the user of the catalog but it also prevents unnecessary handling of slides. The "illustrated catalog" would soon develop into a major institutional reference tool as a key for all the pictorial material available in the collections. Filed in the general dictionary catalog, the illustrated card would serve as a signal to the reader that the entry he is looking at is not for a book but for an illustration in the collection.

New and imaginative ways of library service such as the mixing of books and audiovisual media in close physical proximity have been tried with apparent success in other than typical college library situations: for instance in the University of Pennsylvania Museum in Philadelphia, and more recently in the Library and Museum for the Performing Arts at Lincoln Center, New York City. The Center Library has absorbed the music and dance collections of the New York Public Library. It now provides different levels of service, reading nooks in the exhibition galleries which are equipped with listening stations, slide, filmstrip, and loopfilm projectors, all of rear screen projection type. A complete "stop-look-listen and read" education is achieved, a total learning environment which could also be created in many college libraries, particularly in smaller ones where the problems of control and supervision can be solved more easily. The objection that might be made to this arrangement is that it offers only a limited choice of prepared programs and that it may have to be supplemented by another more general collection of audiovisual materials arranged according to encyclopedic principles.

Faculty and library staff members should always be greatly encouraged to correlate print and nonprint materials. However, the idea of storing slides either in the open stacks in bookshelf binders or in little cassettes resembling book boxes seems to require a belief in the innate orderliness of the undergraduate mind which, though creditable, most librarians have not been able to preserve in the course of their years of working experience.

PROCUREMENT

Unlike some of the newer media whose use is currently revolutionizing educational practices and influencing educational philosophy, the problems raised by slides in the college library seem more acute in matters which have little to do with the intellectual side of their use but which relate to procurement, processing, and storage.

Slides are available commercially from a great number and variety of sources as well as from many educational organizations and institutions. Publications such as *Educational Media Index, Audiovisual Market Place, AV Index, Educational Screen and Audio-Visual Guide Magazine,* and the *Educators Guide to Free Filmstrips* (one in a series of lists of audiovisual aids published by the Educators Progress Service) are the principal selection aids and are too well-known to need elaboration.[10] The ambitious 14-volume *Educational Media Index* published in 1964, which was intended as the most comprehensive selection tool for all media, failed to live up to its claim. The University of Southern California personnel engaged in an automated catalog project of educational media which eventually resulted in an anticipated national media data bank (NICEM). This bank includes all the entries in the *Educational Media Index,* and subsequently published indexes of NICEM.

Also in 1964, Celestine Frankenberg, of the Picture Division of the Special Libraries Association, edited the second edition of *Picture Sources,* an excellent reference and picture-finding tool, listing 703 entries of which 33 are sources outside North America.[11] Although not all of these sources are specifically engaged in the production and sale, or in the collection and circulation of slides, many that do not list slides at all will lend their flat pictures for slidemaking purposes to educational institutions, or have slides made on their own premises from material in their collections. The great value of *Picture Sources* lies in its excellent organization by subject and in the clear description of the scope, purpose, and terms of use for each source listed. An alphabetical and a geographical list of the sources and a fine detailed subject index increase the usefulness of this basic selection tool.

There are also many subject-oriented slide selection aids available from scientific, scholarly, and educational organizations in this country and abroad. On the elementary and secondary school level the Educator's Progress Service is the publisher of a number of such subject lists. These, in contrast to its main series, do not list materials on a variety of subjects available in one medium but, conversely, materials in many media on one broad subject. Journals that have book review sections in which the latest additions to the literature of a given field are reviewed do frequently also review films, records, tapes, and slides. The commercial producers of nonbook media are advertising more and more in the pages of these scholarly journals. It seems that organizations concerned with foreign area studies are among the most energetic propagandists of the audiovisual approach to instruction and research.

Fairly typical of what is available from area studies in a booklet by the Asia Society entitled *A Guide to Films, Filmstrips, Maps, Globes and Records on Asia; Supplement Including a New Section on Slides* (New York: Asia Society, 1967).[12] The *Guide* lists fifty-nine commercial and nonprofit agencies from which slides documenting the geographical, historical, artistic, and cultural aspects of Asia may be obtained. Under each entry are found notes describing in some detail the nature of the collections and their regulations for use.

A French publisher of audiovisuals (Publications filmées d'art et d'histoire, 44 rue du Dragon, Paris) has started a series of slide-books which contain approximately two dozen slides each on a given topic. Each of the slides is documented on two or three pages of descriptive text written by an authority. Each set is prefaced by a general introduction. Some of the books in this series are based on important monographs, for instance those in the *Art of the World* series; but there are also original sets like the sequences on the history of World's Fairs or the cultural activities of the Council of Europe, which have been conceived, photographed, and written by the publisher starting with an original idea.[13] These are not the only books with slides in plastic pockets that are intended for individual study use. There are many American and European publishers that do include some slides in pockets in lieu of color plates in their books. But those are merely illustrated books whereas Publications Filmées produces slide programs with explanatory text. The basic philosophy underlying their enterprise is not unlike that of *The Carnegie Study of the Arts of the United States* and its sets documenting the history of American art produced in the early sixties for distribution to hundreds of American college libraries.

Among the specialized selection aids for slides, the predominant subject is of course, art. *Slides and Filmstrips on Art,* published by the National Art Education Association, and *Sources of Slides: The History of Art,* published by the Metropolitan Museum of Art, New York, stand on opposite ends of the spectrum of popular instructional, scholarly and research-oriented lists of this kind.[14] The latter lists some 150 sources, many of which are aboard; it is updated periodically, approximately every two years.

The Slide and Photograph Librarians group of the College Art Association has compiled a *Slide Buyer's Guide,* distribution of which began in 1972 with plans for it to be updated annually.[15] It is in essence an expanded list of the commercial slide sources given in the guide put together by the Metropolitan Museum.

There is now also a separate directory that deals with noncommercial sources exclusively. It represents the effort of the Slide Library of the University of California at Santa Barbara. Entitled *A Handlist of Museum Sources for Slides and Photographs,* it contains information supplied by four hundred museums, libraries, and archives on available 35mm color slides and black and white photographic prints.[16] Since museums usually charge only a fraction of what commercial photographers charge for the same slide, and since museum slides are often quite superior in quality to those with which the big slide companies flood the educational market, the *Handlist* can become an important tool in the hands of the quality conscious slide buyer with limited acquisitions fund at his disposal. Each entry gives detailed information on prices and quality and topical lists available from the institution. The value of the *Handlist* is enhanced by additional information pertaining to special orders for original photography, how to get cataloging information, and regulations regarding private photography.

Regardless of the source used for the purchase of slides, it is always a good policy to order them on approval. Color fidelity to the original is extremely important in art slides and very difficult to attain in copies made from original slide positives. Many factors cause variations in color reproduction, necessitating the examination of each slide to determine its suitability for the study of art and some of the life sciences.

PRODUCTION

Most institutions find it necessary to produce large numbers of slides on campus, either from photographs taken directly from objects in the college art museum, the natural history and science collections, or from illustrations found in books. This undertaking should be preceded by careful planning for space, materials, equipment, and procedures.

Negatives may be used for the making of black and white slides which come in the old format of 3¼″ x 4″ or in the new 2″ x 2″ format. However, most of the schools contacted for this study do not make negatives of their black and white slides; it is certainly not a prerequisite for the production of 35mm slides. If Panatomic-X Direct Positive film is used, then negatives are not made. This is a faster and less expensive method. Nevertheless, there are obvious advantages to having negatives for student duplication purposes and the replacement of lost or damaged slides. Although some of the older institutions still use 3¼″ x 4″ glass slides, probably only Oxford University, Harvard University, Howard University, Oberlin College, Smith College, the University of Minnesota, the University of Iowa, Vassar College, and Yale University are also still regularly producing them for their own use. These large glass slides are still unexcelled for their resolving power resulting in greater sharpness and brilliancy, particularly in the rendering of halftones, and the monochromatic reproduction of color. The images on them are permanent, much more so than on 2″ x 2″ color slides made from color reversal film, a factor often overlooked by the modern slide curator. But glass slides have their disadvantages, the principal one being that they break easily. They are also bulky and heavy to carry around, and since only the older institutions have the proper projection equipment for them, lecturers cannot take them freely about which severely limits their usefulness.

The creation of slide negatives requires a photographic department which in larger institutions will be part of the central agency on campus where other instructional media, such as films, television programs, taped lessons, and other programmed instruction sequences are also produced. Smaller universities and colleges without such a central agency, which need a more economical setup for the production of slides taken from illustrations found in books, will have to forego the many advantages which negatives can bring.

An inexpensive outfit for the making of slides is available in the *Eastman Ektagraphic Visualmaker.* It consists of an Instamatic camera and two copy stands—one for 3″ x 3″ material and one for 8″ x 8″ material—plus a flash attachment. This system is economical but has its limitations. Every picture takes a fresh flashbulb and it works only for Kodachrome X film which is below the quality of Kodachrome II, a film that is slower and which produces sharper images. A third handicap is the inability to photograph anything larger than 8″ x 8″. Color fidelity with this method leaves much to be desired, too, which may be less important when slides are made to illustrate historical subjects, but it is a serious dificiency when copying art reproductions or when photographing biological or other scientific specimens.

A system found to be satisfactory and inexpensive, costing less than $25.00, consists of the following:

1. The body of a Pentax single-lens reflex camera model H1a with Macro-Takumar f 1:4/50 mm. This lens not only has a fine resolution, but also, most importantly, a range from infinity to 8.25 inches. At the latter distance a large postage stamp fills the entire picture format. It is possible to observe exactly what is actually being photographed through the excellent viewfinder of the single lens reflex camera.
2. An angle viewfinder for the above camera, also made by Pentax. This is not absolutely necessary but a great convenience since it bends the picture in the view finder 90 degrees, so one can look at it from the side rather than from above when the camera is pointed downward.
3. A simple copying stand consisting of a platform, vertical column, and movable arm extending from that column which ensures that the film plane is always parallel to the picture plane.
4. Two simple stroboscopic flash units. It is quite sufficient to use the smallest and weakest type on the market, the kind that also works with house current of 110 volts as well as batteries.

5. Two table tripods to which the strobe units are attached in such a way that they point downward toward the center of the platform at an angle of 45 degrees or less.

Once this system is set up one has to try out the correct opening for the strobe exposure. The experience of many users of the installation is that on Kodachrome II (ASA 25) the lens opening should be f-11. The exposure remains always the same; it depends only on the distance of the two strobes from the platform and on the angle of the light. The important thing is that the strobe light is balanced exactly for the Kodachrome daylight color film. No filters are ever needed.

When taking slides it should be remembered that only those taken on a horizontal plane may be utilized for films. Therefore, if it is envisioned that slides may be utilized for making filmstrips they should always to taken on a horizontal rather than vertical plane.

APPENDIX 1: MINIMUM EQUIPMENT NEEDS FOR SLIDE SERVICES

Type of Equipment	Specifications	Manufacturer or Supplier
A. Photographic Equipment		
Camera body	Pentax H1a single-lens reflex camera	Honeywell Pentax Corp., 2701 4th Ave., Minneapolis, Minn. 55408
Lens	Pentax Macro-Takumar f 1:4/50 mm.	Honeywell Pentax Corp.
Angle viewfinder	Pentax Right Angle Finder	Honeywell Pentax Corp.
Copying stand	Bogen Copy Stand, Model SS-2	Bogen Photo Corp.
Stroboscopic lights (2)	Ultima 40M Electronic Flash (AC operated)	Smith Photographic Equipment Co., Boston, Mass. 02109
Table tripods (2)	PIC Standard. Aluminum 4-section light stand, 22″ to 7′	Smith Photographic Equipment Co.
Slide duplicator	Honeywell Repronar. Will copy color or black and white slides. Completely self-contained unit which includes a specially designed 35 mm. camera.	Honeywell Corp.

Type of Equipment	Specifications	Manufacturer or Supplier
B. Storage and Procession Equipment		
Slide Files	Each unit comprised of 3 sections containing 15 drawers each, pull-out shelf, legs, top; capacity 144 slides per drawer, 6,480 per unit (wood)	Remington Rand Library Bureau, 801 Park Ave., Herkimer, N.Y. 13350
	GF 12 drawer no. 54 12 BB., 13″ x 28″ x 56″ (metal)	General Fireproofing Co.
	Neumadé SF-S Five Drawer Slide Cabinet, 15½″ x 13″	Neumade Products Corp., 720 White Plains Rd., Scarsdale, N. Y. 10583
	Remington Rand Aristocrat Slide File #23148.421 for 2″ x 2″ slides, 8 drawers, 13″ x 28″ x 40″	Remington Rand Library Bureau
	Steelcase Slide File #1821 10 drawers, 12″ x 28″ x 52″ (metal)	Steelcase, Inc., 1120 36th St., SE, Grand Rapids, Mich.
Sorting trays	Remington Rand steel sorting tray without cover; flexifile interior. Cat. no. 9900ff	Remington Rand Library Bureau
Illuminated sorting table	Flat Stacor tracing table, 29½″ x 25″	Stacor Corp., 285 Emmet St., Newark, N. J. 07102
Previewer	Macbeth Airlite Viewer, 25″ x 24″ or 10″ x 10″	Macbeth Daylighting Corp., Newburgh, N. J. 12550
	Slide-X Desk Viewer, 7″ x 7″ screen	Lester A. Dine, Inc., 2080 Gericho Turnpike New Hyde Park, N. Y. 11040
Binding frames	Perrocolor Slide Binders with cover glasses treated to prevent Newtonian rings	Leitz Perrot of Switzerland
Cutter	Perrocut filmstrip cutter	Leitz Perrot of Switzerland

Type of Equipment	Specifications	Manufacturer or Supplier
Frame locking device	Prolock metal binderlocking clamp and Prolock quick fastener for sealing mounts	Leitz Perrot of Switzerland
Anti-static glass cleaning brush	Staticmaster IC 50	Nuclear Products Co. El Monte, Cal. 91731
Special lamp for binding slides	Dazor Floating Fixture Model M-1470 with magnifying lens No. M-1400	Dazor Mfg. Co., St. Louis, Mo. 63155
Slide labels	Avery labels: 1⅞" x 7/16" strips of 14 ea. Pressure sensitive, adhesive backed	Avery Label Co., Park Square Bldg., 31 St. James, Ave., Boston, Mass. 02109
Label typewriter	IBM Electric with "Microgothic" type face	IBM Corp., Parson's Pond Rd., Franklin Lakes, N. J. 07417
C. Equipment for Viewing Slides in the Library		
Fully equipped specially designed electronic carrell	IBM-1500 Electronic Learning Carrell	IBM Corp.
Simpler random access projectors to be used in custom-made carrel	These come in a variety of models taking from 50 to 500 slides. The MAST 136-Su and the MAST RAP 132 allow random selection of about 250 slides by direct dial access. It is possible to project the slides into a closed circuit TV system and to display them on a cathode-ray tube.	Smith Photographic Equipment Co.
Customized standard library carrels	Any standard piece of furniture can be adapted. Desk surface must be extended in depth and shelf must be raised to allow positioning of projector and screen.	Herman Miller, Inc., 140 W. McKinley St., Zeeland, Mich. 49464 Herman Miller is known to have successfully changed the design of his carrel line to accommodate slide viewing equip-

Type of Equipment	Specifications	Manufacturer or Supplier
		ment for the Metropolitan Museum of Art.
Projector	Kodak Carousel No. 850 with remote control, self focus. Takes Kodak Carousel Universal Slide Trays.	Eastman Kodak Co., 343 State St., Rochester, N. Y. 14650
Screen	HPI rear projection cabinet with 14" x 14" screen. Will permit use of projector and slide viewing in fully lit library reading areas on tables or in carrels.	Hudson Photographic Industries, Inc., S. Buckhoust and Station Rds., Irvington-on-the-Hudson, N. Y. 10533

APPENDIX 2: SELECTED SOURCES FOR ART COLOR SLIDES

Ancora Productions
Consejo de Ciento
160 Barcelona 15, Spain

Blauel Kunst-Dias
Mr. E. A. Arnold
Rottenbucher Strasse 52
8032 Graefelfing, Germany

Barney Burstein
10 Branch
Boston, Mass. 02118

Budek Films and Slides Inc.
P.O. Box 307
Santa Barbara, Cal. 93102

European Art Color Slide Co.
Peter Adelberg, Inc.
120 W. 70th St.
New York, N. Y. 10023

Francis G. Mayer
Art Color Slides Inc.
235 East 50th St.
New York, N. Y. 10022

Frederick Teuscher, Inc. (Portable Gallery)
P.O. Box 146
Planetarium Station
New York, N. Y. 10024

Joseph P. Messana, photographer
5574 Lakewood
Detroit, Mich. 48213

Miniature Gallery
60 Rushett Close
Long Ditton, Surrey, England

Museum Color Slides Assn.
Mr. Donald Outerbridge
190 Marlborough St.
Boston, Mass. 02116

Philadelphia Museum of Art
Parkway at 26th St.
Philadelphia, Pa. 19101

Prothmann Associates Inc.
2787 Milburn Ave.
Baldwin, Long Island, N. Y. 11510

Sandak Inc.
4 East 48th St.
New York, N. Y. 10017

Saskia
Photographic Services for
Historians of Art
Mrs. Renate Wiedenhoeft
P. O. Box 440
North Amherst, Mass. 01059

Scala
via Gioberti, 34
Florence, Italy

Seebamil Sales Corp.
555 Ashland Ave.
Baldwin, L. I., N. Y. 11510

Taurgo Slides
154 East 82nd St.
New York, N. Y. 10028

Film

Dwight F. Burlingame
Herbert E. Farmer

Dwight F. Burlingame is Acquisitions Librarian, Saint Cloud State College, St. Cloud, Minnesota. Herbert E. Farmer is Professor, Department of Cinema, University of Southern California.

The film is but one of the many forms of materials that is now gaining a place on the shelves and in the catalogs of academic libraries. This chapter will briefly explore the history of motion pictures, particularly as they relate to the academic community; survey holdings of film in academic libraries; and examine current film library processing procedures.

HISTORY

The history of those discoveries and developments which finally led to the invention of motion pictures has been the subject of many disputes. The principle of the Camera Obscura appears in the works of Aristotle published about 350 B.C., and the fact that a manuscript of Leonardo da Vinci from some time prior to 1519 does not refer to it as an invention, may imply that the principle was already well understood.

The law of persistence of vision, the principle on which the motion picture is based, was also well-known for centuries, probably long before it was more formally described. Many individuals at different times experimented with the recreation or simulation of motion through animated pictures and drawings. Most of the early approaches seemed to utilize direct viewing of the images and might be considered the forerunner of the peep shows, but there were also many attempts at projecting images on a screen using the principles of the magic lantern.

Even the evolution of the principles of photography, the recording of images using light and chemistry, covered several centuries and included such names as Johann Schulze, Carl Wilhelm Scheele, Thomas Wedgewood, and Humphrey Davy. Between 1825 and 1839, Joseph Niepce and Louis Daguerre in France were able to develop practical processes for recording photographic images and in the following decades it was entirely logical that numerous attempts were made to record sequential images photographically. These became more and more practical as photographic emulsions became more sensitive and as the exposure times were reduced.

There is considerable conjecture as to the exact chronological development of materials and equipment during the late 1800s leading to motion picture films as they are known today. With photographers in various parts of the world utilizing rigid support materials such as glass and metal for their photographic emulsions, it is logical that many individuals were working, perhaps simultaneously, on flexible, nonbreakable, lighter photographic films. The result was, of course, the invention of transparent celluloid film and its application as a film base by George Eastman and others.

Motion pictures had, however, been in existence during this period in a crude form. Penny arcades with peep shows, where a person could revolve a drum and get a picture in motion effect, were quite common. The principle of sequential pictures viewed in register had been established.

With the development of the transparent, flexible film base and with the principles of the magic lantern and picture projection widely known, it was logical that numerous inventors were working on schemes to put these ideas to use. Among the well-known names involved in the development of motion picture projection equipment were the brothers Louis and Auguste Lumière, Thomas Armat, Thomas Edison and Robert Paul, to name but a few.[1]

It is generally accepted that the first public showing in America of a motion picture before a paying audience took place on April 23, 1896, at Koster and Bial's Music Hall in New York City.[2] It should be noted that this was but one of many similar performances in Paris, London, and other cities at about this time.

By the end of 1903, motion pictures were well on their way to becoming a people's art. Throughout the history of photography and the film, there has been a tendency toward realism on one hand and artistic creation on the other as shown by Siegfried Kracauer's revealing history of these developments.[3] During the first twenty years of the present century, the art of the silent film went through significant refinement by such men as George Melies, Edwin S. Porter, and D. W. Griffith.

Shortly after the turn of the century, enterprising showmen found that their performances were enhanced by the addition of sound accompaniment, probably first on a piano and later with organ and instrumental groups. By the mid-1920s, a number of different inventors and organizations were seriously working on methods for recording synchronized sound with motion pictures and by the early thirties practically all production was sound film.

Efforts to add color to the black and white images practically paralleled the development of sound technology. Many early silent films contained tinted stock and toned images. On some early films, each individual frame was laboriously hand-painted. Again by the mid-twenties, a number of companies were commercially offering color processes, the best known being Technicolor.[4] By the early 1930s, the techniques and technology of motion picture production required only refinements to produce the motion picture as we know it today.

This brief history leads one quite naturally to the historical background of the educational film and its use in the academic community. George Kleine's publication of a *Catalogue of Educational Motion Pictures* in 1910 is one of the first references in the literature to instructional film, although many of the films listed were in part entertainment films.[5] During the decade between 1910 and 1920, the value of film in education and training was the subject of much speculation and some activity. The government did become directly involved as early as 1914 with a film program in the U. S. Department of Agriculture.[6] In 1917, the Signal Corps of the U. S. Army made several instructional films, including one on the control of venereal disease that became the subject of later studies on the effectiveness of films in education.[7] The Yale University press produced *The Chronicles of American Photoplays* in 1919, a series of dramatic enactments of episodes in American history that was widely shown in the schools of the United States.

Practically all early films were produced on highly flammable 35mm cellulose nitrate film. Because of the danger of fire and because the projection equipment was clumsy, heavy, and expensive, the use of film in the classroom was adopted slowly. A number of types of smaller projectors were developed, using 32mm,

28mm, 20mm, 17.5mm, and 9.5mm film widths but there were none that gained any measure of general acceptance.

In 1923, the Eastman Kodak Company announced the development of a safety, cellulose, acetate film and a new 16mm format along with its associated equipment. Two papers were presented in May 1923 by Dr. C.E.K. Mees before a meeting of the Society of Motion Picture Engineers. These were entitled *A New Substandard Film for Amateur Cinematography* and *The Cine Kodak and Kodascope*.[8] This was the first formal announcement of what was to become the 16mm standard for education as well as for the amateur. It is also perhaps significant that shortly after this announcement, agreement was reached between the major manufacturers of film and equipment (Eastman, Alexander Victor, Albert Howell, Herman DeVry) that only safety film would be manufactured in this format, and the dimensional specifications were standardized so that interchangeability would be possible. Shortly after this time Eastman established a company division to encourage the use of films in education and between 1927 and 1929, a large number of silent films designed specifically for education were produced by Eastman Classroom Films.[9]

In 1929, the Western Electric Company, through one of its subsidiaries, Electrical Research Products Incorporated, organized ERPI Classroom Films, Inc., to produce 35mm sound educational motion pictures. While these were to demonstrate the value and potential of the educational film with sound, general acceptance was not to be achieved until the introduction of truly portable 16mm sound motion picture projectors in the early 1930s.

By the mid-1930s, the findings of research and the waning of the depression stimulated a decided growth of the audiovisual field. By 1940, an estimated ten thousand schools had acquired 16mm sound motion picture projectors; hundreds of school systems and universities had established audiovisual libraries; and many commercial organizations had entered into the production and distribution of educational films. The entry of the United States into World War II, however, focused the need and brought with it the infusion of necessary funding to move films in education from an experimental to an operational force.

In the academic world a number of colleges and universities became involved in film production and distribution as early as the second decade of this century. Concurrent development of instructional film distribution agencies and instructional film libraries in extension divisions during the period from 1920 to 1940 is of major significance, since these two agencies still represent the primary organizational pattern of film utilization in the academic community today.

FILM COLLECTION IN ACADEMIC LIBRARIES

To ascertain when the first film collection was established in an academic library can be most frustrating. Apart from a few exceptional cases, one is fairly safe in concluding that major film collections were not established in academic libraries until the 1950s. Even the Library of Congress was not actively involved in film selection and storage until 1945 when the Motion Picture Project was formed.

The Library of Congress made no effort to collect and preserve films prior to this date because the 1912 Copyright Law waived the requirement to deposit copies at the Library of Congress, due to the protests of the producers and to the danger of storing nitrate films. Further development took place in the 1960s, as the concept of the Instructional Resource Center, Learning Resource Center, or Media Center filtered into the organization of academic libraries, resulting in the combination of traditional libraries and audiovisual services. Thus film collections became identified with academic libraries to a greater degree.

The typical place of films within university and college library collections throughout the United States and the world, for that matter, still appears to be peripheral in nature. Although few academic librarians presently place nonprint media in a role comparable with that of the book, many do generally agree that films, videotapes, and other newer media will increase in importance within the academic library.

There appear to be three main reasons why the growth of film collections within the academic library has been retarded. The advent of the audiovisual center upon the university and college campus is the first reason. Film libraries were established in extension units of colleges as another means of conveying knowledge to the public. This was in the same spirit as was the earlier development of Lyceum and Chautauque series, and correspondence instruction. (A conference of university extension directors, held in 1915, discussed five methods of instruction, one of which was "visual instruction".) It was natural that the equipment required for projection and the skills to handle the highly inflammable nitrate film and complicated equipment were centered in a unit which was placed in direct relation with the teachers in whose classes the films were to be projected, and with the administration. In the early stage of development, only the farsighted could envision the time when individuals could examine films for knowledge. Film centers, established usually as integral parts of the instructional program of parent institutions, undertook the acquisition, processing, and distribution of films and the provision of projection services. For many academic libraries, the division of labor based upon the different formats of the media was welcomed; for others the division was created by default of the library; and still others viewed the new audiovisual organization as an infringement on the library's domain. The services offered by the audiovisual center became more and more comprehensive. In 1955, a National Education Association publication, *Audio-Visual Centers in Colleges and Universities,* listed suggested functions of such centers.[10] Interestingly enough, the functions described are almost identical to those used to characterize the necessary activities of libraries.

A second factor was the cost of the material itself. Cooperative efforts to establish regional film centers and the existence of rental programs throughout the country seem to support this contention. The disparity between the cost of a book and the cost of a film is still a deterrent to many libraries.

While the cost of the material was a major factor in retarding the growth of films in the academic library, the format of the material provided the third major factor, since films and videotapes must necessarily be viewed and heard through supporting equipment. The equipment has been expensive, requiring continuous maintenance and a trained operator for effective results. In addition, special equipment and trained personnel are needed for the inspection and repair of films. Few librarians have budgets to absorb the cost of film and equipment and there is little evidence that they have actively sought additional funds to implement such programs.

SURVEY OF FILM HOLDINGS

Large collections of film in this country include the Library of Congress, which has approximately 100,000 reels and adds some 2,500 to 4,000 reels (1,000 titles) each year; the American Film Institute; and the U.S. National Archives, which has the responsibility for the collection of all government films. The latter's National Audiovisual Center has a sales and circulating collection of government film as well as some archival materials. Other large holdings are located at the Museum of Modern Art in New York, which is especially important to students of the art of cinema and film history; the University of Southern California film library upon which the NICEM catalogs were initially based; the George Eastman House, which stresses the history and development of film; the Sherman Grinberg Film Library; and the Television News Archives, established in 1968 at Vanderbilt University and which is a permanent collection of the daily news broadcasts of the three national television networks. In addition, a number of major universities have extensive collections of instructional films. However, a .search of library statistics for colleges and universities through 1968 revealed no reference to film holdings in academic libraries.[11] On the other hand, a survey by the Junior College Section of the Association for College and Research Libraries revealed that of the 185 two-year college respondents, 31 percent of the libraries owned some films.[12]

To assist the author in determining the extent of film and/or videotape collections in academic libraries today, a survey was made using a random sample of academic libraries across the country. Eighty-six questionnaires were mailed in January of 1971 to college and university libraries to determine (1) if they had a film collection in their library, (2) the extent of the collection, and (3) if they knew of any other film collection in neighboring or other institutions of higher education in the United States. Of the sixty-four responses received, thirteen replied that they had film collections within the library—one had videotapes. In this group of thirteen only six had collections that numbered over two hundred prints. Of the replies indicating that there was no film collection within the library, twenty indicated that all films on campus were handled by the audiovisual center or audiovisual extension service. In the remaining institutions that responded negatively, there was in all probability some form of audiovisual center or extension service that administered the film needs of the campus.

FORMS OF FILM

To this point, emphasis has been placed on the 16mm film and its role in the academic library. However, the 8mm and super 8mm loop films and cartridges are also assuming much importance in the academic community. It is perhaps in this area that the academic library will play the greatest role in the immediate future. The projection equipment is not terribly expensive nor does it require a trained operator. The development of the magnetic sound track on the film has enhanced the versatility of the loop and cartridge presentation. The cost of the film units in this format is also within reason.

At the other extreme is the sophistication of television equipment. Although units are becoming less complex when compared to earlier models, the care and knowledge needed to view videotapes still seems to require a trained operator, who is not normally found in the library. The lack of compatibility of videotapes and videotape recorders is almost more of a problem than with films, due to varying formats of tapes and types of equipment on which the tape must be played. One cataloging code specifies that an element in the descriptive cataloging data for videotape is the type of equipment upon which is was produced.

Further development of new television storage systems (i.e. Electronic Video Recording, Selectavision, and cassette videotape recording) may further complicate the role of the library that includes "television" within the organizational framework.[13] At the present, the single most important problem facing potential television utilization is one of lack of compatibility. However, as video cassettes are developed so that they can be used without a trained operator and as formats are standardized it seems certain that they will find a place in many libraries.

SELECTION AND ACQUISITION

Selection of the right film for the right occasion takes an experienced individual. One of the best methods of selecting a film for purchase still appears to be by committee. The selection committee often consists of a subject specialist, a production (technical) specialist, an audience or utilization specialist (e.g., instructor), and occasionally some members of the intended audience. An evaluation form suited to the needs of the local situation should be utilized when previewing the film for purchase. One widely used form is that published by the Educational Film Library Association (EFLA). In addition to selection by committee, the acquisition department should apply its basic criteria and procedures used for book selection. Of importance in the selection of films are technical qualities and timeliness. Needless to say, the overall purpose of the film and the relevance of its content to the curriculum are of prime importance. One good example of a selection policy which includes films is the "Instructional Materials Selection Policy" of the Northampton County Area Community College (Bethlehem, Pennsylvania).[14]

Today, an acquisitions librarian can order films from many creditable sources. Over thirty-five commercial distributors serve film users in America. A list of these distributors is found in *Feature Films on 8mm and 16mm,* second edition published by the Educational Film Library Association.[15] For an international directory of agencies dealing with, or concerned about films, the *World Film Directory,* UNESCO, 1962, is a good source. NICEM has separate catalogs for both 8mm *(Index to 8mm Cartridges,* 1969) and 16mm (*Index to 16mm Educational Films,* 2nd ed., 1969) films. Another valuable guide is the Library of Congress printed catalog volumes, *Motion Pictures and Filmstrips,* which are issued on a continuing basis. A number of leading universities also have outstanding collections of instructional films that are available for rental and in some cases for purchase.

Whether it is best to have a single budget for the purchase of all media materials (print and nonprint) or several budgets (i.e., film, book, serials, etc.) will depend on local policy, as well as on the regulations in public institutions. Some administrators operating under one budget are now questioning the advisability of following this procedure. Through experience librarians have found that several smaller budgets do not appear to be as large or vulnerable as one large combined amount. There is less chance that the several budgets will be pared. Some administrators operating under several budgets contend that a single budget for media materials would be best because it would allow for the purchase of materials in the formats that are needed at the time. Ideally, the latter would seem to be the more desirable although in practice, it may not be true. It is a perplexing problem, and only consideration of circumstances at the local level will lead to a wise decision.

To complicate matters further, one must take into consideration whether rental of films would not be more economical. Permanence of film content, style of treatment, frequency of local use, inspection and repair, specialized storage space, and staff time must all be considered. In view of these factors most film specialists agree that for 16mm film, rental is more practical than purchase, except for frequently used titles.

CATALOGING AND PROCESSING

In the literature on the processing of audiovisual materials, several methods for cataloging and classifying films are given. Chapter 12 of the *Anglo-American Cataloging Rules* provides for the use of various entries.[16] The rules put forth reflect generally how films can be cataloged in academic libraries. The recent publication of the Canadian Library Association, *Non-Book Ma-*

terials: The Organization of Integrated Collections, is worthy of mention to serve as an example for academic libraries, even though the publication is written specifically for school libraries.[17]

Although some libraries still use color-coding of catalog cards it is not a recommended practice since new methods of catalog reproduction make color coding impractical. Book catalogs do not utilize color, photocopying cards with color film is prohibitive in cost, and centralized cataloging is generally done on white cards. Likewise, development of numerous types of media makes it difficult to find distinctive colors.

For classification, the same system of subject analysis should be used for films as for books and other materials. This will put emphasis on content rather than form, and one system prevailing throughout the library makes for easy use by the library patron. Classification necessitates flexible storage and trained personnel for subject analysis; however, if materials are organized by accession number, this is not necessary. Each method has its strengths and weaknesses and both are used in academic libraries today. It appears that an adaptation of the two systems might be the most practical. For example, at Saint Cloud State College in Minnesota, all films are catalogued as are books, using the Library of Congress subject headings as well as classification. The reason given for this is that films are placed in a special collection as are reference volumes, rare books, and archival materials. This allows for easier and safer handling, and it solves the difficulty of shelving unlike materials in a single collection. By cataloging the films in the same manner as books (even if they are in separate collections), the user is provided access to all formats of material under one subject entry in a single catalog. This seems to be a most important consideration for the user.

While some general rules for the cataloging of films are worthy of mention, detailed information may be found in chapter 12 of the *Anglo-American Cataloging Rules*. The main entry for motion pictures is the title. Imprint information should contain the sponsor and producer. The sales distributor may also be added for this is frequently the source of descriptions and teacher guides, as well as the source for purchase. Dates, while very important, are often difficult to assign because of the variance between the release date and production date. The release date is normally given, but if it is not known, the copyright date of the film is used. If neither date can be established, the probable date of release is used. The basic collation information given is the length, sound or silent, color or black and white, and width of film. Notes are important in the cataloging of films, and are used to include a further extension of the physical description of the film. Acting and production credits, when significant, and the name of the academic authority (author) who was responsible for the content in instructional films are also given. The summary should describe the content of the film succinctly and objectively. Further physical description of the film would include such things as three-dimensional film, magnetic or optical sound track, and special equipment necessary for projection.

Two difficulties present themselves in the cataloging of films. First, the difficulty of turning to a "chapter" or "page" in a reel, e.g., a ten-minute segment on Baltimore architecture which exists in a thirty-minute film on the subject of architecture. The second difficulty is the "outcome-of-seeing" and "issues" orientation of films, often multi-disciplinary by traditional subject classification. Apparently only massive and continuous bibliographic efforts can help the teacher or discussion leader locate suitable film materials. This demand is particularly acute for archivists, television collectors, and special collection librarians. Italian representatives to the UNESCO International Television Committee have stressed the need for sufficient cataloging to allow segment retrieval of film and videotape.

Due to continued developments in the field of videotapes, there are as yet no official cataloging rules constructed for this medium. Two projects worthy of note are those of Joan Troutman and Brigitte Kenney, who have attempted to develop standards for cataloging tape material and indexing psychiatric videotapes.[18] It appears that the basic rules developed for motion pictures may be adapted for videotapes. The general rules for motion pictures can be applied to motion picture loops with minor changes. Because of their specificity and brevity, detailed cataloging is not essential.

Regardless of the system used for the cataloging of films and other audiovisual materials, one should consider a system that can be easily converted to computer storage and retrieval. The Machine-Readable Cataloging (MARC) system for cataloging and classification of films is one example that might be looked forward to in the future. The computer-based statewide film library network developed in New York state is an example of what might be expected in the area of film cooperation during the next decade.[19]

As yet, no single organizational pattern for film service seems preferred enough to be followed by all university and college libraries. Regardless of the path followed, however, Gerald McDonald's statement made in 1942 is still relevant:

> No matter who handles the films however, there should be mutual agreement on the methods of distribution so that film collections will not develop into segregated, closely guarded units. When administrative tradition lodges the film collection outside the library, close cooperation should exist between the distribution center and the services of the library. The library should make every effort to correlate the use of films with its printed materials, provide information on them, and be ready to circulate films, too, if campus needs indicate its responsibility to do so.[20]

Filmstrips

Dennis Fields
Tony Schulzetenberg

Dennis Fields is Associate Professor of Library and Audiovisual Education, Saint Cloud State College, St. Cloud, Minnesota. Tony Schulzetenberg is Associate Professor of Library and Audiovisual Education, also Saint Cloud State College.

The filmstrip as a communications medium takes its place with the book, the film, and the other sources of recorded information as a vital and integral part of the library collection. As a relatively new media form, it does not enjoy the rich heritage of the book, but its usefulness as yet another means of presenting information is perhaps the criterion by which its inclusion should be judged; for if the library is indeed to be the most important learning resource for the academic community, then it is imperative that each resource within the entire range of print and nonprint media be included.

HISTORY

The filmstrip as we know it today has been in existence less than a half century. Included in its lineage are both the early lantern slide and photographic film for it was the linking of these two that led to the development of the filmstrip shortly before 1920. At that time the Underwoods of New York, in working with their extensive photographic collection, placed the collection on 55mm film. This procedure has been heralded as being comparable to the introduction of the Eastman roll film in photography. The Stillman Company built on this idea by expanding the strips of photographs to include not merely captions, but as Falconer pointed out, "teaching" titles for each frame.[1] The impetus for the development of the 35mm filmstrip was provided by the Society for Visual Education (SVE) in 1920, and it is this company that commonly receives credit for its development.[2] However, Dorothy Dent in her history of SVE relates the story of four men who "formed a Chicago-based business called The American Graphic Company, an occurance that was eventually to alter radically the entire future of SVE" which was at that time dependent on slow selling motion picture projectors and films.[3] This new company developed a unique projector, the Sellograph, "a device that projected several still pictures, one frame at a time, from one strip of film." Throughout these early years, and in the years to follow, the filmstrip was known by a variety of names. Commonly listed are names like slide film, strip film, film slide, film rolls, stereoptican films, picturol, and filmstrip.[4] The latter is, of course, the term most commonly used.

Falconer indicated extensive usage of the filmstrip during the 1920s in the educational field, a falling off as educational movies gained in popularity during the 1930s, and then a renewed but more purposeful use during the early 1940s. Ellsworth Dent reported that the filmstrip had gained acceptance not only in education, but also in churches, industry, and among all types of training institutions during the early years. Writing in 1946 he stated that "thousands of different filmstrips and tens of thousands of projectors have been used during the past five years for defense, pre-induction and war training."[5]

The filmstrip continues as an effective medium in all types of educational and training programs. Its purposeful educational use has helped to retain its popularity as one of a wide range of educational media available for use in directed group or individual learning situations. From the nature of that use, filmstrip collections have more often grown as separate entities rather than as a part of library collections, but that concept has changed greatly in the last two decades. The greatest impetus for change has perhaps come from the public school field where the appearance of media centers and the subsequent centralization of all resources led to an integration of all material in the center.

FILMSTRIPS AND COLLEGE USE

The increased emphasis on independent study at the college level has led to a greater use of the filmstrip, for the sound filmstrip is ideally suited to this type of activity. With the use of all media for independent activity, it has become imperative that bibliographic control be established and that filmstrips be accessible to all students. The development of newer and better listening and viewing units, designed specifically for library use, have made it much easier to incorporate filmstrips into the library collection.

The use of the filmstrip in the academic community is not, however, limited to independent study. One of its foremost uses still is as an integral portion of the instructional program in the classroom. It must remain as one of a variety of materials available to the college instructor so that he can include this medium in his repertoire of teaching techniques. Both large and small groups can benefit from filmstrips, for illustrative materials on almost any subject are available in this form. Filmstrips lend themselves to use in discussion or study groups. The use of filmstrips for the student teacher as he works in teacher preparation cannot be overlooked in those institutions offering teacher training programs, and certainly this format of media can serve as resource information for both faculty and students in research. If the college library is to carry out its mission in meeting the curricular and research demands of its clientele, the filmstrip must be an integral part of its collection.

Filmstrips are used extensively on college campuses, but the manner in which they are collected and made available varies from institution to institution. On some campuses filmstrip collections are departmentalized with no central bibliographic control; on others some attempt at bibliographic control is made although the filmstrips are not housed centrally within the library; on others the filmstrips are centrally housed, often in the curriculum collections, with a central catalog of all materials on the campus; and on still others separate audiovisual collections exist, some under library management while others are not. Combinations of all variations also exist, since in some instances curriculum libraries are included in the school of education while remaining a branch of the library; in others the curriculum area is a part of the main library. It is difficult to establish a policy for the development of filmstrip collections and equally difficult to define guidelines for their housing. It does seem imperative, however, the guidelines developed reflect the needs of the institution and that accessibility to all information users be considered one of the prime factors in determining policy.

A telephone survey of state colleges and of other private and public educational institutions in Minnesota revealed that there is hardly a consistent pattern for the handling of filmstrips at these institutions. Since the state colleges evolved from teacher training institutions, the housing of filmstrips in curriculum areas is common; however, these curriculum collections are handled differently at the various colleges. Most have initiated, or are planning initiation, of some type of bibliographic control of this medium. The authors' personal experiences at other institutions in Wisconsin and Texas reveal similar methods of handling filmstrip collections; yet each institution had developed its own particular method for providing some level of bibliographic control. The size of filmstrip collections varies, and it is difficult to determine the holdings of a library because of the various methods used in building collections. Quality studies on the handling of filmstrips are rare, and access to them is limited. Of the sixty-four college and university libraries responding to the survey conducted by the Special Committee on the Bibliographic Control of Audio-Visual Materials in 1958, only twenty-seven indicated that they owned filmstrips. These figures included replies from the extension divisions or audiovisual centers which existed independently of the academic libraries.[6]

NATURE OF THE FILMSTRIP

One of the underlying factors in the acquisition, processing, and handling of the filmstrip in academic libraries is the nature of the filmstrip itself. The words by Falconer best express the nature of filmstrip use: "A sequence of still pictures can combine the dramatic stimulation of the motion picture with the academic integrity of the carefully prepared instructional diagram, painting, or photograph."[7] Edgar Dale, long recognized as a leader in the audiovisual field, substantiates Falconer's statement.[8] With this fortification for the value of the filmstrip, attention should be directed toward the physical nature of the medium.

There is a great deal of similarity between the 35mm slide series and the filmstrip. Both utilize the same photographic source, the 35mm film, with the major difference being that the filmstrip has a fixed sequence by nature of its physical form. The slide series offers more flexibility in sequencing, but in so doing it proves more difficult in handling and storage. The comparison is made here not only to emphasize the similarity of the 35mm slide series and the filmstrip, but also, and perhaps more important, because the difference in the physical properties of the two demand attention from the academic librarian in preparing to work with the filmstrip. It is also of importance to note that the strip film is used in the production of microfilm, and microfilm should not be confused in the reference here to the term filmstrip.

A physical description of the filmstrip can be found in almost any book on audiovisual materials and techniques, or on technology. Falconer in 1948 published what was then the most extensive work on the filmstrip. He devoted much of one chapter to the kinds and varieties of filmstrips and to a description of their physical properties.[9] While the filmstrip has improved greatly in technical quality since then, its form has not undergone any major changes. The most significant improvements have come not in form but in manner of projection, packaging, and use of the filmstrip with other materials. Falconer still remains as one of the more descriptive works on the filmstrip but as indicated previously, physical descriptions by others are readily available. More recent works which quite clearly and succinctly present this aspect of the filmstrip are those of Rudy Bretz and Jerrold Kemp.[10]

It has previously been pointed out that the most common type of filmstrip is the 35mm; however, it should be remembered that 16mm filmstrips have also been produced. The latter have not achieved the popularity of the 35mm and, therefore, attention here will be directed to the 35mm filmstrip which is generally produced in color and is relatively inexpensive. Prices vary, but it is safe to make the assumption that filmstrip prices are comparable to those for books, a criterion which is perhaps most meaningful to academic librarians.

The filmstrip is arranged in motion picture form, with frames (pictures) commonly placed in a vertical rather than a horizontal sequence. When they are placed in horizontal sequence, the nature of each frame is such that it is nearly twice the size of a vertical frame and thus is referred to as a double frame. While black and white filmstrips are still produced, the use of color film and the production of color filmstrips with its resultant impact in realism and attractiveness has led to a decrease in the use of those limited to monochrome. Filmstrips rarely exceed one hundred frames (that number being unusually large) and strips of less than twenty frames are not common; generally, filmstrip rolls will vary in length from two to five feet and will consist of thirty to sixty frames. Plastic containers have replaced the early tin type, and many filmstrips are produced with accompanying printed texts or guides. Likewise, many filmstrips are accompanied by sound recordings, either in tape or record format. Of importance to the user is the fact that the size of the film (35mm or 16mm) and the size of the frame (single or double) will require different projection equipment. It should be noted that the 35mm single frame filmstrip outnumbers any other type so greatly that most librarians, general users, and media specialists will probably not realize other types exist, except possibly for historical reasons.

EQUIPMENT

The criteria for selection of equipment used in viewing filmstrips will vary and depend to some degree on the user and the type of installation, educational or otherwise. The general criteria for equipment selection used by Brown and Norberg are still viable and relevant.[11] The "Criteria for Combination Filmstrip and 2 x 2 Inch Slide Projectors" listed in Erickson are more specific and therefore useful to the potential buyer.[12]

A common practice has been to purchase projectors which will accommodate both filmstrips and slides. This practice is not nearly so popular now as in the past, since the single purpose, remote, automatic slide and filmstrip projectors have in many cases dominated the market.

The cost of viewing equipment is directly proportional to its degree of sophisticaton and specialization. Individual filmstrip viewers can be purchased for less than $20.00, whereas remote control, single-purpose filmstrip projectors may exceed $130.00.

Filmstrips serve as adequate instructional materials both in and out of the college library; however, preview equipment and space must be supplied if the user is to realize this medium's fullest potential. Moreover, filmstrip collections which are intended for checkout by patrons must be realistically supported through a liberal equipment lending system. Some provision must also be made for previewing filmstrips before checkout and for utilizing filmstrips as instructional materials within the academic library.

A popular and efficient solution to the problem of utilization and preview in academic libraries lies in the learning carrel. Carrels offer the user isolation, while providing the rest of the library clientele insulation from distraction. Learning carrels vary in degree of sophistication from desks with shelves and sides to the type with 115 volt electrical power and dial access capability. Those used for preview of the filmstrip and other media are usually minimally equipped with 115 volt outlets and a small front or rear screen area for preview.

On the other hand, some colleges elect centralized preview and listening facilities. Some advantages and disadvantages are forthcoming with this alternative. Centralization offers unity of function, supervision, access to records, and the opportunity of physical requirements for necessary electrical capacity in one location. However, this space, like any specialized area, is less usable for other service functions within the academic library.

Maintenance of the filmstrip projector is similar to that of other projectors, and the simplistic design of the manual types make them easier to maintain. Many of the suggestions listed by Brown and Norberg as purchase criteria have lost their application, since the filmstrip has been sufficiently integrated into most curriculums.

It is suggested by Erickson and many others that the care and inspection given to filmstrips is inferior to that of other media,[13] which is especially unfortunate in view of the fact that the filmstrip seems to have, in many libraries, the distinction of having the highest circulation volume of any nonprint media. With this popularity, the filmstrip has the propensity for disillusioning and disappointing the user if its condition, when received from the library, is poor.

The filmstrip does require less care than many other media; however, there are a few precautions which can improve the condition of filmstrips for use:

1. Inspect visually after use (being careful to handle by the edges).
2. Check to see that the filmstrip is wound in the proper order, beginning to end (do not cinch).
3. Apply sparingly the same cleaning fluid as used on 16mm film.
4. Remove jagged corners of torn perforation with a film notcher or scissors.[14]

Filmstrips can be repaired using a 35mm film splicer, but this practice is not recommended. A far superior practice for both the library and user is to make arrangements and contracts with producers and distributors to replace damaged filmstrips at a reasonable percent of the original cost.[15]

STORAGE AND CIRCULATION

The physical quarters for storing filmstrips vary, even though there are some general procedures and methods which many libraries have adopted and which can serve as useful guidelines. The commercially produced cabinets containing shallow drawers with metal or wire dividers are one of the most popular methods for storing filmstrip collections. There are a myriad of other storage cabinets, drawers, boxes, and wall storage devices each with its own merits and disadvantages.

Many libraries find the cabinet-drawer method of storage inadequate and unsuitable for their use due to rental or checkout procedures. Personnel in these libraries inspect the filmstrip and return it to a cardboard package; and then return the package to a marked shelf, thus making it ready for checkout and avoiding the problem of repackaging for the next checkout or rental.[16] As indicated, a potpourri of storage methods exist. Adoption of any one of these should be predicated upon a valid assessment of the library, existing methods, and the library's user needs.

Filmstrip collections may be arranged in a variety of ways. They are quite often arranged by subject headings which may be assigned by the local library, or taken from Dewey, the Library of Congress, or any other useful and consistent schemes. Accession numbers are usually given to filmstrips where a given number grouping is assigned to the defined subject headings. A common practice is one where sets of filmstrips on any given subject are assigned consecutive numbers, and the entire set is checked out as a unit, rather than checking out individual filmstrips from the set. This practice is useful to both the user and the library since it provides an in-depth look at the subject, allows for ease of handling in checkout and circulation, and curbs losses of individual filmstrips from a set. The value of using the accession number as a location symbol is perhaps offset by the possible advantages of a recognized classification scheme whereby filmstrips on like subjects may be brought together. A classification scheme provides a means for user browsing, an activity that seems to be becoming more popular as nonprint materials are placed on open shelves.

The difficulty in determining the proper place to house filmstrips and other media is evident in the variety of ways that it is presently being done. One of the primary considerations must be bibliographic control if a collection of filmstrips is to be properly handled and utilized by its library clientele. A prerequisite to the processing and handling of filmstrips as a part of the library collection is the selection and acquisition of this medium.

ACQUISITION AND SELECTION

The building of a good filmstrip collection is based upon the application of good selection principles, and success in good collection development lies in extending the principles of book selection to this medium. One immediate problem confronting the academic librarian interested in building a good filmstrip collection as a part of the regular library collection is the lack of selection tools for nonprint. While it is relatively easy to find sources that merely list available filmstrips (i.e., in the manner that *Books in Print* does for books) or that list them by subject area (e.g., *Subject Guide to Books in Print*), it is quite another thing to locate evaluative lists. Filmstrip selection in the past has been accomplished basically through individual preview; it is only in recent years that some tools in the book selection field have turned to the evaluation of other media. Typical among these are such selection aides as *Booklist* and *Library Journal.*

Being forced then to utilize individual selection methodology rather than relying on good selection tools, the academic librarian must be aware of the many pitfalls for the evaluator. It has been a common premise and practice that librarians evaluate as few materials as possible with items in hand, since library selection is based on review sources where the materials have already been evaluated. There is a distinct difference between selecting from materials previously evaluated by a reputable source and actually evaluating the materials themselves.

When the evaluation of filmstrips is necessary for selection, the academic librarian must have an established, systematic procedure for this purpose. The following list of criteria is one example of a systematic design which can enable the librarian to evaluate and select better filmstrips:

1. Are the goals and objectives clearly defined either in the filmstrips or in accompanying teacher's guides so they can be communicated to the intended audience?
2. Is the audience defined in terms of grade level and/or reading level?
3. Is the filmstrip presented in a logical sequence with an identifiable predesign to the sequence?
4. Is it evident in the filmstrip that the visual mode has been followed since filmstrips are a visual medium?
5. Is the content authentic and accurate?
6. Is the material presented in an understandable fashion for the identified audience?
7. Are concepts clearly defined with enough consideration of each to communicate its complete meaning?
8. Does the filmstrip require involvement and interaction with the audience?

9. Does the filmstrip provide enough reinforcement through repetition and review?
10. Are the transition frames from one idea or concept to another merely attractive pictures or do they provide adequate progression?
11. Does the photographic balance and composition enhance the ideas presented?
12. Are the captions readable, suitable, and descriptive of the ideas contained in the visuals?
13. Are the dress, fashion, automobiles, etc., predominant enough to detract when they are out of style? Does the filmstrip contain faddish fashions and language?

This list may be useful for the purposes of previewing and producing filmstrips. Similar lists can be found in Erickson, Brown and Norberg, and Frank Holmes.[17] The reader should be cognizant of the fact that the above list contains many of the same criteria found in common works on selection tools, such as that by Carter and Bonk.[18]

Also of interest to the academic librarian is the similiarity between the traditional selection criteria (authority, authenticity, scope, treatment, arrangement, format, and special features) and those listed above as criteria for the evaluation of filmstrips. This similiarity should encourage academic librarians to engage actively in evaluating filmstrips where adequate review information is not yet available. The absence of review sources should also motivate professionals in several related fields of study to establish and support nonprint review sources.

One substantial list of available filmstrips can be found in the *Index to 35mm Educational Filmstrips* issued by NICEM.[19] The volume contains an alphabetical listing by title along with a complete entry for each filmstrip. An added fringe benefit of the NICEM index is that it contains a separate subject index and a directory of producers and distributors. Bibliographies of filmstrips on almost any subject can eventually be located. Easily accessible books like Rufsvold's and Guss' *Guide to Newer Educational Media* are extremely useful to patron, librarian, and audiovisual specialist alike.[20]

CATALOGING AND CLASSIFICATION

The academic librarian who determines that the filmstrip is a part of his library collection realizes that to maintain bibliographic control, proper cataloging and classification are necessary.

In order to establish a modus operandi for filmstrips, the librarian is confronted with some problems not unlike that faced in the cataloging and classification of books. Basic principles underlie any course of action, but final decisions should be made from options viewed by the librarian for a particular collection. In the final analysis, a procedural manual for technical services should take into consideration the needs of the particular institution and clientele.

The work by the Hamman Committee in 1956 can serve as a fairly realistic guide for the academic librarian searching for guidelines in cataloging and classifying audiovisual materials.[21] Foremost among the committee's recommendations were that some standardization of the essential elements in cataloging audiovisual materials be maintained, that rules be flexible enough to allow for expansion as the collection grows, and that information on the cards be complete enough so that the user doesn't have to consult the film or filmstrip. These rules seem relatively stable for the librarian today although some changes may be needed for cooperative endeavors between librarian, vendors, and patrons.

The first decision facing the academic librarian is whether he will follow the classification scheme already employed by the library for the handling of other materials, i.e., books, or whether he wants to employ a simplified approach such as accession numbers for location symbols in a closed collection. The use of some recognized classification scheme has many advantages in the open collection, among which are that it brings materials on like subjects together, allows for browsing, and brings duplicated material together. Although based on experience rather than any type of research, it is these authors' contention that library patrons will browse in nonprint collections when housed in open collections by subject. The actual housing facilities and collection arrangement are not the only factors to be considered in the choosing of a scheme or shelf arrangement of nonprint media in general and filmstrips in particular. A classified catalog, usually in printed format, if skillfully developed and properly utilized can be an invaluable bibliographic reference.

Librarians confronted with the cataloging and classification of filmstrips can turn to a standard repertoire of tools for assistance, e.g., *Anglo-American Cataloging Rules, Dewey Decimal Classification, the Library of Congress Classification, Sears List of Subject Headings, LC Subject Headings*, and *LC Rules for Descriptive Cataloging*. Especially helpful is the *LC Rules for Descriptive Cataloging: Motion Pictures and Filmstrips* found in the *Anglo-American*

Cataloging Rules (published by the American Library Association).

Hamman also stressed in the committee report that a standardized manual of procedure be prepared for handling of audiovisual materials. Some works in this category which may be consulted are Akers, Riddle, Harris, Hicks and Tillin, and the recently published manual by the Association of Educational and Communications Technology (AECT).[22] The latter seems to provide the best assistance to date although it is not yet an accepted standard.

Also an indispensible tool and one that will save the librarian countless hours of work is the *Library of Congress Catalog: Motion Pictures and Filmstrips*.[23] This can be used as a reference tool in original cataloging or as a source for printed cards and should not be overlooked. Library of Congress cards are available on the same basis as those for books. A few commercial companies also provide printed cards and printed cards may accompany the material purchased. Whatever type of card the librarian develops or chooses, it is paramount that the descriptive cataloging be as complete as possible, for, as pointed out before, it is perhaps more important for audiovisual materials than for books in view of the limited physical access to determine the specific content of an item. The following specific aspects of descriptive cataloging are given to emphasize their importance for nonprint media:

1. *Main Entry*. It is generally recommended that filmstrips be cataloged by title, although at times the author could serve as the main entry (i.e., when the author is responsible for the intellectual content. The advantages of always using the title entry are consistency and less confusion for the library patron.
2. *Imprint*. The type of medium, i.e., (filmstrip), follows the main entry and is in parentheses. Also included are the producer, the date, and if appropriate, the releasing agency. It is suggested for sake of clarity and uniformity that the type of nonprint media be spelled out just above the call number for each entry rather than employing letter symbols or color coding.
3. *Collation*. The collation includes the number of frames, whether in color or black and white, the size of the film, the accompanying sound recording with a description (e.g., and phonodisc: 1s., 12 in., 33⅓ rpm, 18 min.), and a series note in parentheses, if appropriate.
4. *Notes*. Immediately following the collation are notes of importance to the user. Examples are whether the filmstrip in-

cludes a teacher's guide, is issued as a part of a particular set in a series of sets, includes a manual, is issued with a script, or is based on some book or other production.

5. *Credits.* These follow the notes and include such information as the individual producer, educational collaborator, director, narrator, cast, photography credits, and accurate description of the contents. This is not an evaluative description and is often provided by the producer or taken from the guide.
6. *Subject Headings.* Subject headings assigned should be consistent with those used for other materials in the collection, with some adaptation for pecularities in the local collection.
7. *Added Entries.* With some discretion the same general rules used with other materials are applicable and appropriate for filmstrips. Included are such added entries as alternate titles, the producer, and a well-known individual author. A series entry when applicable should be included.

There are several other items of a general nature that merit consideration. For the cataloging of filmstrips in a series, it may be advisable to follow the LC Rules in chapter 12 of the *Anglo-American Cataloging Rules*, which indicate that there be descriptive cataloging for each strip in the series. The option here is to enter the entire series under a series entry and have a contents note listing the individual strips. When the filmstrip is one item in a kit, it may be advisable, as recommended by the AECT manual, that the various parts of the kit be kept together; the same would be true of the filmstrip accompanied by a record or a guide which is cataloged as a filmstrip rather than a kit. All items in a kit should have the same classification number. Color coding seems to have lost its popularity, especally with the emphasis on subject matter—rather than on the medium—and the advent of automated records.

The processing of filmstrips presents many options to the academic librarian. Some procedural rules of thumb, based on empirical evidence rather than on specific research, include the following: (1) mark both the can and the filmstrip; (2) try not to destroy contents information on the top of the can by placing the classification label there; (3) if the filmstrip is part of a filmstrip-record set, place the circulation card with the record; (4) if the filmstrip stands alone the circulation cards can be placed in an in-out box; (5) store records and guides near the filmstrip cabinets; (6) take precautions in the use of adhesives for marking the filmstrip since this may lead to problems in the maintenance of viewing equipment.

The cataloging, classification, and processing of filmstrips is a highly individualistic procedure for the academic library; however, procedures ultimately selected should follow studies and research of the various options available. The decisions finally made must be based on their relevance to the library clientele, the institution to be served, and the agreement of the best judgement of one's professional peers.

This is also true of other procedures for handling filmstrips. Storage containers appropriate to a variety of locations and uses are beginning to appear in the commercial market. Although most experimentation in design is currently being undertaken by business and industry, there are notable exceptions. The difficulties faced by academic librarians, with resultant frustrations, must be overshadowed by the fact that they are making yet another valuable information resource available to the academic community.

Maps and Map Collections

Mary Galneder
Alberta Koerner

Mary Galneder is Map Librarian, Department of Geography, University of Wisconsin, Madison. Alberta Koerner is Assistant Map Librarian, University Library, University of Michigan, Ann Arbor.

As reference and source material in a library, maps have two functions. First, facts about the earth's surface may be recorded on them. Second, and more important because it is an unique characteristic, they are a medium for expressing special relationships, especially distance, pattern outlines, and density distributions. The first of these functons may be performed by books also, but in many cases maps are still a more economical medium. A few lines on a map may record what several pages of text would require. In contrast, the second of these functions can be performed by books only in an extremely limited manner. Words may be sufficiently descriptive of a simple pattern, but a complex one in most cases is lost to all except the most imaginative reader. The pictorial aspect of a map expresses to the mind a multitude of spacial facts and relationships at a glance which could not otherwise be comprehended. A map is, therefore, an integral piece of source and reference material in a library.[1]

The value of maps in libraries may be judged by the prominent place which atlases (collections of maps in book form) have in almost every reference collection. Individual sheet maps, however, cannot be handled in the same way as books and have earned the reputation of "problem children" in libraries. For the most part they have been neglected as information sources. This is unfortunate, for when map collections are adequately maintained and serviced by knowledgeable personnel they may "provide students and faculty members with an important research tool equal to books in stature."[2]

HISTORY

With the exception of the Harvard University map collection, very little is known about the early history of academic map collections. The nucleus of the Harvard collection was gathered by Christoph Daniel Ebeling, a German scholar, for use in writing his major work, *Erdbeschreibung und Geschichte von Amerika* (seven volumes, 1793–1816). It contained some ten thousand maps and charts and thirty-two hundred books dating back to the sixteenth century; many rare historical works on America were included. After Ebeling's death in 1817, the collection was purchased by Israel Thorndike and donated to Harvard.[3] In 1877, Justin Winsor became the university librarian. Winsor realized the importance of maps as primary historical sources and, in 1884, he appointed Henry C. Badger as the first Map Curator. Badger produced a four-volume manuscript index of the map collection.[4] In what may have been the first published article identified with an academic map collection, Badger reported: "The collection of maps was a large one, probably far surpassing both in size and value that of any other university library in the world."[5] He gave the size as about fourteen thousand sheets, from approximately eight thousand publications.

About the turn of the century a number of articles about maps in libraries were published, but the authors were associated with public or governmental libraries rather than academic. These early papers are summarized in "Maps in Libraries," by Walter Ristow, who also "points out some of the factors which have delayed the formulation of a generally accepted system for filing and cataloging maps."[6] He attributes the delay to Philip Lee Phillips, first chief of the Library of Congress Map Division, who had stated earlier that "the cataloging of maps and atlases differs very little from the cataloging of ordinary books." Ristow emphasizes the impression, still evident, that the statement apparently made on librarians.

Some interest in maps was aroused by the requirements of World War I, but the period following the war saw a return to isolationism and a decline in such interest. Nevertheless, scattered articles on maps in libraries, particularly governmental libraries, appeared. An impetus for map library growth was the establishment of separate departments of geography, with the associated need for maps, in various universities. In 1934, the Department of Geography at the University of Chicago announced a plan to develop a map library with an ultimate size of 400,000 sheets and briefly described the types of maps to be included.[7] By 1968, the size of that map collection was just over 210,000 sheets.[8] Two years after the University of Chicago's announcement, Edward B. Espenshade, then Curator of Maps, wrote a paper entitled "Building a Collection of Maps."[9] He lists the factors to be considered in the selection of maps, for example, area, scale, date, and acquisition sources; and presents lists of representative maps for Africa, Great Britain, and the United States. Housing, filing, and the classification of maps are also briefly discussed.

During the same period, a cartography textbook by Erwin Raisz included a short chapter on the "Preservation and Cataloguing of Maps" in a university department of geography.[10] Raisz suggests that only the newest maps should be kept in the geography department and each superceded edition should be donated to the library immediately. He also designed a built-in case for the storage of maps and other materials and recommended arranging the maps by region, maintaining a catalog, and mounting commonly used maps on cloth.

During World War II the shortage of maps and sparsity of information about the location of available maps in the United States became evident.[11] Academic and public libraries loaned or donated maps, which had previously been considered archival material, and other sources of geographic information to the United States Army Map Service to aid in the production of newly required military maps.[12] At the same time a number of qualified geographers, librarians, and other specialists entered the map library field and maps began to be accepted as legitimate materials for libraries.[13] In 1941, nine map librarians petitioned the Washington Chapter of the Special Libraries Association (SLA) to establish a Geography and Map Group. Early meeting were centered on discussions of topics related to maps. Dorothy Lewis, in an article entitled "Maps: Problem Children in Libraries," reported on one meeting held in 1944.[14] That same year, the group became a division of SLA with a membership of over fifty. A year later, the New York group was established.[15]

The Geography and Map Division began publication of its *Bul-*

letin as a four-page newsletter in November 1947; in 1953, the *Bulletin* became a quarterly. It has developed into the major source of information about geography and map librarianship and currently averages seventy-two pages per issue. Usually featured in each issue are three major articles, shorter contributions, a Division and professional news section, lists of new books, atlases, maps, book reviews, and miscellaneous items of interest to readers.

In 1950, members of the Geography and Map Division volunteered to prepare a special issue of *Library Journal* entitled "Maps in the Library."[16] The series of papers includes articles on acquisitions, cataloging, maps in public and academic libraries, historical maps, reproduction of maps, and gazetters. Since these topics still concern map librarians, the articles continue to be useful.

Another early project of the Division was the publication of a directory of map collections in the United States and Canada.[17] The *Directory* lists holdings in 527 separate collections, selected from more than 1,100 replies to a questionnaire distributed to educational centers and private collectors.

Following the war, the U.S. Army Map Service distributed a set of approximately 5,000 maps to 45 institutions in order to demonstrate its appreciation for their generosity in loaning source material. A favorable response to these gifts led to the establishment of the Army Map Service depository program. By 1950, " . . . 150 universities and colleges received 20,000 maps; [forty-three of these also received] . . . copies of captured German and Japanese maps."[18] The number of members had risen to 163 when the depository program was temporarily suspended during the Korean War. It was reinstated in 1959. At that time 169 libraries accepted membership; in 1971, 195 institutions (of which only 20 were public libraries) were members.

The libraries which received the Army Map Service maps were forced to accommodate the large number of maps; and space, personnel, and funds were sought and found to organize existing or newly acquired map collections.

In "What About Maps?," a 1955 review of the status and literature of maps in libraries, Walter Ristow discusses progress in the field since 1946, and closes on an optimistic note:

> In summary, it is gratifying to report that the foundations of map librarianship have been greatly strengthened during the past ten years, largely as a result of the energetic and enthusiastic work of a small group of specialists. Continued cooperative

action should result in further progress toward the standardization of processes, techniques, and equipment and in the compilation of additional reference tools and aids.[19]

PRESENT STATUS

In a third summary and literature review, "The Emergence of Maps in Libraries," Ristow writes:

> Many of the proud hopes and objectives of 1955 are, however, largely unrealized. Two factors have, I think, contributed most significantly to the slowdown. First, the Army Map Service depository program, such a powerful stimulus to action in the postwar decade, has had no counterpart in the years here under review. Lacking such a compellant, most library administrators have continued to give low priority to map library problems. Their policies have all too often been influenced by the problems maps pose as nonbook-format materials. . . .
>
> An even greater deterrent has been the heavy manpower drain from the profession's "small group of specialists." By various types of attrition map librarianship has lost, within the past ten or fifteen years, some forty or fifty of its most experienced, knowledgeable, and dedicated professionals.[20]

Ristow's three articles provide a useful historical survey and introduction to the field and literature of map librarianship; however, events in the past few years seem to counter his somewhat pessimistic assessment of the slowdown of progress in map librarianship.

For example, where there had been only one organization devoted to the subject of maps in libraries, there are now three in North America, one in Great Britain, and one on an international level. Since 1966, the Geography and Map Division of SLA has been joined by the Western Association of Map Libraries (WAML), the Association of Canadian Map Libraries (ACML), the Map Curator's Group of the British Cartographic Society, and the Geography and Map Subsection of the International Federation of Library Associations (IFLA).

The Western Association of Map Libraries was formally established on July 1, 1967. It has held semiannual meetings since then and began a *Newsletter* in 1969.[21] Subsequently retitled and now appearing three times a years, the *Information Bulletin* publishes proceedings of WAML meetings, papers contributed by or of particular interest to west coast map librarians, book reviews, lists of maps of western North America, and Association news.

An article by Joan Winearls, "Map Libraries in Canada," may have acted as the catalyst which led to the formation of the Association of Canadian Map Libraries in 1967.[22] The first annual conference was held that year and the *Newsletter* has appeared since 1968. It serves basically as an information source for ACML, while another publication, *Proceedings,* contains the papers delivered at each annual conference meeting. A committee of ACML has begun preparing a *Manual of Standards and Procedures for Map Libraries.* The first two chapters, "Basic Public Relations for the Map Library" and "Physical Requirements: Planning the Map Area," were printed in the March, 1972, *Newsletter.* Other chapters were also included so that members could comment and enable the final publication to represent a consensus of opinion concerning standards and procedures of map librarianship.

After an initial meeting in 1966, a Map Curator's Group was formed as part of the British Cartographic Society. This group has conducted several workshops on map librarianship and has featured tours of map collections for its members. News of its activities are reported in the *Cartographic Journal,* sponsored by the parent organization.[23]

In 1969, the Geography and Map Libraries Subsection of the Special Libraries Section of IFLA held its organizational meeting in Copenhagen.[24] A year later, a second meeting was held in Moscow, although future meetings will be scheduled every other year. Because of its affiliation with IFLA, only library associations may join.[25] Papers presented at the sessions are usually published in *INSPEL,* the journal of the Special Libraries Section.

Among the first needs noted by each organization and completed by three has been the compilation of a directory of map collections in each of their respective areas. The *Directory of Canadian Map Collections* was published in 1969.[26] It lists eighty-seven collections and briefly outlines holdings, facilities, acquisition policy, map coverage, and cataloging and classification information. An appendix shows catalog card styles for twenty-seven different libraries. The Western Association of Map Libraries *Directory* was also published in 1969, and lists 111 collections in the eight westernmost states and two Canadian provinces.[27] Information given for each is similar to that in the Canadian directory. A few private collections are included. The second edition of *Map Collections in the United States and Canada,* compiled by the SLA Geography and Map Division, appeared in 1970. Six hundred and five collections are listed, although the private collections in the 1954 edition have been omitted. Entries also contain information similar to those of the Canadian and Western compilations.

The IFLA directory is in the planning stage; it is anticipated that the first mailing of questionnaires will go to about three hundred libraries.[28] The need for a directory of British map collections has been recorded but no further information is known.[29]

BIBLIOGRAPHIC LITERATURE

In addition to the lengthy bibliographies which accompany "The Emergence of Maps in Libraries," "What About Maps?" and "Maps in Libraries" by Walter Ristow, two separate lists, both now in second editions, are available. One, *Selected Bibliography on Maps in Libraries*, by Jessie Watkins was compiled to aid the "person with the responsibility for organizing and developing a map collection."[30] *Map Librarianship* was developed by Bill M. Woods for a course on carto-bibliography and updated for use in a one-day workshop designed as a brief introduction to the varied aspects of map librarianship.[31] Each is subdivided by subject and covers such topics as map libraries, introductory material on maps, classification and cataloging, acquisitions, mapping agencies, and map use.

Although it is not a bibliography, another guide is the *Index* to numbers 1 through 70 of the *Bulletin* of the SLA Geography and Map Division.[32] Because the *Bulletin* has been a primary source of information on maps in libraries since its beginning, the *Index* is very useful.

Two other publications dealing with maps in libraries are available. The first, *Recent Practices in Map Libraries*, contains papers delivered as a Map Workshop Panel during an SLA Geography and Map Division conference program.[33] The papers, which cover map librarianship, sources of information, map cataloging, equipment, automation, and repair and preservation, were published in *Special Libraries* (vol. 61, 1970) and then reprinted in pamphlet form. The second, a compilation of papers on nonbook librarianship by Jean Kujoth, includes papers on the problems of maps, map collections in university geography departments, and cataloging and classification.[34]

MAP LIBRARIES

Based on figures from the late 1960s, the largest academic map libraries are those at the University of California at Los Angeles, with nearly 300,000 sheets; Louisiana State University School of Geoscience, over 250,000 sheets; and the University of Illinois, almost 250,000 sheets.[35] Descriptions of these and other large and small academic map collections vary from historical summaries to handout sheets for users of the library with most briefly describing the contents of the library, acquisitions, cataloging, facilities, and usage. Among the collections which have been described are those of Cornell, Dartmouth, Florida State, Harvard, Laval, Louisiana State, Northwestern University, Texas A & M, and the Universities of California at Berkeley and Los Angeles, Illinois, Michigan, Oregon, Toronto, Wisconsin at Milwaukee, and Western Illinois. One survey has studied map libraries larger than a certain size in Michigan and offers some generalizations about the field of map librarianship in that state.[36] Another surveys map libraries in the Chicago metropolitan area, their character, and the nature of their holdings.[37] A recent article by John Bergen analyzes map collections of universities and colleges in the Midwest.[38]

In comparison with the academic map collections, the largest map library in the United States, that of the Geography and Map Division, Library of Congress, contained 3,450,356 sheets on June 30, 1972.[39] The U.S. Defense Mapping Agency, Topographic Center (prior to July 1, 1972, the Army Topographic Command, which superceded the Army Map Service in 1969) map collection reported 1,600,000 maps and the U.S. National Archives, 1,500,000 maps. Smaller map collections in government agencies are those of the U.S. Geological Survey, 100,000 maps, and the U.S. Naval Oceanographic Office, 62,000 charts.[40] The largest private map library, that of the American Geographcal Society, listed 310,000 maps and the New York Public Library totalled 287,000 sheets.[41]

Information about the status, services, areas of specialization or special holdings of federal, public, archival, society, and foreign map collections is also important to the academic map librarian. In 1953, Arch Gerlach reviewed government libraries in terms of their potential for geographic research and because of their value in such research, maps were discussed in most cases.[42] Five years later, Catherine Bahn reviewed map libraries in the District of Columbia, the majority of which were administered by the Federal Government.[43] Aspects of three different government map libraries, those of the Library of Congress, the Army Map Service, and the Cartographic Records Branch of the National Archives have also been described in various articles and reports. Additional background information about the beginning of map collecting by Federal agencies and some of the notable items in these collections are presented in papers by Mary Murphy, "History of the Army Map Service Collection;" Richard Stephenson, "Congress, First Map Collection;" Clara LeGear, "Early Years in the Map Division, Library of Congress;" and Herman Friis, "The National Archives of the United States." These papers were delivered at a meeting of the Geography and Map Group of the Washington Chapter of Special Library Association and published under the title *Federal Government Map Collecting.*[44]

Public, archival, and other map collections are important since they frequently contain maps which are no longer available for purchase. Among the collections which have been described are the Rucker Agee Collection, which was donated by Mr. Agee to the Birmingham, Alabama, Public Library; Detroit Public Library; Los Angeles Public Library; New York Public Library and its early maps; the Toronto Public Reference Library; the Illinois State Archives; Louisiana State Library; and the Wisconsin State Historical Society. The James Ford Bell Collection, now a part of the University of Minnesota Library, gathered material relating to the history of discoveries and exploration and has many rare items.[45] The map department of the American Geographical Society, together with the society's library, forms an extensive bibliographic system of geographical publications.[46] As part of this system, the map department maintains an extensive catalog which includes selected maps from books and periodicals as well as separate maps. Reproductions of these cards are available in the society's *Index to Maps in Books and Periodicals.*

To consult copies of rare maps, it may be necessary for a scholar to visit foreign map collections or arrange for photoreproductions from their holdings. Descriptions have appeared for the National Map Collection of Canada; the British Museum Map Room and its resources; the Map Room of the Royal Geographical Society; the Bibliotheque Nationale, Paris; the Deutsche Bücherei in Leipzig; the Saltykov-Shchedrin Public Library in Leningrad; and for a number of map libraries in Denmark, the Netherlands, the Soviet Union, and the Democratic Republic of Germany. Other important map collections, such as the Kartenabteilung of the Deutsche Staatsbibliothek in Berlin and the Kartensammlung of the Institut für Landeskunde in Bonn-Bad Godesberg, are listed in *Orbis Geographicus.*[47]

MANAGEMENT

The day-to-day functions of a map library are comparable to those of a book library. That is, the librarian is concerned with building the collection, organizing it for use, and providing reference service. The librarian should also see that the library has a definite purpose and direct all efforts to fulfilling that purpose.[48] Difficulties in performing these functions stem from the unique format of maps, lack of centralized order facilities, and lack of agreement on standardized cataloging.

Recently, several general articles on the operation of map libraries have appeared. In "Map Librarianship," Robert White discusses the responsibilities, qualifications, and duties of the map librarian. D. S. Rugg, in "Developing the University Map Library," also outlines the responsibilities of the map librarian, as well as the specific details of planning for the collection and the functions of the librarian. A. M. Ferrar, "The Management of Map Collections and Libraries in University Geography Departments," directs his remarks to collections in geography departments and explores the duties of the librarian as they are applicable to smaller collections.[49]

Long range goals for the map library are important both for planning the library and for gaining administrative support. Although it was meant to be prepared prior to consulting an architect about designing new facilities, a useful checklist of points to cover in such a plan was written by Stanley Stevens.[50] The plan for the establishment of the map library at the University of California, Santa Cruz, serves as an example.[51] A written plan for the development of a smaller map collection is also stressed by John Fetros.[52] Emphasizing the role that modern maps play in modern society and pointing out the lack of alternate community sources for maps are methods suggested, also by Fetros, to gain administrative support for the development of map collections.

ACQUISITIONS

As part of its long range plan, an academic map library should have an acquisitions policy that places primary emphasis on the teaching needs and research interests of the academic community it serves. Priorities should be determined for the scope of coverage and geographical areas to be collected. Space, equipment, staff time, budget, and administrative support must also enter into the determination of a philosophy and establishment of a program to assure its fulfillment.

Recent correspondence with representatives of thirty academic map libraries indicates that while most have a philosophy for acquisition, it is seldom a written one. Articles previously cited that describe academic map libraries and their acquisition policies include those for Harvard, the University of Oregon, the Universities of California at Berkeley, Los Angeles, and Santa Cruz, Dartmouth, Cornell, Laval, Western Illinois University, Northwestern University, and the University of Michigan. Robert C. White, former map librarian at the University of Illinois at Urbana, includes a discussion of acquisition policy in his 1970 article cited earlier.

With a clearly established philosophy of acquisition in mind, the map librarian may then turn to the actual task of where to acquire the desired maps. As funds for map collections in academic libraries are usually limited, methods for obtaining free maps are very important. A majority of maps in many academic libraries are obtained through depository agreements with the U.S. Defense Mapping Agency, Topographic Center (small to medium scale topographic and world maps) and the U.S. Geological Survey (topographic and geologic maps for the United States). The U.S. Defense Mapping Agency, Topographic Center, has a fixed number of depository libraries and has a list of about a dozen map libraries waiting to join the program.[53] Similar arrangements may often be made with the U.S. National Ocean Survey (nautical and aeronautical charts), U.S. Agricultural Stabilization and Conservation Service (county soil surveys), and individual state government agencies.

City and county government agencies may also send maps free upon request. Other possibilities include the arranging of duplicate exchange programs with other map libraries, participation in the Library of Congress summer map processing project in exchange for some of its duplicate maps, participation in the Public Law 480 program handled through the Library of Congress, and written requests to chambers of commerce, boards of trade, and tourist groups. Lists of the latter organizations are found in the annual *Worldwide Chamber of Commerce Directory* and *Thomas Register of American Manufacturers.*

Additional listings for sources of free and inexpensive maps appear in articles by Sandra Satterlee, "Sources of Free Maps from Central America, South America, and Africa," and by John Fetros, the bibliography from "Free and Inexpensive Maps for the Public Library."[54]

The most important sources of information about materials which may be purchased (and occasionally obtained free of charge) are journals in the fields of geography and cartography. The Geography and Map Division *Bulletin* of SLA and the WAML *Information Bulletin,* mentioned previously, are of special relevance. Other journals in these fields which often either list or mention new maps are: *Canadian Cartographer, Surveying and Mapping, Cartographic Journal, World Cartography, Professional Geographer,* Association of American Geographers *Newsletter, Imago Mundi,* and Society of University Cartographers *Bulletin.* These and other geographical journals are briefly described by Richard Stephenson in his "Published Sources of Information about Maps and Atlases."[55] Another introduction to the bibliography of cartography was written by Roman Drazniowsky: he discusses bibliographies for maps, atlases, and globes, emphasizing catalogs, annual reports, and lists of maps prepared by various map publishers.[56] In his 1967 article, Ristow also has a section about cartographic production in which he describes many of the above mentioned journals and other acquisition tools.[57] Map materials are occasionally mentioned in journals in other fields such as history, economics, and anthropology.

Stephenson also discusses and lists seventeen cartographic accession lists from various types of map libraries in Australia, Brazil, Canada, Ethiopia, Great Britain, the United States, and Mexico. His bibliography includes lists published by academic map libraries, such as the Map and Geography Library of the University of Illinois. Not mentioned in his selective list are Illinois State University or Northern Illinois University. On the other hand, two regularly appearing lists of special note are cited, the Royal Geographical Society's *New Geographical Literature and Maps* and the American Geographical Society's *Current Geographical Publications.*

Stephenson has lengthy and informative sections on catalogs and lists of map publishers, sellers and secondhand dealers, and gives, by geographical area, their names and addresses. He cites an even longer list containing addresses of about 250 agencies which was produced by the Map Library of the Canadian Department of Energy, Mines and Resources in Ottawa. Now available in a third edition, this list has grown to include 460 references and two new supplements: "Out of Print Maps and Atlases" and "Dealers in Three Dimensional Maps and Globes."[58] Each gives addresses for commercial as well as governmental agencies.

Articles concerned with sources of information about maps are included in Watkins' bibliography; of these Edward Espenshade's article is of special relevance.[59] Another source, for maps and aerial photographs, is *Sources of Information and Materials: Maps and Aerial Photographs.*[60] Although it was compiled for teachers needing sources of cartographic information, it is also useful for map librarians. Items of particular use are the bibliography of "Maps and Mapping;" and chapters titled "Sheet Maps and Other Cartographic Materials from Government and Society Sources;" "Atlases;" and "Aerial and Space Photography." Addresses are included for government agencies, dealers who distribute the U.S. Geological Survey's topographic quadrangles, and commercial agencies named in the text. Information about films, filmstrips, slides, globes, relief models, and map transparencies is also provided.

As mentioned previously, government agencies are a major source of map publications. Stephenson's article gives addresses of many such agencies, and the Watkins' publication references articles pertaining to the acquisition of maps from government sources. Important U.S. Government publications that are usually accessible to the map librarian include the *Monthly Catalog of Government publications,* published by the U.S. Superintendent of Documents, Government Printing Office, and its various price lists, such as *Price List 53: Maps, Engineering, Surveying*; the *Monthly Checklist of State Publications,* issued by the Library of Congress; the *New Publications* list of the Geological Survey; the proof sheets for "Maps" (now only atlases are listed although the term "Maps" is still used) which are available by subscription from the Library of Congress; and the *Catalog of Copyright Entries . . . Maps and Atlases.* Joseph Rogers, retired chief of the Copyright Cataloging Division at the Library of Congress, discusses the types of maps included and information available from the *Catalog of Copyright Entries . . . Maps and Atlases* in "Copyright Catalog Is Useful Tool."[61] The copyright catalog is especially useful for its listings by copyright claimant, subjects, areas, editors, and compilers. Renewal registrations are separately listed. A "Publishers Directory" in each issue lists all publishers represented in the Current Registrations section and gives the latest address for each.

Academic map librarians should not overlook the *Bibliographie Cartographique Internationale,* an international bibliography of maps, or the national bibliographies which are regularly used in library acquisition departments.[62] Although publication is usually several years late, the *Bibliographie Cartographique Internationale* is still the most complete bibliography of maps. It is "published annually by the Comité Nationale de Géographie and the Union Géographique Internationale. Each volume has an author and subject index and is arranged according to the major geographical divisions beginning with the world, then progressing to continents, which in turn are subdivided by individual countries in alphabetical order."[63] A descriptive list of twenty-four national bibliographies, which have sections on maps and atlases, is included by Stephenson in his article on map sources.[64] He lists the bibliographies by geographic area, making special note of those for Austria, East Germany, New Zealand, Poland, Switzerland, Turkey, France, West Germany, and Australia. Such bibliographies are especially important since most of them give prices, an item of information which is sometimes difficult to obtain for maps.

Some of the previously mentioned acquisition tools help the map librarian decide if a map is worth adding to the collection by descriptive annotations. Only rarely are reviews available to aid in map selection. Three references which may be of assistance in evaluating maps and atlases are: "Evaluation of Modern Maps" by Richard Harrison; *Keys to Map Evaluation* by the SLA Geography and Map Division; and J. Patrick Walsh's *General World Atlases: A Comparative Analysis* (an up-dated version is included in his *Home Reference Books in Print*).[65]

After an academic map librarian has decided on a map to acquire, it must be ordered, a task requiring specialized knowledge and systematic procedures. Some map librarians handle this procedure themselves while others submit their orders through a central library ordering department. Both processes involve sending the order to the publisher itself or to a dealer through whom maps (or books) are regularly obtained. Since map librarians, with the assistance of the aforementioned acquisition tools, will be most familiar with map dealers and publishers, it may be advantageous for the map librarian to place orders. However, it is often possible for the map specialist to indicate for a central order department the source from which a certain map may be obtained. Problems common to both methods of handling map orders are the time involved in verification of orders, record control, handling of invoices and dealers, maintaining budget accounts, avoiding duplication of orders, and assuring the receipt of items. It is debatable as to which method provides for the handling of these problems in the most effective manner. Advantages of a central ordering department to the map librarian are no handling of payments, invoices, claims, or order forms, and less unintentional duplication in library systems having a number of divisions or branches for which maps may be ordered.

The Western Association of Map Libraries' *Information Bulletin* for June, 1970 (volume 1), contains résumés from a panel on map acquisition control. Two of the participants, Robert Sivers of the University of California at Santa Barbara, and Evelyn Percival of the University of California at Los Angeles discuss methods of direct control by the map librarian, while Sheila Dowd of the University of California at Berkeley covers the procedure of dealing through a central acquisitions department.

Regardless of the method utilized for ordering maps, each academic map librarian will have to retain a file of orders outstanding, received, and cancelled. A separate file for each category, arranged either by main entry of cartographer, compiler, and publisher, or by area, seems to be most efficient. A periodic review of orders outstanding should be undertaken to make sure materials are obtained. It may be necessary to initiate claims or follow-up letters to receive wanted materials. These problems are discussed by Sivers, Percival and Dowd.

When a map has been received, the next step in the process of making it available to readers is to indicate receipt of the map on the order file record or to file a slip in the orders received file. Depending upon the backlog of maps to process, the next steps will vary somewhat. The map may be added to a group of materials awaiting processing. Then, depending on the type of map, it may be given an ownership stamp, accessioned, indexed, classified or cataloged, and filed.

CATALOGING AND CLASSIFICATION

There are many different opinions as to methods of classification and cataloging for maps. Since a collection of maps is not very useful unless it is organized, there is general agreement that some method is necessary. The academic map librarian may read about the reasons for and the necessity of classification and cataloging in the publications by Ristow and White given above. Many other authors have discussed the topic, and references to pertinent articles are found in Watkins' *Selected Bibliography* and the *Cumulative Index* of the *Bulletin*.[66] Of special note to academic map librarians are articles by O. C. Anderson, Arch C. Gerlach, T. R. Smith, M. E. Fink, Bill Woods, and Roman Drazniowsky.[67]

Commonly used classification schemes in published form are those of the Library of Congress, American Geographical Society, Universal Decimal Classification, and Boggs and Lewis.[68] A modification of the Dewey Decimal Classification is used for the wall map collection at the United States Air Force Academy; this scheme is described by Thomas Hinckley.[69] Other classification schemes or subject heading lists for maps may be borrowed or photocopies purchased from the collection maintained by the SLA Special Classifications Committee at the School of Library Science of Western Reserve University. The guide to the collection lists twenty-two items which deal with maps.[70]

In selecting a classification scheme it is important to consider whether it can encompass an expanding collection, be applied readily by people not necessarily experienced in map classification, retain its currency, provide easy and rapid access to maps, and result in maps of the same areas or subjects being located in close proximity.

Cataloging methods often followed are found in the chapter on "Maps, Atlases, etc." in the *Anglo-American Cataloging Rules,* and in books by Samuel Boggs and Dorothy Lewis and the American Geographical Society. A major controversy involved in cataloging methods for maps is the use of a standard main entry as used in book cataloging or an area designation as the main entry. In "The Emergence of Maps in Libraries," Ristow presents an interesting discussion of the topic.[71] Important considerations in determining how detailed the cataloging will be are the number of staff members available and able to do it, the amount of time they can expend on this activity, and the size of the collection. A small staff and collection may necessitate less detailed cataloging.

A relatively recent development which may eventually serve to standardize and expedite the cataloging process is the use of automated techniques. It is discussed by Ristow who cites four references on the topic.[72] The Library of Congress has developed a Machine-Readable Cataloging (MARC) format for map cataloging which is described in detail in the LC publication, *Maps: A MARC Format,* and discussed in the article, "Machine-Readable Map Cataloging in the Library of Congress;" another manual from the Library of Congress illustrates how catalog data is prepared for conversion to machine-readable form.[73] Mary Murphy's "Map Collection Prepares to Automate" gives a detailed description of the process at the U.S. Army Topographic Command library, makes recommendations to libraries considering automation, and provides thirteen items in its bibliography; Carlos Hagen discusses an information retrieval system for maps for application at UCLA and stresses the importance of automated cataloging.[74]

Verification of spellings or form for place names, authors, cartographers, etc., is common to all cataloging methods. An academic map librarian, following cataloging rules and a standard main entry, can follow the same verification procedure used by other catalogers in the library. This may require consulting the library's book catalog, as well as the map catalog, various book publishing information sources, such as *Books in Print, Cumulative Book Index,* telephone directories, Library of Congress cards, government directories, the LC *Copyright Catalog,* and published map catalogs such as the *British Museum Catalog,* and catalogs of the American Geographical Society, the Bancroft Library, New York Public Library, and the William L. Clements Library.

Verification of place names is simplified by keeping an alphabetical record of all names used. For a place name where the country is known, the standard authorities are the gazetteers of the U.S. Board of Geographic Names.[75] General gazetteers such as *Columbia-Lippincott* and *Websters,* accepted as standard references, may have to be consulted if the country is not known. Since there is no single comprehensive gazetteer of the United States, the *Rand McNally Commercial Atlas and Marketing Guide,* with its state by state place and physical feature indexes, is the best source of information for domestic names. Postal and shipping guides may also be consulted.

Old, rare, and manuscript maps bring to cataloging the difficult task of determining whether the map is separately published or from an atlas, and sometimes determining the cartographer, engraver, and publisher of the map. Lloyd Brown, in his *Notes on the Care and Cataloging of Old Maps,* gives detailed instructions concerning classification and cataloging, especially for determining the cartographer and the various editions of a map.[76] He also provides examples of typed cards and indicates items on old maps which should be described as notes on the cards. Important aids for solving problems involving early maps are the lists of geographical atlases in the Library of Congress, compiled by Philip Lee Phillips and Clara LeGear; *Atlantes Neerlandici* by Cornelis Koeman; and the Map Collectors' Circle series. Occasionally regional bibliographies will prove useful, for example, the volumes produced by Cumming, Wheat, and Karpinski.[77]

Important for helping users find the maps they need is the analysis of maps for pertinent subject and added entries. For example, maps with insets of cities or thematic maps cataloged only under the area or subject of the main map will hide potentially useful information. Noting this data on the catalog card and providing subject cards for the subjects with which it deals will make the information readily accessible. An advantage of computerized cataloging is the ease of providing numerous approaches to the areas, subjects, individuals, or agencies represented by a map.

Lists useful for assigning subject headings to maps will be found in Boggs and Lewis, the Library of Congress list of *Subject Headings,* Sears, and the publication American Geographical Society. Two of the MARC map project publications indicate how to assign headings.[78] Added entries for compilers, publishers, and printers may be made to the extent permitted by the amount of staff time available for cataloging, typing, and filing.

The types of card catalogs that are found in academic map libraries vary not only according to differences in classification and cataloging, but also in the arrangement of cards in the catalog. Staffs of some map libraries follow the standard dictionary catalog system, while others have divided catalogs which group together various categories such as subjects or areas, main entries (cartographers, compilers, publishers, printers), or dates. In some libraries, where detailed cataloging is not attempted, a shelflist by area or subject may be used to locate maps that will satisfy particular user needs. A dictionary catalog eliminates the necessity of remembering which file to check for a topic, area, cartographer or date, but requires more complicated filing rules. It may slightly reduce time spent in organizing cards for filing. A divided catalog is advantageous when one is concerned only with maps of a certain area, subject, or date. It will require looking in both such files should one be seeking maps published by a governmental agency of a certain area and also for maps of the area, while a dictionary catalog will usually group such entries together.

EQUIPMENT

After a map has been processed, it must be physically added to the files. The choice of storage equipment is a major decision. Most map librarians now agree that horizontal cases, in steel or wood, with large shallow drawers offer the best combination of accessibility to and protection for the maps. These cases, originally designed as drafting room equipment, consist of five drawer units with separate tops and bases. Units may be stacked as high as the weight of the floor will support, although a height of only two sections provides a convenient work area on top of the cases and offers expansion space for the future. Mary Galneder discusses some of the features found in various units and the differences between wood and steel cases.[79]

Drawer sizes are not standardized but may be characterized as small, medium, large, and extra large. The medium size, with interior dimensions of about 42 x 30 x 2 inches, seems most useful. Most maps may be stored without folding and wasted space is minimal. For special purposes, other size drawers may be more desirable. For example, the U.S. Geological Survey topographic quadrangles which comprise a large part of most collections, can be stored in two stacks within a drawer if a large size is chosen. Extra large drawers, 72 x 42 x 2 inches, are useful for storing oversize materials, which should not be folded, e.g., air photo enlargements and navigation charts.

Within the drawers most maps are housed in paper folders which should be made of nonacid paper with a pH factor of 4.5 or higher.[80] Folders, in addition to offering added protection from dust, serve to keep maps of one area or one set in the same place. Open edges of the folders may face the front or the back of the drawers. If the open edge is at the front, the map may be seen before it is removed; if the open edge is at the back, it is necessary to remove the folder first, but it offers more protection for the map.[81] An ideal but costly arrangement except for rare or expensive material is to have one folder for each map.

Methods of labeling folders vary a great deal. Barbara Christy, in "Critique of Pure Labeling for Map Collections," presents a rationale for using labels and discusses the amount of information to give, style to follow, and materials to use for drawer and folder labels.[82] Walter Ristow and David Carrington in "Machine-Readable Map Cataloging in the Library of Congress" describe the use of catalog work sheets as folder labels which provides an easily visible detailed description of each map.[83] The greater the amount of information provided on the folder and the fewer the number of maps in the folder, the easier the access to desired maps will be.

Other types of storage units are briefly described by J. Douglas Hill.[84] Vertical units are generally not as satisfactory as those with horizontal drawers, at least for a large collection. Portfolios and buckram covered boxes offer more protection from dust, but more time is needed for removing and refiling the maps. Therefore, their use is not economical except for archival collections, where maximum protection and the preservation of maps in their original condition is a primary function.

An extensive report on equipment and space needs for map libraries was prepared by a committee of the SLA Geography and Map Division under the chairmanship of Catherine Bahn.[85] The weight of filled map cases and the number of maps per unit have been determined and are extremely useful figures when new equipment or a new physical location for cases is under consideration. Other types of equipment and supplies are also described and a list of manufacturers, at that time, is included. Equipment needed in a map room but not ordinarily found in a library includes drafting and light tables, a projector for enlarging or reducing the size of the map, large carts on wheels with a top surface of approximately twelve square feet, and work room space with a sink. Special attention is given to the space needed by readers for consulting maps. Bahn cites at least ten square feet while Clara LeGear suggests sixteen square feet.

The descriptions and floor plans of two recently opened map rooms, at Northwestern University and the University of Michigan, illustrate different ways of arranging map collections.[86] The arrangement usually varies with the types and sizes of map cases, the types of materials, the needs of users, other equipment in the map room, and architectural limitations of the space available.

Rolled wall maps may also be a part of the library map collection. Shallow slanted bins with each map labeled and listed on the doors offer satisfactory storage at the University of Wisconsin. Other types of storage for these maps have been described by Roepke, Collier, and Doerr.[87]

REPAIR AND PRESERVATION

The repair and preservation of maps must also concern the map librarian. Clara LeGear's article, "Maps: Their Care, Repair, and Preservation in Libraries," is a comprehensive and useful guide to the care of maps.[88] It guides one along progressive steps from the unwrapping of a package of maps through mounting and proper storage. Preservation and repair are also covered. Temperature and humidity controlled facilities are as important for maps as they are for books. Richard Smith has tested the deterioration rate of United States Geological Survey topographic maps and concludes that relative humidities lower than the recommended 50 percent are more conducive to a long life expectancy.[89]

For the repair of older materials, Boak writes "not to do anything which cannot be undone."[90] He recommends repairing rips with reinforcing materials affixed by a water soluble or nontoxic solvent. For preserving an entire map, lamination of the map after it has been deacidified is probably the best process.

REFERENCE SERVICE

The objective of reference service for the map collection is the same as it is for the book collection—the provision of needed information. This objective, however, is made more difficult by the lack of bibliographic control for maps, by the lack of knowledge about the information on maps which may be of value to the prospective user, the format of maps which makes it more difficult to examine individual maps than books, and the large number of maps at different scales and published at different times for the same area.

Four types of sources are needed for reference service: a map catalog, a collection of reference materials, a file of information about map publishers and dealers, and information about how maps are and have been made.[91] Since many map collections are not adequately cataloged, the librarian must be aware of the type of information apt to be found on maps of different publishers.

Books which are useful in map collections are listed in the section on cataloging and in the bibliography by Woods.[92] The author also advocates the collection of information, in the form of dealers' and publishers' catalogs, about where maps may be obtained as an important part of map reference service. From such information, the user can determine which map or which sheets of a series of topographic quadrangles he requires and order them for himself.[93]

A recent publication is Muriel Lock's *Modern Maps and Atlases*.[94] This book attempts to describe current mapping on a worldwide scale. Separate parts discuss international maps and atlases, national and regional maps and atlases according to geographic areas, and thematic maps and atlases. Other parts cover modern cartographic techniques and map librarianship from the British viewpoint. Lock's book is a useful tool containing information not combined elsewhere or readily available but it should be used with care.

EXHIBITS AND PROMOTION

Because maps are unique library material, a good way to inform library users about the existence and the services of the map collection is through the use of exhibits. Whether it is a comprehensive history of mapping, commemoration of an historic cartographic event, the development of a city, or a fanciful Christmas case, a map display attracts attention.

Useful information on the planning and designing of cartographic displays is contained in "Cartographic Exhibits" and

"Map Exhibits—Panel Discussion."[95] Ways of using maps in connection with books and other library material are outlined by Dalphin and English, and Hammond.[96]

Other means of promoting interest in maps include traveling exhibits, magazine articles, and offers to lecture to interested groups. A successful program to introduce students to the resources of the Map Library at the University of Kansas has been established; it includes library tours and orientation, class assignments using the library, cross references in the public card catalog, and a special bibliography.[97]

MAP LISTS AND USE STUDIES

There is no basic list of maps for college libraries. However, the articles "These Maps Are Essential" and "Building a Collection of Maps" list some types of maps that should be considered as a basic part of any map collection.[98]

Only two surveys on the use of map collections have been published; both were directed to the clients who use the map library rather than the types of maps which are requested. Carlos Hagen found that the use of the UCLA map library is not limited to geographers but includes users from a variety of campus departments as well as from off campus. At the University of Oregon, Harry Bach's survey was designed to determine the academic year of users.[99] Results showed that only five percent of the student body used the map room, and that more than twice as many upper classmen used the collection as did lower classmen. A year long circulation count at the University of Wisconsin, where the Map Library is housed and administered as part of the Geography Department, revealed 2,479 maps and air photos charged out to members of the department or students using them for departmental assignments and 2,425 items charged out to faculty and students from other campus departments.

TRAINING AND EDUCATION

Training for map librarianship has been a neglected field of library education.[100] Western Michigan University recently instituted a program for map librarians which combines standard library school courses with geography courses; integration between the two is provided through an internship under the University map librarian. Other courses have been offered at Columbia, Illinois, Toronto, and the Graduate School of the U.S. Department of Agriculture on an irregular schedule.[101] The need for more training has been stressed by Woods and the contents of educational programs examined by Woods and Hagen. Louis Kiraldi also reviews methods for training map librarians and suggests an internship program in preference to formal classes.[102]

In the absence of formal training, various universities and organizations have presented programs, workshops, or institutes on maps in libraries. One of the first was conducted at the University of Illinois in 1955.[103] Since then, a workshop has been conducted at the Free Library of Philadelphia in cooperation with the Drexel Institute of Technology and an institute has been held at the University of California at Los Angeles. The New Jersey Library Association conducted day-long workshops for map librarians in 1970, 1971, and 1972, and the Geography and Map Group of the SLA Washington Chapter held a conference at LC Geography and Map Division.[104]

The Summer Processing Projects of LC Geography and Map Division have also provided prospective and working map librarians with an introduction to the way maps are handled in that organization. These projects are basically designed to help the Library of Congress dispose of its backlog of surplus maps. In exchange for their work at the division, participants may select maps from the surplus files for shipment to their respective institutions. Pros and cons of the project have been explored by Ristow, Hagen, and Otness.[105]

CIRCULATION

Rules for the circulation of maps in academic library collections vary greatly, depending primarily upon the orientation of the map collection toward the academic community as a whole, to a number of schools or departments, to a specific department, or to specific types of maps, e.g. rare, geologic. The previously cited articles about specific academic libraries may be consulted for examples of policies and procedures. Other articles of interest are those by Alonso, "Conservation and Circulation in Map Libraries: A Brief Review," and Winearls, "To Loan or Not to Loan."[106] In general, it appears that some circulation is desirable provided rules are established regarding procedures for handling maps and the length of the loan period. Loans for on campus office or classroom use should be permitted. The lending of maps for field use should be discouraged. Some map libraries have collections intended for field use, but most are geared to library reference use. The availability of increasingly larger paper sizes in the various quick copying devices should encourage the reproduction of needed maps for field use.

Photographs, Pictures and Prints

H. Joanne Harrar

Ms. Harrar is Associate Director of Libraries, University of Georgia, Athens

INTRODUCTION

The three media, photographs, pictures and prints, share certain characteristics: they are two-dimensional in form, and visual representations, either of abstract ideas and concepts or of concrete objects, places, or people, imagined or at some time real. The means of creation give photographs and prints their distinctiveness; yet their differences may at times be blurred. For example, an early etching of a painting by Rembrandt may be both a fine print in its own right as well as a reproduction of an important work of art. Recent technological developments enable fine prints to be mass-produced by modern lithographic methods; such a print then becomes a picture, as does an original photograph undergoing the same process.

The importance of such distinctions may exist in direct relation to the size and scope of the collections in which these media are found, as well as the ways in which the collections are used, and the degree of scholarly sophistication of their users. In any event, photographs and prints may be distinguished by definition. Photographs are pictures or images produced on specially coated papers through the action of light upon sensitized surfaces; they are paper prints derived from negative film. Prints are pictures on paper lifted from cut, etched, greased or otherwise prepared surfaces which usually have been inked and against which the paper has been pressed.

According to the Print Council of America, an original print (or fine print) is a work of art whereby the artist himself has created the picture or design upon the appropriate surface, then has pulled (or supervised the pulling of) the print from that surface, and finally has approved the print, generally by numbering and signing the product.

Since photographs and prints are considered to be broad categories of pictures, it is obvious that pictures encompass a variety of graphic representations, even including drawings, charts, and graphs. A clear distinction between even the print and photograph is becoming increasingly difficult in view of the work of contemporary artists. Pictures as referred to here are largely published (printed) reproductions of images other than works of art, for the most part, published reproductions of photographs. Perhaps one should make a clear distinction between the medium and the content in one's use of words: i.e., between (1) the subject category to which an image belongs, and (2) the medium in which that image is preserved. The problem probably derives from the fact that presently the work of art has a very specialized purpose and is appreciated only for its own sake, whereas, before the invention of photography, images now thought of as works of art had a much broader purpose, that of recording "life." A historian might use a painting as a visual record of an event in Renaissance history, but he probably would not think of using a twentieth-century work of art in this way; he would use a photograph. Thus art and nonart categories become muddled. While this fact should not bother one too much when organizing a "picture file" for a public library or a school library, a college librarian in an institution that offers history as well as art history or art appreciation courses must keep the dual function of the work of art (and of reproductions thereof) clearly in mind.

While pictures on two-dimensional surfaces have been extant since the Egyptians first put reed pen-brushes to papyrus, prints emerged later, with the invention of printing from wooden blocks in China, probably during the seventh century. Photographs, of course, constitute a relatively new medium, appearing in the early nineteenth century with the development of a basic photographic process by the French physicist, Joseph Niepce.

The formalized collection of works in these media appears to have first taken place, on the Continent, at least, in the great museums. Fine prints, of course, constituted an art form worthy of preservation. Photographs were used as early as 1855 to inventory the contents of museum collections; only later did photography itself gain recognition as a distinctive art form.[1]

In the United States the collecting pattern initially followed that of Europe. It was not until the waning of the nineteenth century that collections were developed in libraries. The first known picture collection was begun in 1889 by John Cotton Dana at the Denver Public Library; he later expanded upon the concept in the Newark, New Jersey, Public Library.[2] By 1915 picture collections existed in many public libraries, including New York, Boston, Chicago, and Washington.[3] Today outstanding collections are located at the New York Public Library, as well as at such municipal libraries as those of Boston, Chicago, and Cleveland.

These collections have become important concomitants of museums, either as integral parts of their holdings of original works of art, or as adjuncts, housed in the museums' libraries, and used primarily for scholarly study and research. The first instance is exemplified by the graphics collection held by the Museum of Modern Art, or the Print Department of the Metropolitan Museum of Art; the latter by the collections of the Frick Art Reference Library in New York City.

Private business, industries, and organizations have amassed large quantities of visual resource material of potential value to the academic community. A single periodical publisher, "*Look* Magazine recently turned over its files of 17½ million black and white photograph negatives, 1½ million color transparencies, 450 thousand contact sheets, and 25 thousand movies stills to the Library of Congress. Filling more than 100 five-drawer filing cabinets, the collection's card index will enable LC's Prints and Photographs Division to make these resources immediately available for research by scholars without restriction and generally for other noncommercial purposes."[4]

While collections have developed within a significant number of American universities, their location and administration varies. Thus the major print collection at Harvard falls within the province of the university museum, while the photograph collection is under the jurisdiction of the Fine Arts Library of the Harvard College Library.[5] The Fine Arts Library is not, however, the exclusive repository of photographs at Harvard. There are many photograph collections in the University, all more or less specialized. The Fogg Museum and the Carpenter Center for Visual Studies contain photographs as works of art. There are, in addition, collections of photographs on astronomy, anthropology, social history, and many other academic subjects elsewhere in the Harvard libraries.

Most institutions are not confronted with the administration of the complexities of material which obtains at Harvard, however; it is common to find graphics collections attached either to university museums or to university libraries, as is the case at Yale, Princeton, and the University of California at Berkeley.

College libraries have not, as a rule, developed graphic arts collections of any magnitude approaching that of universities in this country. Virtually all college libraries possess picture files of some kind in support of various phases of the curriculum, and some have adopted the public library-initiated activity of lending or renting art works or reproductions for home or dormitory use and appreciation. Large collections are limited; an outstanding, though atypical, example is that located in the Smith College Library. As with some university collections, college graphics collections may be attached to the institution's museum, as is the case at Bowdoin, or to an instructional department, as at Bryn Mawr.

Picture collections, while not so varied in scope, size, or purpose, have been traditional features of school libraries, where they have been used to support units of classroom instruction.

Special libraries, too, have recognized the value of graphics collections for a variety of reasons: some provide visual histories of the businesses or companies with which the libraries are affiliated; others are collections of pictures which have been used, or may possibly be used, in publications issued by these organizations, e.g., the picture collections of the National Geographic Society Library, or the Time-Life, Inc., publications library. Such collections may also be oriented to the promotion of the companies they serve, or some specific aspects of those companies' endeavors or products.

Particularly noteworthy of recognition are the collections housed in the U.S. National Archives and in the Library of Congress, two of the most important special and research libraries in the United States. While the National Archives holdings may be deemed largely historical in nature and use, those of the Library of Congress are not only historical, but also important aids to the full range of scholarly pursuits.

Picture collections have reached different levels of development with different emphasis and for different purposes, depending on the user needs as perceived by the institution. From elementary school through graduate school, the major function is to support instructional programs. Elementary, junior, and senior high schools rely almost solely on pictures garnered from diverse and free sources; while college and university collections may include paintings, prints, and photographs, with many being purchased from dealers, that are used not only in the classroom on a collective basis, but in the individual pursuit of study and research. All institutional (school, public, and college) collections are usually also designed to inculcate in the beholder an appreciation of the visual arts. Although such appreciation may be a similar intent of museum collections, the use of visual materials for scholarship is often their primary concern. Special libraries may include museum collections and specialized departmental libraries within academic institutions that provide their visual materials for the use of scholars studying specialized subjects or aspects of the several media themselves.

Regardless of the type and size of libraries in which collections of photographs, pictures, and prints are found, those responsible for collection development are confronted with certain common problems. These include the selection, acquisition, processing, housing, and use of the various forms. Although techniques, particularly those of organization and use, may be similar from form to form, the size of the collection being treated as well as its use and the sophistication of the user groups substantially influence the level of detail and quality of treatment given a collection. The smaller the collection, the more simple its organization tends to be; while the converse requires a more complex arrangement to provide adequate data for effective retrieval of specific items.

Though the modes of treatment of a small picture collection in a school library might closely parallel those in a college library collection of similar size, those modes would probably differ substantially for a medium to large size collection in a college or public library. The treatment of the three media in the pages which follow is indicative of either suggested or commonly followed practices for collections in college libraries today.

PICTURES

Although picture collections may constitute separate entities in themselves, they may, in smaller academic libraries, encompass photographs, plans, charts, and other two-dimensional representations as well. In university and larger college libraries, picture collections may be administered and housed in conjunction with an art department or museum. In smaller colleges, they are often located under the jurisdiction of the library's reference department staff and used in support not only of the institution's art and art appreciation program, but of general liberal arts courses, such as history, geography, and teacher education. Thus the college library picture collection is apt to be broad in scope and simple in organization and administration.

Additions to picture collections should be selected on the basis of their subject value, or, if a file of representations of important art works is being created, on the basis of fidelity to the originals, especially in the quality of color reproduction and registration. Clarity of the images depicted is important. Whether the pictures are in black and white or in color may be important considerations to the user; for certainly color, if of high quality, lends a visual perception of reality unmatched by black and white illustrations.

Sources for obtaining pictures are limited only by the imagination of the staff responsible for maintaining the collection. Heavily illustrated magazines such as *National Geographic* or *Realités* are excellent and readily available. The cutting of more expensive art journals, where preservation and easy retrieval of the pictures is important, may take precedence over the retention of issues in their entirety. Other standard sources are: illustrated volumes withdrawn from the library's circulating collection, travel literature, chamber of commerce publications, calendars, and, of course, items listed as available gratis in such sources as *Library Journal's* "Checklist" or the *Wilson Library Bulletin*'s column, "Information Exchange." Ireland's *The Picture File in School, College and Public Libraries*[6] is a well-known guide which lists a variety of sources. Although somewhat out of date, this publication still yields numerous leads which should prove productive. Other useful and more current aids are the three titles published by Bruce Miller Publications: *Sources of Free Pictures, Sources of Inexpensive Pictures*, and *Sources of Free Travel Posters.*[7]

It may not always be possible or wise to bring all pictures together in one location; yet it is helpful to have an index, by subject, to pictures available in volumes on the library's shelves. Indexes to pictures in books and magazines are important adjuncts to the picture collection itself. Four particularly valuable titles are Clapp's *Art in Life 1936–1956* and *Art in Life 1957–1963*,[8] Havlice's *Art in Time*,[9] and Vance's *Illustration Index.*[10]

Once pictures have been acquired, it is usually necessary to mount them so that they may be uniformly preserved, and housed. Mounting may be simple: attaching the picture with rubber cement or glue to a standard-sized backing, either heavy wrapping paper, mounting paper, or cardboard. However, it should be known that both glue and rubber cement deteriorate and discolor in time. Drymounting is the best for preservation purposes, but is more expensive. Again, Ireland provides specific instructions for cutting and mounting, and suggests brands and weights of papers. Hicks[11] gives alternative modern methods of recent development: coating the pictures with a plastic spray or inserting them in envelopes of transparent plastic, forms of protection which, while sturdy, are somewhat more expensive and apt to cause glare. Plastic envelopes should not be used without discrimination, as some kinds are safe and others are not; there are some that attract moisture and give off harmful chemicals. Lamination, using the proper plastic material and equipment, is likewise possible but costly. This process is economically feasible for very large collections where long-term or permanent retention is anticipated. Heavy use of pictures may also make it imperative that they be laminated.

Whether mounted or not, pictures may be filed in manila folders, either standard or legal size, and housed in vertical filing cabinets. Standard or letter-sized vertical files will accommodate mounts up to 9″ by 12″; legal-sized files will house mounts up to 10″ by 15″. Unless mounts are packed fairly tightly in vertical files, they are apt to bend and warp. For that reason, the horizontal map cabinet, in which pictures may be laid flat, is preferred in some libraries. Larger pictures may be housed flat in map or chart file drawers. These are available in five-drawer units, each drawer equipped with an interior fabric dust cover. A recommended cabinet size which should accommodate most mounted pictures is 43″ wide by 32″ front-to-back, with 2″ deep drawers.

All picture collections require at least one means of retrieval. This may be nothing more than the use of subject headings, whereby one appropriate to each picture is added in a standardized location on the face of the mounting or the verso of the picture itself. Pictures entered under one specific heading are housed in manila folders or envelopes similarly marked and alphabetically filed by subject. A library may choose to develop its own list, or to use a recognized tool, such as *Sears' List of Subject Headings.*[12] On the other hand, there are available lists of subject headings specifically geared to picture collections. These include the one devised by Ireland in *The Picture File in School, College and Public Libraries,*[13] as well as the Newark Public Library list, updated by Dane.[14]

Picture collections are not, as a rule, given full cataloging and classification in the average college library. Ireland suggests that a card file be kept of headings used and of cross references employed to aid the library staff and users in location of desired subjects. Thus cataloging is less common, perhaps because of the expense which would be incurred for what in many libraries is a relatively ephemeral collection.

Pictures, of the kind discussed here, may circulate for out-of-library use or may be examined only in the library building; policies regarding use differ widely. Where pictures do circulate, however, a simple charge card indicating the borrower, the due date of the items borrowed, the number of pictures taken, and the subject categories from which they are drawn may be prepared. The pictures, when checked out, may be placed in manila envelopes, plastic sleeves, or even cylindrical containers, for protection and transportability.

Collections of art reproductions should also be mentioned in conjunction with general picture collections. These vary from copies of famous works of art found in books and periodicals and on post cards to full-sized facsimiles suitable for hanging. These reproductions may serve as an inventory of an existing collection or collections, provide the means to study and compare particular works when the originals are not available, and offer an opportunity for aesthetic pleasure either within the library or within the viewer's own home. Image clarity, quality of color reproduction, and fidelity to the original work, which are the criteria for picture collections, also apply to collections of art reproductions, generally to an even more rigid degree.

The source of the "picture" and the name of the photographer are extremely important when picture collections are considered finding devices for sources of images not merely for enjoyment and study, but for reproduction for publication. This, however, brings up the sticky and largely unsolved pictorial copyright problem. The legal and ethical problems connected with the use of images should be weighted in each instance and appropriate action taken to ensure no direct loss of royalties or value to the creator or owner of the original work. Single copies of material within an educational institution for student and faculty on campus use in connection with an established curriculum is a currently acceptable procedure. The abuse of this liberty should not be tolerated and no resale or extension of this privilege considered if it will infringe on the rights of the creator or owner.

A variety of selection aids for art reproductions are available. Many in themselves constitute catalogs of reproductions, while at the same time providing the sources from which to purchase full-size or near full-size copies of the originals. Four volumes stand out: the two UNESCO catalogs,[15] Bartran's *A Guide to Color Reproductions*,[16] and the latest edition of New York Graphic Society's *Fine Art Reproductions of Old and Modern Masters*.[17] The UNESCO catalogs, with a black and white reproduction of each work included, cover reproductions for sale by publishers from several countries, while the New York Graphic Society catalog is limited to works, small colored versions of which are included, which the society itself offers for sale. The Bartran guide is particularly useful for its index of titles.

Even though the availability of reproductions is increasing, it is often helpful to be able to locate copies of major works in volumes held within the library's book collection. Of particular value for older works are Monro's *Index to Reproductions of American Paintings*,[18] and her *Index to Reproductions of European Paintings*.[19]

Reproductions may be mounted and housed in the same fashion as pictures; however, the larger or more costly the item, the more advisable it is to employ horizontal rather than vertical storage.

Although reproductions may be categorized by subject, they are more frequently associated with the artist than with the content depicted. Thus, in contrast to pictures, they are usually arranged alphabetically by artist or by some combination of subject, country of origin, and style or period of the artist. If sufficiently large, the collection may be catalogued, with the main entry under the artist and an added entry under the title of the work itself. The description should then include the size of the actual reproduction, the method of reproduction (if known), the publisher, and the date of the reproduction. A relatively recent innovation in cataloging art reproductions is the use of miniatures of the works in question on the catalog cards. Due to the cost of such illustrations, however, only the most sophisticated collections have begun to employ this means of browsing and retrieval.

A practice traditionally more common to public than to academic libraries, but one which is growing in popularity among the latter, is the lending of framed reproductions. The cost of full-size copies, together with the expense of framing, tends to limit the scope of such collections. Still, where they do exist, they may be cataloged in the same fashion as two-dimensional reproductions, and circulated using the simplest of identifications; e.g., either medium and accession number, or medium, artist, and title.

While unframed reproductions may be temporarily mounted in any commercial adjustable frames currently available, the unit cost and the degree of permanency permitted by preframing suggest that ready-to-hang art work is more desirable for the small academic library. Preframed reproductions may be procured from several standard library supply houses, as well as from art reproduction dealers.[20]

PHOTOGRAPHS

When photograph collections are maintained separately from general picture collections, they are developed to constitute works of art in themselves (the oeuvre of photographers who are or aspire to be artisans in this medium), art reproductions (explicit copies of original works of art) offering the opportunity for study and comparison, albeit second hand. The works photographed form an archival record of the institution in which the collection is located, or its environs, its photographs rendering a visual history that documents specific places and events.

College libraries tend to preserve those photographs or collections of photographs which it receives as gifts, although most, particularly smaller college libraries, do not produce original photographs nor collect original photographs deemed to be works of art. Reproductions of the latter are more readily available in published volumes of the collected works of major photographers in the United States and abroad.

Photographs differ from other visual media in that they are in fact comprised of two parts: the negative film and the positive print. Ideally, the library should possess both, although the average college library will own only the latter. Where negatives are available, they should be given an identifying number and placed in glassine or similar transparent envelopes and filed in a vertical or horizontal file, depending on size. Ostroff questions the use of glassine envelopes and gives more details in the "Preservation of Photographs."[21] The paper used to separate photograph negatives should be acid-free. Photographic prints should bear the same identifying number as their negatives, or an individual identifying number when the negative is absent. The prints may be either mounted or unmounted, and housed in manila folders or envelopes in filing cabinets; where more than one print must be held in a single container, it is desirable to separate each from the others by sheets of light-weight paper, thereby eliminating the possibility of two or more prints adhering to one another.

It is suggested that in addition to the identifying number, which is usually the accession number, the verso of the print should carry the name of the photographer together with the title of the photograph. The nature of the collection will determine its arrangement. A general collection can be indexed or classified by subject categories as picture collections are; reproductions of works of art might be indexed or catalogued by the artists; art photographs by the photographers; reproductions of buildings by their architects.

The larger the collection, the greater the need for cataloging and classification, while the smaller the quantity of materials, the less vital and perhaps economical it is to provide a detailed treatment. Where cataloging of photographs is deemed necessary, an author–title–subject arrangement is recommended. Additional information of value to potential users are an indication of black and white or color pictures and their physical dimensions. Classification schemes have been developed by large libraries for their collections; among the more prominent are those of the Metropolitan Museum of Art and New York University. However, classification is generally an unnecessary luxury for the small collection unless it is highly specialized.

Photographs may be circulated, employing simple procedures; nevertheless, library policy tends to restrict their consultation to use within the library building. This practice might be questioned if negatives and equipment were available, thereby making possible inexpensive replacement of lost or damaged items.

PRINTS

Fine prints, as distinguished from photographic prints or mass-produced reproductions, are original works of art in themselves. They differ from original works, such as paintings, for there can be but one original painting, while there may be a multiple number of originals of a given print. Four basic forms of prints exist: (1) those produced by relief processes, including woodcuts and wood engravings; (2) those produced by incised processes, including engravings and etchings; (3) those created by lithography; and (4) those created by stencil processes, including the presently popular silk-screen printing process.

Collections of fine prints are less apt to be the responsibility of the smaller academic library than of the art museum or art department. Large university libraries, however, may have separate print rooms to provide special processing and housing for their collection which serves research and appreciation needs, as well as a source of long-term investment. With the increase in recent years of original graphics, and with the rush to collect the output by both institutions and individuals, prices are being driven steadily higher, giving fine prints a tangible monetary value that may have relatively little to do with the artistic merits of the works themselves.

Prints may be selected for the library collection according to the reputation of the creators, the forms involved, the content depicted, or the general aesthetic appeal. Print dealers often issue catalogs from which selections may be made and include such commercial galleries as the Association of American Artists, Ferdinand Roten Galleries, Graddock and Barnard. These and other print dealers advertise in art-related periodicals, among them *Studio International*, *Museum News*, and *Antiques*, as well as in the fine art pages of the *New York Times*.

The processing of fine prints is a rather more delicate matter than that of the average picture; for details, Dudley's *Museum Registration Methods*[22] or Zigrosser's *Guide to the Collecting and Care of Original Prints*[23] should be consulted. Basically, however, fine prints should be hinged to mats of rag paper or mat board, using Japanese paper and library paste. The mats themselves should be hinged, with window fronts, so that the surface of the print will be protected over all but the image area. This may be protected by a sheet of glassine paper or Japanese mending tissue inserted between the hinged cover and the print. Each print should be placed in an individual acid-free folder and housed either in horizontal filing cabinets or in print boxes specially designed for the purpose.

The physical arrangement and the cataloging of the print collection will depend in large measure upon its size, with the artist constituting the main approach in both instances. Since, in earlier times, prints were often reproductions of paintings, it is necessary, for such prints, to provide entry by means of the artist of the original work, as well as by the printmaker and the titles of both the print and the original work, if the titles differ. Dudley[24] suggests that even the smallest collection be provided with a variety of records, indicating catalog information on the one hand, and source information as to donor, vendor, and the like, on the other. Again, there being available no standardized techniques for cataloging prints, local needs should dictate the degree of control required. In most instances simple artist–title–subject cataloging should suffice, with indications of the medium and the size of the print. Where more detailed coverage is required, the volume by Dudley and Wilkinson may serve as a basic guide.

In libraries where prints are looked upon as materials for study and research, their circulation may be limited; where, however, they are considered as works of art to be lived with and enjoyed, they may be framed and circulated as are art reproductions. Permanent framing, while perhaps the more desirable method, is costly; therefore many libraries are using more adjustable frames which are usually stocked by library supply houses, and which may be provided only when prints are to be placed in circulation.

Prints, like art reproductions, should be loaned for periods long enough to permit the borrower to absorb and enjoy the work in question. Some libraries have chosen to circulate these works for the duration of a quarter or a semester, in some instances charging a deposit which is returned to the borrower when the work is returned undamaged.

TRENDS

While collections of two-dimensional visual representations are becoming ever more essential in this McLuhanesque age, it does not appear that these collections will, within the foreseeable future at least, constitute more than a modest segment of the average college library's holdings. It would appear that large col-
as pictures; however, the larger or more costly the item, the more
lections will, in the future, be maintained primarily in museums or museum libraries and major research institutions as is the current practice.

In very large collections, where storage space becomes a major consideration, it may be necessary to reduce portions of the collection to microform or to eliminate photographic prints, retaining the negatives only, and reproducing positives upon demand. Another possibility is the development of centers where negatives may be pooled. From these, positive prints or slides could be made available as needed. At least one such center presently exists for this purpose: Taurgo, Inc., in New York.[25]

Future academicians may realize the need for more detailed and relevant classification schemes with specialized subject-heading lists; these, as with the cataloging data of large print and nonprint media collections will eventually be manipulated via computer. As the technology of telefacsimile transmission improves and the costs decreased, it is conceivable that librarians and their patrons located anywhere may have access to reasonably faithful reproductions of individual works and collections hitherto available in only the largest or most lavishly supported institutions.

Relatively few college libraries have entered into the collection of photographs, pictures, and prints to any appreciable degree. Even fewer have available the skills to produce such materials, relying primarily on commercially available materials. Yet these forms are becoming of sufficient importance to warrant more concentrated attention to their value in library programs. By so doing the basic knowledge of sources, handling modes, uses, and values should become as commonplace among librarians working with them as the similar knowledge for traditional forms of library material.

Finally, standards for collection initiation, development, and utilization should be devised and incorporated into the American Library Association standards for college and junior college libraries, for only by so doing may these forms be recognized as the important elements of education, both formal and life-long, which they are.

SELECTED BIBLIOGRAPHY

Administering Collections of Photographs, Pictures and Prints

General

Asheim, Lester. "Fine Arts," in his *The Humanities and the Library*, pp. 100–50. Chicago: American Library Assn., 1957.

Broxis, Peter F. *Organizing the Arts*. Hamden, Conn.: Shoe String (Archon), 1968, 132 pp.

Carson, Doris M. "Cataloging Nonbook Materials," *Wilson Library Bulletin* 39: 562–64 (Mar. 1965).

Clarke, Virginia. *Non-Book Library Materials*. Denton, Texas: North Texas State College, 1953. 154 pp.

Collison, Robert L. *The Treatment of Special Material in Libraries*. London: Aslib, 1957. 104 pp.

Corbett, Edmund V. *The Illustrations Collection: Its Formation, Classification and Exploitation*. London: Grafton, 1941. 158 pp.

Dudley, Dorothy H. and Irma B. Wilkinson. *Museum Registration Methods* rev. ed. Washington, D. C.: American Assn. of Museums and Smithsonian Institution, 1968. 294 pp.

Freitag, Wolfgang M. "Art Libraries and Collections," in the *Encyclopedia of Library and Information Science*, vol. 1, pp. 571–621. New York: Dekker, 1968.

Hicks, Warren B. and Alma M. Tillin, *Developing Multi-Media Libraries.* New York: Bowker, 1970. 199 pp.

Hill, May D. "Prints, Pictures and Photographs," *Library Trends* 4(2):156–63 (Oct. 1955).

Lewis, Stanley T. "Experimentation with an Image Library," *Special Libraries* 56:35–38 (Jan. 1965).

Milhollen, Hirst. "Pictures Invade the Catalog," *Library Journal* 71:803–4 (June 1, 1946).

"Pictures, Designs, and Other Two-Dimensional Representations," in *Anglo-American Cataloging Rules,* North American text, pp. 329–42. Chicago: American Library Assn., 1967.

Processing Manual for Books and Non-Book Materials. Glen Ellyn, Ill.: College of DuPage, Instructional Resources Center, 1970 .

Weihs, Jean Riddle; Shirley Lewis, and Janet MacDonald. *Non-Book Materials: The Organization of Integrated Collections* (Ottawa: Canadian Library Assn., 1973), 107 pp.

Williams, Catherine M. *Use and Care of Flat Picture Materials.* Columbus: Ohio State Univ., Teaching Aids Laboratory, 1956 . 21 pp.

Photographs

Crozet, R. "Cataloguing a Photograph Library," *UNESCO Bulletin for Libraries* 18(3):127–29 (May–June 1964).

Howe, Jane. "Cataloguing a Photograph Collection," *Oklahoma Librarian* 13: 8–12 (Jan. 1963).

Luecke, Camilla P. "Photographic Library Procedures," *Special Libraries* 47: 455–61 (Dec. 1956).

Mitchell, Eleanor. "The Photograph Collection and Its Problems," *College and Research Libraries* 3:176–82 (Mar. 1942).

Reinhardt, Phyllis A. "Photograph and Slide Collections in Art Libraries," *Special Libraries* 50:97–102 (Mar. 1959).

Vanderbilt, Paul. "Filing Systems for Negatives and Prints," in *The Complete Photographer,* 5:1722–34. New York: National Educational Alliance, 1942–43.

Pictures

Dana, John Cotton, ed. *The Picture Collection,* by Marcelle Frebault under the direction of Beatrice Winser. 5th ed., rev. New York: Wilson, 1943. 86 pp.

Dane, William J. *The Picture Collection: Subject Headings.* 6th ed. Hamden, Conn.: Shoe String, 1968. 103 pp.

Gould, Geraldine N., and Ithmer C. Wolfe. *How to Organize and Maintain the Picture/Pamphlet File.* Dobbs Ferry, N.Y.: Oceana, 1968. 146 pp.

Ireland, Norma O. *The Picture File in School, College and Public Libraries.* rev. and enl. ed. Boston: Faxon, 1952. 136 pp.

Javitz, Ramona. "Put Accent on Pictures," *Library Journal* 74:1235–37+ (Sept. 15, 1947).

Keck, Caroline K. *How to Take Care of Your Pictures.* New York: Museum of Modern Art and the Brooklyn Museum, 1954. 54 pp.

Kelly, Matilde. "Chicago Public Library Combines Picture Files," *Library Journal* 75:1453–57 (Sept. 15, 1950).

Miller, Bruce. *So You Want to Start a Picture File.* Riverside, Calif.: Bruce Miller Pubns., 1954. 28 pp.

Parker, John Austin. "A Brief History of the Picture Collection," *Wilson Library Bulletin* 30:257 (Nov. 1955).

Picturescope. New York: Special Libraries Assn., Picture Div. quarterly, 1953– .

Underhill, Charles S. "Sketch for a Picture Collection," *Wilson Library Bulletin* 30:539–42 (Mar. 1956).

Williams, Catharine M. *Learning from Pictures.* 2d ed. Washington, D.C.: National Education Assn., Dept. of Audiovisual Instruction, 1968. 166 pp.

Prints

Cain, Robert E. "The Original Print," *Library Journal* 91:5323–26 (Nov. 1, 1966).

Fisher, Elizabeth M. "The Fine Arts Picture Collection," *Library Journal* 64:784–87 (Oct. 15, 1939).

Foster, Donald L. "A Picasso in Every Library," *Wilson Library Bulletin* 37: 58–60+ (Sept. 1962).

Print Council of America, *What Is an Original Print?* ed. by Joshua B. Cahn. New York: The Council, 1964. 31 pp.

Zigrosser, Carl and Christa M. Gaehde. *Guide to the Collecting and Care of Original Prints.* New York: Crown, 1965. 120 pp.

Selection Sources for Photographs, Pictures, and Prints

Bartran, Margaret. *A Guide to Color Reproductions.* 2d ed. Metuchen, N.J.: Scarecrow, 1970. 625 pp.

Bennett, Edna. *Pictures Unlimited*. New York: Photographic Trade News Corp., 1968 .

Bettmann, Otto, ed. *Bettman Portable Archive.* New York: Picture House, 1966. 229 pp.

Brooke, Milton, and H. J. Dubester. *Guide to Color Prints.* New York: Scarecrow, 1953. 257 pp.

Miller, Bruce, Publs. *Sources of Free Pictures, Sources of Inexpensive Pictures, Sources of Free Travel Posters.* Bruce Miller Publications, Box 369, Riverside, CA 92502.

Clapp, Jane. *Art Reproductions.* New York: Scarecrow, 1961. 350 pp.

Frankenberg, Celestine G. *Picture Sources.* 2d ed. New York: Special Libraries Assn., 1964. 216 pp.

International Directory of Photographic Archives of Works of Art. vol. 1. Paris: Dunod, 1950; vol. 2. Paris: UNESCO, 1954.

New York Graphic Society, *Fine Art Reproductions of Old and Modern Masters*. 8th ed. Greenwich, Conn.: The Society, 1968. 420 pp.

——— *Reproductions of American Paintings*. Greenwich, Conn.: The Society, 1962. 132 pp.

O'Connell, Catherine. "Art Sources for the Library," *Library Journal* 85:1285–88 (Mar. 15, 1960).

The UNESCO Catalogue of Colour Reproductions of Paintings—1860 to 1969. New York: Unipub, 1968. 450 pp.

The UNESCO Catalogue of Colour Reproductions of Paintings 1860 to 1969. New York: Unipub, 1969. 549 pp.

Indexes to Photographs, Pictures, and Prints in Books and Periodicals

Clapp, Jane. *Art in Life 1936–1956*. New York: Scarecrow, 1959. 540 pp.

——— *Art in Life 1957–1963*. New York: Scarecrow, 1965. 379 pp.

Ellis, Jessie Croft. *Index to Illustrations*. Boston: Faxon, 1967. 682 pp.

Havlice, Patricia P. *Art in Time*. Metuchen, N.J.: Scarecrow. 1970. 350 pp.

——— *Costume Index: Supplement*. New York: Wilson, 1957. 210 pp.

Monroe, Isabel. *Index to Reproductions of American Paintings*. New York: Wilson, 1948. 731 pp.

——— *Index to Reproductions of American Paintings: First Supplement*. New York: Wilson, 1964. 480 pp.

——— *Index to Reproductions of European Paintings*. New York: Wilson, 1956. 668 pp.

———, and Dorothy E. Cook. *Costume Index*. New York: Wilson, 1937. 338 pp.

Vance, Lucile E., and Esther M. Tracey. *Illustration Index*. 2d ed. New York: Scarecrow, 1966. 527 pp.

Selected References on the Acquisition, Organization, and Dissemination of Nonprint Media in Academic Libraries

Mary B. Cassata

Mary B. Cassata is Assistant Director of University Libraries for Public Services, State University of New York at Buffalo.

GENERAL

"Alphabetical Listing of Terminology." In *National Conference on the Implications of the New Media for the Teaching of Library Science,* pp. 208–26. Urbana: Univ. of Illinois Graduate School of Library Science, 1963.

"Audiovisual Materials and the Library." *Wisconsin Library Bulletin* 66:65–98 (March 1970).

"Audiovisual Practices Among Colleges and Universities." *American School and University* 36:26–27 (July 1964).

Balanoff, Neal. "James M. Wood Learning Center." *Audiovisual Instruction* 8:226–29 (April 1963).

Barnes, E. A. "Learning Center Dramatizes Use of Latest Technical Developments." *College and University Business* 35:53–56 (Sept. 1963).

Bathorst, Leonard H., and Bruce Klein. *A Visual Communications System*. Dubuque, Iowa: W. C. Brown Book Co., 1966.

Bennett, Fleming, and Jane L. Culler. *ACRL Audio-Visual Directory*. Chicago: American Library Association, 1956.

Bergeson, Clarence O. "Relationship of Library Science and Audio-Visual Instruction." *Audiovisual Instruction* 12:100–3 (Feb. 1967).

Bertrand, John L. "Media Reference Center." *Audiovisual Instruction* 12:16–22 (Jan. 1967).

Bidwell, Charles M. "The Information Problem: Codes for Media." *Audiovisual Instruction* 12:325–28 (Apr. 1967).

Brahmo, S. "Role of Maps in Library Service." *Herald of Library Science* 5:203–9 (July 1966).

Brong, Gerald R. "Library Networks and Non-Print Resources." *Library News Bulletin* 37:165–69 (July 1970).

Brown, James W., Richard B. Lewis, and Fred F. Harcleroad. *A-V Instruction: Materials and Methods.* 2d ed. New York: McGraw-Hill, 1964. 592p.

Brown, James W., and Kenneth D. Norberg. *Administering Educational Media.* New York: McGraw-Hill, 1965. 357p.

Brown, James W., and James W. Thornston, eds. *New Media in Higher Education.* Washington, D. C.: Association for Higher Education, 1963. 183p.

Burkett, J., and T. S. Morgan, eds. *Special Materials in the Library.* London: Library Association, 1963. 179p.

Ceram, C. W. *Archaeology of the Cinema.* Translated by Richard Winston, Jr. New York: Harcourt, 1965.

Cross, A. J., and Irene F. Cypher. *Audiovisual Education.* New York: Crowell, 1961. 415p.

Cummings, Frederick. "Art Reference Library." *College and Research Libraries* 27:201–6 (May 1966).

Curry, R. L., and G. D. Shepherd. "Learning in a Personalized Media Environment." *Library College Journal* 3:28–32 (Spring 1970).

Dale, Edgar. *Audiovisual Methods in Teaching.* Rev. ed. New York: Dryden Pr., 1954. 534p.

Dupuy, Trevor Nevitt. *Ferment in College Libraries.* Washington, D. C.: Communication Service Corp., 1968. 158p.

———. *Modern Libraries for Modern Colleges.* Washington, D. C.: Communication Services Corp., 1968. 122p.

Fine, Benjamin. *Teaching Machines.* New York: Sterling, 1962. 176p.

Edinger, Lois. "Technology in Education." *Wilson Library Bulletin* 41:72–75 (Sept. 1966).

Erickson, Carlton W. *Fundamentals of Teaching with Audiovisual Technology.* New York: Macmillan, 1965. 384 p.

Finn, James D. *Teaching Machines and Programmed Learning, 1962: A Survey of the Industry.* Washington, D. C.: U. S. Office of Education, National Education Association, 1962. 85p.

Fleischer, Eugene. "Systems for Individual Study: Decks, Cassettes, Dials or Buffers?" *Library Journal* 96:695–98 (Feb. 15); *School Library Journal* 18:27–30 (Feb. 1971).

Foltz, Charles. *The World of Teaching Machines: Programmed Learning and Self-Instructional Devices.* Washington, D. C.: Electronic Teaching Laboratories, 1961.

Fry, Edward B. *Teaching Machines and Programmed Instruction.* New York: McGraw-Hill, 1963.

Geller, Evelyn. "The Marriage of the Media." *Library Journal* 93: 2079–84 (May 15, 1968).

———. "This Matter of Media." *Library Journal* 96:2048–53 (June 15, 1971).

Godfrey, Eleanor P. *The State of Audiovisual Technology 1961–1966.* Washington, D. C.: Department of Audiovisual Instruction, National Education Association, 1967. 217p.

Goldstein, Harold. "A/V—Has It Any Future in Libraries?" *Wilson Library Bulletin* 36:670–73 (Apr. 1962).

———. "Audio-Visual Services in Libraries: What One Course at Illinois Attempts To Do." *Illinois Libraries* 45:67–71 (Fall 1963).

Grady, Marion B. "Comparison of Motion Pictures and Books as Resource Materials." Ph.D. dissertation, University of Chicago, 1951. 450p.

Green, Alan C., et al., eds. *Educational Facilities with New Media.* Washington, D. C.: Dept. of Audiovisual Instruction, National Education Association, 1966.

Grove, Pearce S., et al. "Unique Struggle in the Oklahoma Sun: Systems and Standards for Bibliographic Media Control." *Oklahoma Librarian* 20:4–6 (Jan. 1970).

———, and Evelyn G. Clement. *Bibliographic Control of Nonprint Media.* Chicago: American Library Assn., 1972. 415p.

Haas, Kenneth B., and Harry Q. Pacher. *Preparation and Use of Audio-visual Aids.* 3d ed. New York: Prentice-Hall, 1955.

Hart, T. L., ed. "Media for the 70's." *Focus* (Mar. 1971).

Harvey, John F. "Measuring Library Audio-Visual Activities." *College and Research Libraries* 18:193–98 (May 1957).

Hicks, Warren B., and Alma M. Tillin. *Developing Multi-Media Libraries.* New York: Bowker, 1970. 199p.

Hoye, R. E. "Checkpoint to Teaching Splashdown: Design and Production of Instructional Materials Using the Systems Approach." *Wisconsin Library Bulletin* 66:79–82 (Mar. 1970).

Hudson, R. B. "New and Future Trends in the Use of Audio-Visual Materials." *ALA Bulletin* 63:39–42 (Jan. 1964).

Hyatt, O. H., and N. B. Pascal. "Mixing the Media: Audiovisual Publication." *Scholarly Publishing* 1:377–87 (July 1970).

Kemp, Jerrold E. *Planning and Producing Audiovisual Materials.* San Francisco: Chandler, 1963.

Kenney, B. L., and F. W. Norwood. "CATV: Visual Library Service." *American Libraries* 2:723–26 (July 1971).

Kindler, James S. *Using Audio-visual Materials in Education.* New York: American Book Co., 1965.

Knirk, Frederick G., and John Child, eds. *Instructional Technology: A Book of Readings.* New York: Holt, 1968.

Korte, D. A. de. *Television in Education and Training: a Review of Developments and Applications of Television and other Modern Audio-Visual Aids.* Translated by G. du Cloux. London: Cleaver-Hume, 1967. 182p.

Kujoth, Jean Spealman. *Readings in Nonbook Librarianship.* Metuchen, N. J.: Scarecrow, 1968. 463p.

Lawson, John. *Film: The Creative Process: The Search for an Audio-Visual Language and Structure.* New York: Hill and Wang, 1964.

Lieberman, Irving. *Audio-Visual Instruction in Library Education.* New York: Columbia Univ. School of Library Service, 1955. 213p.

———. "Use of Non-Print Media in Library School Instruction." In *Library Education: An International Survey,* pp. 247–72. Urbana: Univ. of Illinois Graduate School of Library Science, 1968.

Lumsdaine, Arthur A., and Robert Glaser. *Teaching Machines and Programmed Learning, a Source Book.* Washington, D. C.: Dept. of Audio-Visual Instruction, National Education Association, 1960.

McIntyre, C. J. "Impact on New Media on College Instruction." *Journal of Higher Education* 34:84–91 (Feb. 1963).

Margolin, Joseph, and James F. Mahoney, "Analysis of the Need for and Feasibility of More Effective Distribution of Government-Supported Non-Written Materials." ERIC Research in Education, (Dec. 1968), EP 011 381.

Miller, E. P., and Barbara Hagist. "Tulsa Adopts Multi-Media Programming." *ALA Adult Services Division Newsletter* 6:56–58 (Summer 1969).

Moriarty, John H. "New Media Facilities." *Library Trends* 16:251–58 (Oct. 1967).

Moses, R. B. "Reaching Out with the New Media." *Connecticut Libraries* 13:17–21 (Summer 1971).

National Education Association. Commission on Definition and Terminology. *The Changing Role of the Audiovisual Process in Education: A Definition and a Glossary of Related Terms.* Los Angeles: the Association, 1963.

New Teaching Aids for the American Classroom. Stanford, California: Symposium on the State of Research in Instructional Television and Tutorial Machines, 1960.

Nolan, John L. "Audio-Visual Materials." *Library Trends* 10:261–72 (Oct. 1961).

Norton, E. S. "Authors on Tape." *School Libraries* 15:35–37 (Mar. 1966).

Pearson, N. P., and L. Butler. *Instructional Materials Centers.* Minneapolis: Burgess, 1969. 345p.

Pringle, Eugene A. "Audiovisual Materials and College Objectives." *Choice* 3:1107–9 (Feb. 1967).

Ristow, Walter William. "The Emergence of Maps in Libraries." *Special Libraries* 58:400–19 (July 1967).

Rossi, Peter H., and Bruce J. Biddle, eds. *The New Media and Education.* Chicago: Aldine, 1966.

Rufsvold, Margaret I., and Carolyn Guss. "Proceedings of a Work Conference on Bibliographic Control of Newer Educational Media." Mimeographed. Bloomington: Indiana Univ., 1960.

———. "A Proposed Method for Establishing Bibliographic Control of the Newer Educational Media for the Purpose of Informing Teachers Concerning Available Materials and Their Education Utility." Mimeographed. Bloomington: Indiana Univ., 1960.

———. "Sources of Information about Newer Educational Media for Elementary and Secondary Education (1950–1960)." Mimeographed. Bloomington: Indiana Univ., 1960. 152p.

———. "Software: Bibliographic Control and the NICEM [National Information Center for Educational Media] Indexes." *School Libraries* 20: 11–20 (Winter 1971).

Saettler, Paul. *A History of Instructional Technology.* New York: McGraw-Hill, 1968.

Scuorzo, Herbert E. *Practical Audio-Visual Handbook for Teachers.* West Nyack, New York: Prentice-Hall, 1967.

Shane, M. Lanning. "Audio-visual Aids and the Library." *College and Research Libraries* 1: 143–46 (Mar. 1940).

Sheviak, M. R. "Message of Media." *School Libraries* 20: 17–20 (Spring 1971).

Shores, Louis. "Audio-visual Dimensions for an Academic Library." *College and Research Libraries* 15: 393–97 (Oct. 1954).

Stolurow, Lawrence. *Teaching by Machine.* Washington, D. C.: U.S. Dept. of Health, Education and Welfare, 1961.

Stone, C. Walter. "Development of Professional Tools for the Materials Center." In *School Library as a Materials Center,* edited by M. H. Mahar, pp. 7–11. Washington, D. C.: U.S. Office of Education, 1963.

———, ed. "Library Uses of the New Media of Communication," *Library Trends* 16: 179–299 (Oct. 1967).

———. "Place of Newer Media in the Undergraduate Program." *Library Quarterly* 24: 368–73 (Oct. 1954).

Strobecker, E. C., ed. *Allies of Books: A Report of the Workshop in Audiovisual Media, July 1–12, 1963*. Louisville: Catherine Spalding College, 1964.

Tauber, Maurice F., and Oliver L. Lilley. "Feasibility Study Regarding the Establishment of an Educational Media Research Information Service." Mimeographed. New York: Columbia Univ., 1960. 235p.

———, and Irene Roemer Stephens. *Conference on the Use of Printed and Audio-Visual Materials for Instructional Purposes.* New York: Columbia Univ., School of Library Service, 1966. 241p.

Taylor, Calvin W., and F. W. Williams, eds. *Instructional Media and Creativity.* New York: Wiley, 1966.

Taylor, Kenneth I. "Instructional Materials Centers and Programs." *North Central Association Quarterly* 40:214–21 (Fall 1965).

Wendt, Paul R. *Audio-Visual Instruction.* Washington, D. C.: National Education Association, 1966.

Wiman, Raymond V., and Wesley C. Mierhenry, eds. *Educational Media: Theory into Practice.* Columbus, Ohio: Charles E. Merrill, 1969.

Wittich, Walter Arno, and Charles I. Schuller. *Audio-Visual Materials: Their Nature and Use.* 4th ed. New York: Harper, 1966.

Wright, C. W. "At Central Washington State College: All Services Under One Roof." *Audiovisual Instruction* 8:222–25 (Apr. 1963).

BIBLIOGRAPHIES

Allison, Mary L. *New Educational Materials 1968.* New York: Citation Pr. 1968. 256p.

American Library Association. Children's Services Division. Library Service to the Disadvantaged Child Committee. *I Read, You Read, We Read.* Chicago: the Association, 1971. 104p.

American Library Association. *Films for Libraries.* Chicago: the Association, 1962. 81p.

Approved Instructional Materials for Secondary Schools, 1968/69, Instructional Materials List. Rockville, Md.: Montgomery County Public Schools, Dept. of Instructional Materials.

Audio-Visual Equipment Directory. Evanston, Ill.: National Audio-Visual Assn., 1953–

Audio Visual Market Place: A Multimedia Guide. New York: Bowker, 1971. 234p.

Audio Visual Source Directory for Services and Products. Tarrytown, N. Y.: Motion Picture Enterprises Publications, Inc.

AV Index: A Guide to Instructional Material Information in Selected Publications. Detroit: Audio-Visual Research Institute, 1961– .

Blue Book of 16mm Films. Chicago: Educational Screen, Inc., 1925– .

British National Film Catalogue. London: British Industrial and Scientific Film Assn., 1963– .

Canadian Film Institute. *Catalogue of 16mm Films on Behavioral Sciences Available from the National Science Film Library.* Ottawa: the Institute, 1967.

Catalog of 16mm Films Available on Rental or Purchase in the United States. Ottawa: National Film Board of Canada, 1968. 64p.

Dale, Edgar, and Greg Trzebiatowski. "A Basic Reference Shelf on Audio-Visual Instruction." Stanford, Calif.: ERIC Clearinghouse, 1968. 17p.

———, et al. *Motion Pictures in Education: A Summary of the Literature.* New York: Wilson, 1938.

Dove, Jack. *Music Libraries: Including a Comprehensive Bibliography of Music Literature and a Selected Bibliography of Music Scores Published Since 1957.* 2v. London: Andrew Deutsch, 1965.

Drazniowsky, Roman. "Bibliographies as Tools for Map Acquisition and Map Collection," *Cartographer* 3:138–44 (Dec. 1966).

Eason, Tracy. "A Selected Bibliography of A-V Media in Library Literature, 1958–69," *Wilson Library Bulletin* 44:312–19 (Nov. 1969).

Educational Film Guide. New York: Wilson, 1936–62.

Educational Film Library Association. *8mm Film Directory.* New York: Comprehensive Service Corp., 1968.

Educational Films and Filmstrips 1969. Whittier, Calif.: Moody Institute of Science, Educational Film Division.

Educational Films 1969. East Lansing: Michigan State Univ., 1969. 568p.

Educational Sound Filmstrip Directory. 4th ed. St. Charles, Ill.: Dukane Corp., Audio-Visual Division.

Educator's Guide to Free Films. Randolph, Wis.: Educator's Progress Service, 1949– .

Educator's Guide to Free Filmstrips. Randolph, Wis.: Educator's Progress Service, 1962– .

Educator's Guide to Free Tapes, Scripts and Transparencies. Randolph, Wis.: Educator's Progress Service, 1955– .

Educator's Purchasing Master. 3 v. Fisher Pub. Co., 1970.

Education Media Council. *Educational Media Index.* New York: McGraw-Hill, 1964.

"Filmstrips and Motion Pictures Useful in Teaching Management." In *Management of Libraries and Information Centers* by M. H. Lowell, pp. 155–62. Metuchen, N.J.: Scarecrow, 1962.

Filmstrip Guide. New York: Wilson, 1948–62.

Frankenberg, Celestine G. *Picture Sources.* 2d ed. New York: Special Libraries Association, 1964.

Freidman, Florence B. *Classroom Teacher's Guide to Audio-Visual Material.* Rev. ed. Philadelphia: Chilton, 1961.

Gillespie, J. T., comp. "Getting Started with Non-Print Media." *Top News* 25:402–05+ (June 1969); 26:262–64 (Apr. 1970).

A Half Century of American Film: 500 Selected Features for Discriminating Viewers. Chicago: Films Inc., 1969. 160p.

Harrison Catalog of Stereophonic Tapes. New York: M. and N. Harrison, Inc., 1955– .

Kone, Grace Ann. *8mm Film Directory: A Comprehensive Descriptive Index.* New York: Educational Film Library Assn., 1969. 532p.

Kula, Sam. *Bibliography of Film Librarianship.* London: Library Assn., 1967. 68p.

Landers, Bertha, ed. *A Foreign Language Audio-Visual Guide.* Los Angeles: Landers Associates, 1961.

Lane, David O. "Basic Collection of Records for a College Library." *College and Research Libraries* 23:295–301 (July 1962).

Learning Directory. 7 v. Westinghouse Learning Corp., 1970.

Levy, P., comp. "Audiovisual Guide: A Multimedia Subject List." *Library Journal* 96:1443–44+ (Apr. 15, 1971); *School Library Journal* 18:45–46+ (Apr. 1971).

Lieberman, Irving. *A Working Bibliography of Commercially Available Audio-Visual Materials for the Teaching of Library Science.* Univ. of Illinois Graduate School of Library Science. (Occasional Papers no. 94). 1968. 77p.

Limbacher, James L., ed. *Feature Films on 8mm and 16mm: A Directory of 8mm and 16mm Feature Films Available for Rental, Sale or Lease in the United States.* 2d ed. New York: Educational Film Library Assn., 1968.

Moldstad, John A. *Sources of Information on Educational Media.* Washington, D.C.: U.S. Dept. of Health, Education and Welfare, Office of Education, 1963.

National Center for Audio Tapes 1970–72 Catalog. Boulder: Univ. of Colorado, National Center for Audio Tapes, 1970. 123p.

National Information Center for Educational Media. *Index to 8mm Motion Cartridges.* New York: Bowker, 1969. 402p.

———. *Index to Overhead Transparencies.* New York: Bowker, 1969. 552p.

———. *Index to 16mm Educational Films.* 2d ed. New York: Bowker, 1969, 1111p.

———. *Index to 35mm Educational Filmstrips.* 2d ed. New York: Bowker, 1970. 872p.

New York State Library Musical Recordings. Albany, N.Y.: Univ. of the State of New York State Education Department. Division of Library Development, 1968. 28p.

Peer, Catherine A. "Reference Sources in Nonprint Media." *Pennsylvania Library Association Bulletin* 25:168–72+ (May 1970).

Reid, Seerley; Carpenter, Anita; and Daugherty, Annie Rose. *Directory of 3,660 16mm Film Libraries.* Washington: U.S. Dept. of Health, Education and Welfare, 1958.

Roach, Helen. *Spoken Records.* 2d ed. New York: Scarecrow, 1966. 206p.

Rufsvold, Margaret I., and Carolyn Guss. *Guides to Educational Media.* 3d ed. Chicago: American Library Assn., 1971.

Schwann Long Playing Record Catalog. Boston: W. Schwann, 1948– .

Selected List of Catalogs for Short Films and Filmstrips, 1963. New York: UNESCO, 1965.

Sgro, L., and R. Munger. "Audiovisual Materials: Purchase or Produce." *Wisconsin Library Bulletin* 66:88–90 (Mar. 1970).

Southeast Suburban Audio-Visual Library Catalogue of Instructional Materials. Wayne, Pa.: Southeast Suburban Audio-Visual Library, 1968. 103p.

Wade, Serena E. "A Basic Reference Shelf on Individualized Instruction." Stanford, Calif.: ERIC Clearinghouse, 1968. 8p.

Yonge, D. L. *Catalogue of Early Globes, Made Prior to 1850 and Conserved in the United States: A Preliminary Listing.* American Geographical Society, 1968. 118p.

CATALOGING AND CLASSIFICATION

Allen, Thelma E., and Daryl Ann Hickman. *New Rules for an Old Game.* Vancouver: Univ. of British Columbia, 1967.

Anderson, Sherman. "Cataloging the Contents of Certain Recordings." *Library Resources and Technical Services* 9:359–62 (Summer 1965).

Archer, Ellinor, and Shirley Gawith. "Cataloging a Film Library." *Australian Library Journal* 11:121–24 (July 1962).

Badten, Jean, and Nancy Motomatzu. "Commercial Media Cataloging—What's Holding Us Up?" *School Library Journal* 15:34–35 (Nov. 1963).

Barnes, Christopher. "Classification and Cataloging of Spoken Records in Academic Libraries." *College and Research Libraries* 28:49–52 (Jan. 1967).

Boaz, Martha Terosse. "Organization and Administration of Audio-Visual Aids in a College Library." A.M.L.S. thesis. Univ. of Michigan, 1950. 53p.

Bradley, John G. "Cataloging and Indexing Motion Picture Film." *American Archivist* 8:169–84 (July 1945).

Brahmo, S. "Processing of Maps; Including a Select Bibliography of Maps Pertaining to India Published During 1683-1853." *Library Herald* 9:117–28 (Oct. 1966).

Carson, Doris M. "Cataloging Nonbook Materials." *Wilson Library Bulletin* 39:562–64 (Mar. 1965).

Chibnall, Bernard, and Antony Croghan. *A Feasibility Study of a Multi-Media Catalogue.* Report to Office for Scientific and Technical Information on Project S1/25/36. Univ. of Sussex, 1969. 57p.

Clugston, Katharine W. "Anglo-American Cataloging Rules: Film Cataloging at the Library of Congress." *Library Resources and Technical Services* 13:35–41 (Winter 1969).

Cohen, Allen. "Classification of Four Track Tapes." *Library Resources and Technical Services* 6:360–61 (Fall 1962).

"Commercial Media Cataloging: What's Around." *Library Journal* 93:4345–51 (Nov. 15, 1968).

Coover, James B. "Computers, Cataloging, and Co-operation," Music Library Association Notes 25:437–46 (Mar. 1969).

Cox, Carl T. "The Cataloging of Records." *Library Journal* 85: 4523–25 (Dec. 15, 1960).

Cox, J. C. "Cataloging and Classification of Slides, Filmstrips, and Films." In *Catholic Library Association Conference Proceedings 1960,* pp. 186–88. New York: Catholic Library Assn., 1960.

Croghan, Antony. *A Thesaurus-Classification for the Physical Forms of Non-Book Media.* Mimeographed. The author: 17 Coburgh Mansions, Handel St., London, 1970.

Crowther, G. "Cataloguing and Classification of Cine Film at the Royal Aircraft Establishment." *ASLIB Proceedings* 11:179–87 (July 1959).

Cunnion, T. "Cataloging and Classification of Phonograph Records." In *Catholic Library Association Conference Proceedings 1960,* pp. 180–85. New York: Catholic Library Assn., 1960.

Davis, L. R. "Punch Card File System" [for slides]. *U.S. Camera* 16:68–69 (Sept. 1953).

DeLerma, Dominique-Rene. "Philosophy and Practice of Phonorecord Classification at Indiana University." *Library Resources and Technical Services* 13:86–92 (Winter 1969).

Dome, John E. "Automation of Media Cataloging." *Audiovisual Instruction* 11:446 (June 1966).

Drake, Helen. "Cataloging Recordings." *Illinois Libraries* 46:145–52 (Fall 1964).

Grenfell, David. "The Cataloging of Films." *Librarian and Book World* 47:62–64 (Apr. 1958).

———. "Standardization in Film Cataloging." *Journal of Documentation* 15:81–92 (June 1959).

Hagen, Carlos B. "An Information Retrieval System for Maps." *UNESCO Bulletin for Libraries* 20:30–35 (Jan.–Feb. 1966).

———. "A Proposed Information Retrieval System for Sound Recordings." *Special Libraries* 56:223–28 (Apr. 1965).

Hallowell, Jared R. "Some Information on the Cataloging of Phonograph Records." A.M.L.S. thesis. Univ. of Michigan, 1960. 30p.

Hamman, Frances. "Bibliographic Control of Audio-Visual Materials: Report of a Special Committee." *Library Resources and Technical Services* 1:180–89 (Fall 1957).

Harris, Evelyn J. *Instructional Materials Cataloging Guide.* Tucson: Univ. of Arizona, Bureau of Educational Research and Services, 1968. 27p.

Johnson, J. T., et al. *AV Cataloging and Processing Simplified.* Raleigh, N.C.: Audiovisual Catalogers, Inc., 1971. 236p.

Kemp, Muriel Louise. "Worcester Free Public Library Gives Discs Full Treatment." *Library Journal* 73:406–8 (Mar. 1948).

Kohn, L. E. "A Photograph and Lantern Slide Catalog in the Making." *Library Journal* 57:941–45 (1932).

Leon, J. L. "How to Catalog Magnetic Tapes." *Audiovisual Instruction* 13:311 (Apr. 1968).

Lincoln, Sister M. Edmund. "Techniques for Handling Phonograph Records." *Catholic Library World* 27:107–10+ (Dec. 1955).

Line, Maurice. "A Classification for Music Scores on Historical Principles." *Libri* 12:352–63 (1963).

Lomer, G. R. "Lantern slide storing and cataloging." Canadian Library Assn. *Bulletin* 4:119–22 (1948).

Lucas, E. Louise. "The Classification and Care of Pictures and Slides." *ALA Bulletin* 24:382–85 (1930).

McPherson, Beryl and Carolyn Berneking. "Phonorecord Cataloging—Methods and Policies." *Library Journal* 83:2623–24+ (Oct. 1, 1958).

Mary Alvin, Sister, and Sister M. Michele. "La Roche College Classification System for Phonorecords." *Library Resources and Technical Services* 9:443–45 (Fall 1965).

Mary Laurenta, Sister. "Classifying and Cataloging Filmstrips, Records, and Tapes." *Catholic Library World* 38:242–43 (Dec. 1966).

"Media Programs: Patterns of Organization." *Audiovisual Instruction* 10:111–14 (Feb. 1965).

Meikleham, Margaret H. C. "Cataloging the Record Collection in McMaster University Library." *Ontario Library Review* 29:154–57 (May 1945).

Milhollen, H. "Pictures Invade the Catalog." *Library Journal* 71: 803–4 (1946).

National Education Association. Association for Educational Communications and Technology. *Standards for Cataloging Nonprint Materials.* Rev. ed. National Education Assn., 1971.

Ogi, Masaaki. "Pattern-matching Technique Applied to Indexing and Retrieving Films for Television Use." *Proceedings of the American Society for Information Science,* pp. 89–93 vol. 5. Information Transfer, 1968.

Palmerlee, A. E. "Automation and Map Libraries: Thoughts on Cooperative Cataloging Through Automation." *SLA Geography and Map Division Bulletin* 49:6–16 (Sept. 1967).

Redfern, Brian. "Arranging and Cataloging Gramophone Records." In *Organizing Music in Libraries,* pp. 67–73. New York: Philosophical Library, 1966. 80p.

Riddle, Jean, et al. "Bibliographical Chaos and Control in the Multi-Media Centre." *Canadian Library Journal* 27:444–47 (Nov. 1970).

Skoog, A. C., and G. Evans. "Slide collection classification." *Penn Library Association Bulletin* 24:15–22 (Jan. 1969).

Somerville, S. A. "Cataloging of gramophone records." *Librarian and Book World* 38:97–99 (July 1969).

Southern Baptist Convention. Church Library Department. *Church Library Classification and Cataloging Guide: Books, Filmstrips, Recordings, Tape Recordings, Slides.* New York: Broadman, 1969. 454p.

Stevenson, Gordon. "Classification Chaos." *Library Journal* 88: 3789–94 (Oct. 15, 1963).

Stiles, Helen J. "Phonograph Record Classification at the United States Air Force Academy." *Library Resources and Technical Services* 9:446–48 (Fall 1965).

Stoops, Betty. "Cataloging and Classification Systems for Instructional Materials." *Audiovisual Instruction* 9:427–28 (Sept. 1964).

———. "Film Titles and Credits—Are They Adequate?" *Illinois Libraries* 48:83–89 (Feb. 1966).

Sunder, Mary Jane. "Organizing of Recorded Sound." *Library Resources and Technical Services* 13:93–98 (Winter 1969).

"Table I Checklist of Items for Physical Description of Non-Book Materials." *Wisconsin Library Bulletin* 66:72–73 (Mar. 1970).

Tillin, Marian. "Treat Records Like Books." *Library Journal* 85: 4518–21 (Dec. 15, 1960).

Wasserman, Morton N. "A Computer-Prepared Book Catalog for Engineering Transparencies." *Special Libraries* 57:111–13 (Feb. 1966).

White, Brenda. *Slide Collections: A Survey of their Organization in Libraries in the Fields of Architecture, Building, and Planning.* Edinburgh: privately published, 1967.

Wolf, R.; L. Stemmle; and F. F. Yonkman. "Filing Lantern Slides." *Science* 114:308 (Sept. 21, 1957).

MANUALS

American Library Association. Division of Cataloging and Classification. *ALA Cataloging Rules for Author and Title Entries.* 2d ed. Chicago: the Association, 1949. 265p.

———. Public Library Association. Audio-visual Committee. *Guidelines for Audiovisual Materials and Services for Public Libraries.* Chicago: the Association, 1970. 33p.

Anglo-American Cataloging Rules. North American Text. Chicago: American Library Assn., 1967. 400p.

Aslib. Film Production Librarians Group. Cataloging Committee. *Film Cataloging Rules.* London: Aslib, 1963. 71p.

Baker, Hazel. "Manual for an Audio-Visual Program for High School Librarians in Ohio." M.A. thesis. Kent State Univ., 1962. 38p.

Bradley, Carol J., ed. *Manual of Music Librarianship.* Ann Arbor, Mich.: Music Library Association, 1966.

Coates, E. J. *The British Catalogue of Music Classification.* London: Council of the British National Bibliography, 1960. 56p.

Croghan, Antony. *Faceted Classification for and an Essay on the Literature of the Performing Arts.* London: privately published, 1968. 120p.

DeKieffer, Robert E., and Lee W. Cochran. *Manual of Audio-visual Techniques.* Englewood Cliffs, N.J.: Prentice-Hall, 1962. 254p.

Gambee, Budd L. *Non-book Materials as Library Resources.* Chapel Hill: Univ. of North Carolina, 1967.

Harris, Evelyn J. *Instructional Materials Cataloging Guide.* Tucson: Univ. of Arizona, 1968.

Hicks, Warren B., and Alma M. Tillin. *Developing Multi-Media Libraries.* New York: Bowker, 1970, 199p.

———. *The Organization of Nonbook Materials in School Libraries.* Sacramento, Calif.: California State Dept. of Education, 1967. 71p.

Joint Committee on Music Cataloging. *Code for Cataloging Music and Phonorecords.* Chicago: American Library Assn., 1958. 88p.

Jones, Emily S. *Manual on Film Evaluation.* New York: Educational Film Library Assn., 1967. 32p.

Keen, Eunice. *Manual for Use in the Cataloging and Classification of Audio-Visual Materials for a High School Library.* Lakeland, Fla.: privately published, 1955. 35p.

Lubetsky, Seymour. *Principles of Cataloging.* Los Angeles: Institute of Library Research, Univ. of California, 1969.

McFarland, Roger B., and Caroline Saheb-Ettaba. *ANSCR: Alpha Numeric Scheme for Classification of Recordings.* Williamsport, Pa.: Bro-Dart, 1968.

Manual for Cataloging and Storage on Non-Book Materials. Winnipeg, Manitoba: Winnipeg School Division no. 1, Library Service Centre, 1967.

Manual for Processing Non-Book Materials in School Libraries, for Use in Course 531: Technical Services. Kalamazoo, Mich.: Western Michigan Univ., Dept. of Librarianship, 1966.

Manual for Organizing Audiovisual Media. Raleigh, N.C.: State Dept. of Public Instruction, Division of Educational Media, 1968.

Marshall, Ralph Thomas. "Organization and Cataloging of Films, Filmstrips and Recordings," M.S.L.S. thesis. Western Reserve Univ. 1952. 39p.

Oral Roberts University Library. "Cataloging Handbook." Tulsa, Okla.: the Library, 1967.

Piercy, Esther J. *Commonsense Cataloging; a Manual for the Organization of Books and Other Materials in School and Small Public Libraries.* New York: Wilson, 1965. 223p.

Processing Manual for Books and Non-Book Materials. Glen Ellyn, Ill.: College of DuPage, Instructional Resources Center, 1970.

Riddle, Jean, et al. *Non-Book Materials: The Organization of Integrated Collections.* Prelim. ed. Ottawa: Canadian Library Assn., 1970. 58p.

Rufsvold, Margaret. *Audio-Visual School Library Service: A Handbook for Libraries.* Chicago: American Library Assn., 1949. 116p.

Sanderson, Jessie Mae. *Non-Book Library Materials, a Cataloging Guide.* Livonia, Mich.: Livonia Public Schools. Department of Instructional Materials Services, 1965.

Scholz, Dell DuBose. *A Manual for the Cataloging of Recordings in Public Libraries.* Baton Rouge, La.: privately published, 1963. 42p.

Scott, Margaret B., et al. *Cataloging for School Libraries.* Rev. ed. Toronto: Univ. of Toronto, College of Education, 1967.

Simons, Wendell W., and Luraine C. Tansey. *A Universal Slide Classification System for the Organization and Automatic Indexing of Interdisciplinary Collections of Slides and Pictures.* Santa Cruz: Univ. of California, 1970. 183p.

Snow, Kathleen M. *Manual for Cataloguing Non-Book Materials.* Calgary, Alberta: Univ. of Calgary Bookstore, 1968.

Steele, Robert. *The Cataloging and Classification of Cinema Literature.* Metuchen, N.J.: Scarecrow, 1967. 133p.

Trainor, Beatrice. *The Canadian Film Institute: The Cataloging and Classification in its Library and Information Service.* Ottawa: Canadian Library Assn., 1960. 52p.

U.S. Library of Congress. *Library of Congress Catalog: Motion Pictures and Filmstrips.* Washington, D.C.: the Library, 1967.

———. *Library of Congress Catalog: Music and Phonorecords.* Detroit: Gale, 1965.

———. *Motion Pictures, Filmstrips, and Other Projected Images: a MARC Format.* Washington, D.C.: the Library, 1970.

———. *Rules for Descriptive Cataloging in the Library of Congress.* Washington, D.C.: the Library, 1949. 141p.

———. *Rules for Descriptive Cataloging in the Library of Congress: Phonorecords.* Prelim. ed. Washington, D.C.: the Library, 1952. 11p.

———. Descriptive Cataloging Division. *Rules for Descriptive Cataloging in the Library of Congress: Motion Pictures and Filmstrips.* Washington, D.C.: the Library, 1965. 20p.

———. Subject Cataloging Division. *Music Subject Headings Used on Printed Catalog Cards of the Library of Congress.* Washington, D.C.: the Library, 1952.

Westhius, Judith, and Julia M. DeYoung. *Cataloging Manual for Nonbook Materials in Learning Centers and School Libraries.* Ann Arbor: Univ. of Michigan, 1966. 35p.

Wetmore, Rosamond Bayne. "A Guide to the Organization of Library Materials in Schools and Small Public Libraries." Muncie, Ind.: Ball State Univ. Dept. of Library Science, 1967.

Wynar, Bohdan S. *Introduction to Cataloging and Classification.* 3d ed. Rochester, N.Y.: Libraries Unlimited, 1967. 306p.

ORGANIZATION AND ADMINISTRATION

Alonso, P. G. "Conservation and Circulation in Map Libraries: A Brief Review." *SLA Geography and Map Division Bulletin* 74:15–18 (Dec. 1968).

American Library Association. Library Technology Project. *Testing and Evaluation of Record Players for Libraries; Report Based on a Study Conducted for the Project by Consumer's Research, Inc.* (LTP pub. no. 5) Chicago: the Association, 1962.

"Audio Services and Facilities, a Panel Discussion." In *Library Environment: Aspects of Interior Planning,* pp. 41–50. Chicago: American Library Assn., 1965.

Bennett, Fleming. "Audio-Visual Services in Colleges and Universities in the United States." *College and Research Libraries* 16: 11–19 (Jan. 1955).

Blair, Patricia O. "Treatment, Storage, and Handling of Motion Picture Film." *Library Journal* 71:333–36 (Mar. 1, 1946).

Calhoun, John M. "Preservation of Motion-Picture Film." *American Archivist* 30:517–25 (July 1953).

Canadian School Library Association. Technical Services Committee. *Organization of Non-Book Materials in School Libraries.* Toronto: the Association, 1968.

Christensen, Ruth. "The Junior College Library as an Audiovisual Center." *College and Research Libraries* 26:121–28 (Mar. 1965).

Clark, Tommy A. "Instructional Materials Center." M.L.S. thesis. Univ. of Mississippi, 1966. 58p.

Cowan, Jean C. "The Care and Treatment of Long Playing Records in Public Libraries." *Librarian and Book World* 47:76–79 (Apr. 1958).

Davis, B. "Control and Storage of a Slide Collection." A.M.L.S. thesis. Science. Boston: Simmons College, 1956.

Day, Dorothy L. "Films in the Library." *Library Trends* 4:174–81 (Oct. 1955).

Ehrenberg, R. "Map Acquisition, Arrangement, and Description at the National Archives." *SLA Geography and Map Division Bulletin* 68:10–13 (June 1967).

Erickson, Carlton, W. H. *Administering Audiovisual Services.* New York: Macmillan, 1959.

Faris, Gene, and John Moldstad. *Improving the Learning Environment: A Study on the Local Preparation of Visual Instructional Materials.* Washington: U.S. Office of Education, 1963.

Giannotta, K. M. "Suggested Plan for Organizing and Administering Audio-visual Services Within a School Library Materials Center (Grades 7–12)." M.S.L.S. thesis. Southern Connecticut State College.

Gould, Geraldine N., and Ithmer C. Wolfe. *How to Organize and Maintain the Picture/Pamphlet File.* Dobbs Ferry, N.Y.: Oceana, 1968. 146p.

Grove, Pearce S., and Herman L. Totten. "Bibliographic Control of Media: The Librarian's Excedrin Headache." *Wilson Library Bulletin* 44:299–311 (Nov. 1969).

Günther, A. "Slides in Documentation." *Unesco Bulletin for Libraries* 17:157–62 (1963).

Havard-Williams, P., and S. Watson. "The Slide Collection at Liverpool School of Architecture." *Journal of Documentation* 16: 11–14 (Mar. 1960).

Hensel, Evelyn Mildred. "Treatment of Nonbook Materials," *Library Trends* 2:187–98 (Oct. 1953).

Hill, May D. "Prints, Pictures and Photographs." *Library Trends* 4:156–63 (1955).

International Association of Music Libraries. *Phonograph Record Libraries: Their Organization and Practice.* Edited by H. F. J. Currall. Hamden, Conn.: Shoe String, 1963.

Ireland, Norma Olin. *The Picture File in School, College, and Public Libraries.* Rev. ed. Boston: Faxton, 1952.

Irvine, Betty Jo. "Slide Collections in Art Libraries." *College and Research Libraries* 30:443–45 (Sept. 1969).

Kocher, Sandra A. "2" x 2" Color Slides of Art." *Art Journal* 23: 42+ (1969).

Lowens, Irving. "Broadside at the Pirates: Law Protecting Recordings Takes Effect This Month." *Music Education Journal* (Feb. 1972).

Lowrie, Jean E. "Organization and Operation of School Library Materials Centers." *Library Trends* 16:211–27 (Oct. 1967).

McIntyre, C. J. "Librarian's Role as an Educator in the Production of Nonprint Materials." *Library Trends* 16:266–73 (1967).

McMurry, Glenn D. "Film Library Uses for the Computer." *Audiovisual Instruction* 12:314–20 (Apr. 1967).

Mitra, D. K. "Maps in Libraries, Their Storage and Preservation." *Herald Library Science* 7:27–32 (Jan. 1968).

Morphet, Edgar, and David L. Jessar, eds. *Planning for Effective Utilization of Technology in Education.* New York: Citation Pr. 1968.

Pearson, Mary D. *Recordings in the Public Library.* Chicago: American Library Assn., 1963. 153p.

Peskind, Ira J. "Organization of an Audio-Visual Unit in a Junior College Library." *College and Research Libraries* 12:62–66 (Jan. 1951).

Pickett, A. G., and M. M. Lemcoe. *Preservation and Storage of Sound Recordings.* Washington, D.C.: Library of Congress, 1959. 74p.

Preggie, W. C. "Local Production Center: A Time and Money Saver." In *Proceedings of the National Conference on the Implications of the New Media for the Teaching of Library Science,* pp. 49–52. University of Illinois Graduate School of Library Science Monograph Series, No. 1. Urbana: Univ. of Illinois Pr., 1963.

Pressler, Joan. "Organizing Library-Based AV Materials." *School Libraries* 14:43–47 (Mar. 1965).

"Producing Slides and Filmstrips." Kodak Publications No. S-8. Rochester, N.Y.: Eastman Kodak Co., 1968.

Quinly, William J. "The Selection, Processing and Storage of Non-Print Materials: Aids, Indexes and Guidelines." *Library Trends* 16:274–82 (Oct. 1967).

Redfern, Brian. *Organizing Music in Libraries.* New York: Philosophical Library, 1966, 80p.

Saunders, Helen E. *Modern School Library: Its Administration as a Materials Center*. Metuchen, N.J.: Scarecrow, 1968.

Smith, Nicholas N. "Film Care." *Bookmark* 27:231–32 (Mar. 1968).

Stone, C. Walter. "Listening Facilities in the Library." In *Library Environment: Aspects of Interior Planning*, pp. 34–40. Chicago: American Library Assn., 1965.

Stripling, E. M. "Technical Organization of Film and Visual Materials in College and University Libraries." M.S. thesis. Columbia Univ., 1951. 115p.

Swann, E. "Problems Involved in Establishing a Slide Collection in the School of Architecture, School of Melbourne." *Australian Library Journal* 9:159–62 (July 1960).

White, Brenda. *Slide Collections: a Survey of Their Organization in Libraries in the Field of Architecture, Building, and Planning.* Edinburgh: privately published, 1967.

White, F. A., and J. Younger. "Slides and Filmstrips Add Service." *Wisconsin Library Bulletin* 62:162–63 (1966).

Yesner, Bernice L. *Administering Filmstrip and Record Collections.* New York: McGraw, 1968.

SELECTION AND ACQUISITION

American Library Association. Library Technology Project. *The Testing and Evaluation of Record Players for Libraries.* Chicago: American Library Assn., 1962.

The Audio-Visual Equipment Directory. Evanston, Ill.: National Audio-Visual Assn., 1953– .

Audiovisual Market Place. New York: Bowker, 1969– .

"Audiovisual Selection Aids." *Wisconsin Library Bulletin* 62-180–81 (May 1966).

Billings, Jane Kelley. "Selection for the Instructional Materials Center." *Wisconsin Library Bulletin* 64:9–12 (Jan. 1968).

Brubaker, Mildred J. "A & P of AV Materials." *Illinois Libraries* 49:129–40 (Fall 1967).

Clark, Joan E. "Selection and Presentation of Films and Film Programs for Adults; With List of Suggested Film Programs." *Bookmark* 27:159–63 (Jan. 1968).

Cox, Carl T. "Filmstrips: Selection, Evaluation, Cataloging, Processing." *Wilson Library Bulletin* 38:178–82 (Oct. 1963).

Daily, Jay E. "The Selection, Processing, and Storage of Non-Print Materials: A Critique of the Anglo-American Cataloging Rules as They Relate to Newer Media." *Library Trends* 16:283–89 (Oct. 1967).

Davis, Chester K. "Record Collections, 1960: LJ's Survey of Fact and Opinion." *Library Journal* 85:3375–80 (Oct. 1, 1960).

Dunnetski, Stanley F. "Principles of Film Evaluation for Public Libraries." *Illinois Libraries* 49:89-92 (Feb. 1967).

Educational Film Library Association. *Film Evaluation Guide, 1946–1964.* New York: the Association, 1965. 528p.

Educational Foundation for Visual Aids. Equipment Department. *Equipment for Audio-Visual Aids.* London: the Foundation, 1968. 27p.

"Film Selection Policy of Special Service Film Library." *Bookmark* 25:203–6 (May 1966).

George, E. A. "Effective Educational Media Committee." *Pennsylvania Library Association Bulletin* 26:261–63 (Sept. 1971).

Golej, Peter. "Selection of Instructional Films for Schools." *Michigan Association of School Librarians* 13:1–5 (Winter 1964).

Hodges, E. D. "Selecting Materials to Support the Curriculum." *Childhood Education* 43:69–72 (Oct. 1966).

Jennings, P. M. *Audio-Visual Aids: A Classical Catalogue.* Centaur Books, 1966. 70p.

Jones, M. L. *Sources of AV Materials.* Washington, D.C.: Govt. Print. Off., 1967.

Lieberman, Irving. "Reference Service and Audiovisual Materials: Recommended Books, Pamphlets and Periodicals for a Library and Audiovisual Materials Information Collections as Well as Tools for Selection of Material." In *National Conference on the Implications of the New Media for the Teaching of Library Sci-*

ence, pp. 164–78. Urbana, Ill.: Univ. of Illinois, Graduate School of Library Science, 1963.

Limbacher, James L. "Film Evaluation and Criticism." *Illinois Libraries* 46:121–25 (Feb. 1964).

Pula, Fred John. *Application and Operation of Audio-Visual Equipment in Education.* New York: Wiley, 1968. 360p.

Quinly, William J. "The Selection, Processing, and Storage of Non-Print Materials: Aids, Indexes and Guidelines." *Library Trends* 16:274–82 (Oct. 1967).

Simons, Wendell W. "Choosing Audio-Visual Equipment." *Library Trends* 13:503–16 (Apr. 1965).

"Some Sources of 2 x 2-inch Color Slides." Kodak Pamphlet No. S-2. Rochester, N.Y.: Eastman Kodak Co., n.d.

Thomas, Robert Murray, and S. G. Swartout. *Integrated Teaching Materials: How to Choose, Create, and Use Them.* Rev. and enl. New York: McKay, 1963. 559p.

STANDARDS

American Library Association. Association of College and Research Libraries, Audio-Visual Committee. *Guidelines for Audio-Visual Services in Academic Libraries.* Chicago: the Association, 1968.

———. Public Library Association, Audio Visual Standards Committee. "Recommendations for Standards for Audio Visual Services in Public Library Systems." Mimeographed. Chicago: the Association, 1969.

———. ———. ———. *Guidelines for Audiovisual Materials and Services for Public Libraries.* Chicago: the Association, 1970. 33p.

———. Resources and Technical Services Division, Copying Methods Section. *Microfilm Norms: Recommended Standards for Libraries.* Chicago: the Association, 1967. 48p.

American National Standards Institute. *Catalog 1970.* New York: the Institute, 1970.

French, J. "Evaluation Gap: The State of the Art in A/V Reviewing, with Special Emphasis on Filmstrips." *Library Journal* 95: 1162–66+ (Mar. 15, 1970); *School Library Journal* 17:104–8+ (Mar. 1970).

Joint Committee of the American Association of School Librarians and the Department of Audiovisual Instruction of the National Education Association. *Standards for School Media Programs.* Chicago: American Library Assn., 1969. 66p.

Meierhenry, Wesley C. "National Media Standards for Learning and Teaching." *ALA Bulletin* 63:238–41 (Feb. 1969).

National Education Association, Department of Audiovisual Instruction. *Quantitative Standards for Audiovisual Personnel, Equipment and Materials in Elementary, Secondary and Higher Education.* Washington: the Association, 1966.

———. ———. *Standards for Cataloging, Coding, and Scheduling Educational Media.* Washington, D.C.: the Association, 1968. 50p.

National Fire Protection Association. *Standard for the Storage and Handling of Cellulose Nitrate Motion Picture Film.* Boston: the Association, 1967. 38p.

Plunkett, Dalton G., and Allan D. Quick. *Cataloging Standards for Non-Book Materials.* Tigard, Ore.: Northwest Library Service, 1968. 54p.

Public Library Association, Standards Committee. *Minimum Standards for Public Library Systems, 1966.* Chicago: American Library Assn., 1967. 69p.

"Quantitative Standards for Audiovisual Programs." *Audiovisual Instruction* 10:462 (July 1965).

Sherman, Mendel, and Gene Faris. "Standards and Evaluative Instruments for Audiovisual Programs." *School Libraries* 15:25–29 (May 1966).

Notes

"Bibliographic Organization of Nonprint Media"

1. Ernest Cushing Richardson, *Classification: Theoretical and Practical,* 3rd ed. (New York: Wilson, 1930), p. 42.

2. Strabo, *The Geography of Strabo* (New York: Putnam, 1917).

3. Dorothy Mae Norris, *A History of Cataloging and Cataloging Methods* (London: Grafton, 1939), pp. 195–96.

4. Jesse H. Shera, *Libraries and the Organization of Knowledge* (Hamden, Conn.: Shoe String, 1965), p. 143.

5. Melvil Dewey, *Dewey Decimal Classification and Relative Index,* 2 vols., 16th ed. (Lake Placid Club, N. Y.: Forest, 1959), introduction.

6. Ibid.

7. Horace Kephart, "Classification (and) Synopsis of Reports from 127 Libraries on Systems of Classification," ed. Melvil Dewey (Papers prepared for the World's Library Congress held at the Columbian Exposition in 1893; Washington, D. C.: Govt. Print. Off., 1896), pp. 861–97.

8. Josephine Metcalfe Smith, *A Chronology of Librarianship* (Metuchen, N. J.: Scarecrow, 1968), p. 123.

9. Melvil Dewey, "Library Pictures," *Public Libraries* 11:10–11 (1906).

10. Henry Evelyn Bliss, "Economics in Libraries," *Library Journal* 28:711 (1910).

11. *Bowker Annual of Library and Book Trade Information,* 16th ed. (New York: Bowker, 1971), p. 179.

12. C. W. Stokes, "Classification and Filing of Photographs," *Printer's Ink* (Aug. 3, 1916), pp. 82–86; James Gillis, "Moving Pictures," *American Library Annual* (1915–16), p. 77; Thomas Edison, "Motion Pictures," *American Library Annual* (1917–18), p. 61; Julia G. Babcock, "How to Handle Slides and Records," *Public Libraries* 24:377 (1919).

13. W. C. Berwick Sayers, *A Manual of Classification for Librarians and Bibliographers* (London: Grafton, 1926), p. 7.

14. Margaret A. Klein, "Government Activities in the Visual Field: A Filing System for Visual Aides," *The Educational Screen* 12:103–4 (Apr. 1933); ibid., 12:128–9 (May 1933); ibid., 12:161–62 (June 1933).

15. Melvil Dewey, *Simplified Library School Rules* (pub. Boston, New York Library Bureaus, 1898), p. 53.

16. M. Lanning Shane, "Audio-visual Aids and the Library," *College and Research Libraries* 1:143–46+ (Mar. 1940).

17. *Post-War Standards for Public Libraries* (Chicago: American Library Assn., 1943), p. 67.

18. "The Cataloging of Materials Other Than Books," *The Library Association Record* 46:78–81 (May 1944).

19. Earl E. Sechriest, "Organization, Administration, Supervision and Mechanical Facilities of Departments of Audio-Visual Aids" (Abstract of a Ph.D. dissertation, Univ. of Pittsburgh), *Bulletin* 41:1–8 (Feb. 10, 1945).

20. Muriel Louise Kemp, "Worcester Free Public Library Gives Discs Full Treatment," *Library Journal* 73:406–8 (Mar. 1, 1948).

21. "Processing Audio-Visual Materials," mimeographed (Bloomington: Indiana Univ., 1948).

22. Virginia Clarke, "Now, Just One Place to Look," *Library Journal* 73:1233–36 (Sept. 15, 1948).

23. Edith Scott, "Cataloging Non-Book Materials," *Journal of Cataloging and Classification* 5:46–47 (Spring 1949).

24. Kenneth C. Harrison, "What English Libraries Are Doing," *Library Journal* 74:676–77 (Apr. 15, 1949).

25. Dilla W. MacBean, "Audio-Visual Materials in the Library," *Wilson Library Bulletin* 23:697–98 (May 1949).

26. Bessie M. Daughtry, *Cataloging and Classifying Audio-Visual Materials* (Tallahassee: Florida State Univ., 1950).

27. Barbara M. Westby, ed., *Sears List of Subject Headings*, 10th ed. (New York: Wilson, 1972).

28. Ira J. Peskind, "Organization of an Audio-Visual Unit in a Junior College Library," *College and Research Libraries* 12:62–66 (Jan. 1951).

29. Pierce Butler, "The Bibliographical Function of the Library," *Journal of Cataloging and Classification* 9:3 (Mar. 1953).

30. "Audio-Visual Board" (Minutes of ALA New York Conference, Chicago: American Library Assn., 1952), p. 123.

31. Edith M. Brainard, "The Use and Administration of Audio-Visual Materials in Colleges in the Pacific Northwest: Report of a Survey," *College and Research Libraries* 14:317–19 (July 1953).

32. Sister Mary Janet, "Cataloging of Nonbook Materials," *Catholic Library World* 24:153–55 (Feb. 1953).

33. Evelyn Hensel, "Treatment of Nonbook Materials," *Library Trends* 2:187–98 (Oct. 1953).

34. C. Walter Stone, "Place of Newer Media in the Undergraduate Program," *Library Quarterly* 24:368–73 (Oct. 1954).

35. "Revised Cataloging Rules," *Journal of Cataloging and Classification* 11:37 (July 1955).

36. "Audio-Visual Board" minutes of ALA Philadelphia Conference (Chicago: American Library Assn., 1955), p. 65.

37. Beverly Hickok "Handling Visual Aid Material," *Special Libraries* 46:358–60 (Oct. 1955).

38. John F. Harvey, "Measuring Library Audio-Visual Activities," *College and Research Libraries* 18:193–98+ (May 1957).

39. H. R. Halvorsen, "Colorful Card Catalog," *Educational Screen and A-V Guide* 37:565 (Nov. 1958).

40. Doris M. Carson, "Cataloging Nonbook Materials," *Wilson Library Bulletin* 39:562–64 (Mar. 1965).

41. Dorothy H. Dudley, et al., *Museum Registration Methods* (Washington D. C.: American Association of Museums and the Smithsonian Institution, 1958).

42. Edith P. Sickney and Henry Scherer, "Developing an A-V Program in a Small College Library," *Library Journal* 84:2457–59 (Sept. 1, 1959).

43. Shirley L. Hopkinson, "The Descriptive Cataloging of Library Materials," San Jose, Cal.: the author, 1963.

44. Maurice Tauber and Oliver L. Lilley, "Feasibility Study Regarding the Establishment of an Educational Media Research Information Service" mimeographed (New York: Columbia Univ., 1960).

45. Margaret I. Rufsvold and Carolyn Guss. "Proceedings of a Work Conference on Bibliographic Control of Newer Educational Media" mimeographed (Bloomington: Indiana Univ., Nov. 5, 1960).

46. Carolyn Guss, "Toward a National Descriptive and Evaluative Cataloging Service for Newer Educational Media," *Bulletin of the School of Education* 36:35–42 (Nov. 1960).

47. Margaret I. Rufsvold and Carolyn Guss, "Sources of Information about Newer Educational Media for Elementary and Secondary Education: 1950–1960" mimeographed (Bloomington: Indiana Univ., Apr. 20, 1960).

48. Carolyn I. Whitenack, "A National Catalog for A-V," *Audiovisual Instruction* 6:510–11 (Dec. 1961).

49. "USC's Film Department Gets Grant for Automated Cataloging Project," *Library Journal* 90:85 (Jan. 1, 1965).

50. Glenn D. McMurry, "What Is NICEM?" *Educational Screen and A-V Guide* 46:21 (July 1967).

51. Judith Westhuis and Julia M. DeYoung, *Cataloging Manual for Non-Book Materials in Learning Centers and School Libraries* (Ann Arbor: Univ. of Michigan, 1966).

52. William J. Quinly, "The Selection, Processing and Storage of Non-Print Materials: Aids, Indexes and Guidelines," *Library Trends* 16:274–82 (Oct. 1967).

53. "Cataloging Handbook" (Manual prepared for the Oral Roberts University Library, circa 1967).

54. *Manual for Organizing Audiovisual Media* (Raleigh, N. C.: State Department of Public Instruction, Division of Educational Media, 1968); *Standards for Cataloging Coding and Scheduling Educational Media* (Washington, D.C.: National Education Association, 1968); Antony Croghan, *A Faceted Classification for an Essay on the Literature of the Performing Arts* (London: the author, 1968).

55. Bernard Chibnall and Antony Croghan, *A Feasibility Study of a Multimedia Catalogue* (Report to Office for Scientific and Technical Information on Project S1/25/36, Univ. of Sussex, Sept. 1969).

56. Fleming Bennett, "Audio-Visual Services in Colleges and Universities in the United States," *College and Research Libraries* 16:11–19 (Jan. 1955).

57. *Standards for School Media Programs* (Chicago: American Library Assn. and Washington: National Education Assn., 1969).

58. James B. Coover, "Computers, Cataloguing, and Co-operation," *Music Library Association Notes* 25:437–46 (Mar. 1969).

59. Richard L. Darling, "Report on Preliminary Considerations of the Committee for the Use of Audiovisual Materials in Libraries," *Resources and Technical Services Bulletin* 13:301 (Spring 1969).

60. Audiovisual Committee, Public Library Association, *Guidelines for Audiovisual Materials and Services for Public Libraries* (Chicago: American Library Assn., 1970).

61. *Maps: A MARC Format* (Washington, D. C.: Library of Congress, 1970); *Films: A MARC Format* (Washington, D. C.: Library of Congress, 1970).

62. Jean Riddle, Shirley Lewis, and Janet Macdonald, *Non-Book Materials: The Organization of Integrated Collections,* prelim. ed. (Ottawa: Canadian Library Assn., 1970).

63. *Processing Manual for Books and Non-Book Material* (Glen Ellyn, Ill.: College of DuPage, Instructional Resources Center, Winter, 1970); Robert A. Veihman, "Cataloging and Processing Non-Book Materials—A True Instructional Resources Center Concept," *Audiovisual Instruction* 15:58–59 (Dec. 1970).

64. Antony Croghan, "A Thesaurus-Classification for the Physical Forms of Non-Book Media" (mimeographed, 1970).

65. ———, *A Manual on the Construction of an Indexing Language Using Educational Technology as an Example* (London: Coburgh Publications, 1971).

66. "A Bill to Preserve, for Purposes of Study and Research, Nationally Televised News and Public Interest Programs," S. B. 1169, 92nd Congress, First Session (Washington, D. C., Mar. 10, 1971).

67. Announcement by Henriette D. Avram, chief, Machine-Readable Catalog Development Office, Library of Congress, Aug. 9, 1971.

68. "Audiovisual Cataloging Automated," *Library of Congress Information Bulletin* 31:7 (Jan. 1972).

69. *Standards for Cataloging Nonprint Materials*, rev. ed. (Washington: Assn. for Educational Communication and Technology, 1972).

70. Pearce S. Grove and Evelyn G. Clement, *Bibliographic Control of Non-print Media* (Chicago: American Library Assn., 1972).

71. "Committee on Moving Pictures and the Library," *ALA Bulletin* 22:133 (June 1928).

72. Clarence E. Sherman, "Relations Between Moving Pictures and Libraries," *ALA Bulletin* 19, no. 4 (July 1925).

73. Frank H. Chase, "Moving Pictures and the Library," *ALA Bulletin* 21:144 (July 1927).

74. "Committee on Moving Pictures and the Library," p. 133.

75. Chase, "Moving Pictures," p. 145.

76. Frances Hamman, "Bibliographic Control of Audio-Visual Materials: Report of a Special Committee," *Library Resources and Technical Services Bulletin* 1:180–89 (Fall 1957).

77. Eunice Keen, "Aids for Use in Cataloging and Classifying Audio-Visual Materials," *Library Resources and Technical Services Bulletin* 1:189–97 (Fall 1957).

78. "Annual Report, Kansas City Conference" (Chicago: American Library Assn., 1957), p. 64.

79. "Teacher's Section," *Proceedings of the American Library Association* (Annual Conference, 1966), p. 91.

80. American Library Association, *Guidelines for Audio-Visual Services in Academic Libraries*, prepared by the Audio-Visual Committee of the Association for College and Research Libraries and ALA Audio-Visual Committee (Chicago: the Association, 1968).

81. "Audio-Visual Commttee," minutes of the ALA San Francisco Conference (Chicago: American Library Assn., 1967).

82. Ibid., p. 18.

83. *Anglo-American Cataloging Rules*, North American Text (Chicago: American Library Assn., 1967).

84. Sayers, *Manual of Classification*, p. 7.

85. Arch C. Gerlach, "Geography and Map Cataloging and Classification in Libraries," *Special Libraries* 52:248–51 (May 1961).

86. Theodore H. Laying, "Problems in the Map Room," *Canadian Library* 18:63–66 (Sept. 1961).

87. A. M. Ferrar, "The Management of Map Collections and Libraries in University Geography Departments," *Library Association Record* 64:161–65 (May 1952).

88. Lloyd A. Brown, "The Problem of Maps," *Library Trends* 13:215–25 (Oct. 1964).

89. Josephine Metcalfe Smith, *A Chronology of Librarianship* (Metuchen, N. J.: Scarecrow, 1968), p. 123.

90. Melvil Dewey, "Library Pictures," *Public Libraries* 11:10–11. (1906).

91. Jane Howe, "Cataloguing a Photograph Collection," *Oklahoma Librarian* 13:8–12 (Jan. 1963).

92. Betty Hale, "Pictures in Your Company's Archives," *Special Libraries* 54:41 (Jan. 1965).

93. Boris W. Kuvshinoff, "A Graphic Graphics Card Catalog and Computer Index," *American Documentation* 18:3–9 (Jan. 1967).

94. Adelheid G. Ladewig, "Routine for the Cataloging and Processing of Slides," *Journal of Cataloging and Classification* 6:67–68 (Summer 1950).

95. Lyle F. Perusse, "Classifying and Cataloging Lantern Slides for the Architecture Library," *Journal of Cataloging and Classification* 10:77–83 (Apr. 1954).

96. P. Havard-Williams and S. Watson, "The Slide Collection at Liverpool School of Architecture," *Journal of Documentation* 16:11–14 (Mar. 1960).

97. Alfred Günther, "Slides in Documentation," *UNESCO Bulletin for Libraries* 17:157–62 (May 1963).

98. Morton N. Wasserman, "A Computer-Prepared Book Catalog for Engineering Transparencies," *Special Libraries* 57:111–13 (Feb. 1966).

99. Brenda White, *"Slide Collections: A Survey of Their Organization in Libraries in the Fields of Architecture, Building, and Planning* (Edinburgh: privately published, 1967).

100. Diamond, Robert M. *The Development of a Retrieval System for 35mm Slides Utilized in Art and Humanities Instruction.* (Fredonia, N. Y.: State University College, Instructional Resources Center, 1969).

101. Wendell W. Simons and Luraine C. Tansey, *A Universal Slide Classification System with Automatic Indexing* (Santa Cruz: Univ. of California, 1969); idem, *A Slide Classification System for the Organization and Automatic Indexing of Interdisciplinary Collections of Slides and Pictures* (Santa Cruz: Univ. of California, 1970).

102. Betty Jo Irvine, "Slide Collections in Art Libraries," *College and Research Libraries* 30:443–45 (Sept. 1969).

103. Sir Arthur Elton, "The Film as Source Material for History," *ASLIB Proceedings* 7:215 (Nov. 1955).

104. Edgar Dale, *Motion Pictures in Education: A Summary of the Literature* (New York: Wilson, 1938).

105. Lorraine Noble, "This Film Publishing Business," *ALA Bulletin* 30:967–73 (Dec. 1936).

106. Ibid., p. 968.

107. Ibid., p. 973.

108. Dorothy Arbaugh, "Motion Pictures and the Future Historian," *American Archivist* 2:106–14 (Apr. 1939).

109. "Visual Methods Committee," *ALA Bulletin* 32:979–83 (Oct. 15, 1938).

110. Ibid., pp. 981–83.

111. John E. Abbott, "Cataloging and Filing of Motion Picture Films," *Library Journal* 63:93–95 (Feb. 1, 1938).

112. "Visual Methods Committee," *ALA Bulletin* 33, no. 11:216–18 (Oct. 15, 1939).

113. "Visual Methods," *ALA Bulletin* 33, no. 9:662 (Sept. 1939).

114. Edwin E. Williams, "A.L.A. Notes," *Wilson Library Bulletin* 14:778 (June 1940).

115. Gerald D. McDonald, *Educational Motion Pictures and Libraries* (Chicago: American Library Assn., 1942), p. vii.

116. Ibid., pp. vii–x.

117. American Council on Education, *Selected Educational Motion Pictures.* (Washington, D. C.: The Council, 1942).

118. John G. Bradley, "Cataloging and Indexing Motion Picture Film," *American Archivist* 8:169–84 (July 1945).

119. Patricia O. Blair, "Treatment, Storage, and Handling of Motion Picture Film," *Library Journal* 71:333–36 (Mar. 1, 1946).

120. "General Sessions and Reports, Audio-Visual Committee," minutes of ALA Buffalo Conference (Chicago: American Library Assn., 1946), p. 93.

121. "Business Meeting," minutes of ALA Chicago Conference (Chicago: American Library Assn., 1951), p. 22–23.

122. "How We Do It," *EFLA Service Supplement* (Educational Film Library Association: ca. July 1952) vol. 8.

123. *Proceedings of the First International Film Cataloging Conference* (1951), convened under the auspices of the Film Council of America at George Eastman House, Rochester, N.Y. Edited by Norman B. Moore and John Flory, June 1952.

124. "The Conference on International Standards for Film Cataloguing," *Library of Congress Information Bulletin,* 12:10–11 (May 18, 1953).

125. "The Cataloguing of Films and Filmstrips: UNESCO Proposals," *UNESCO Bulletin for Libraries* 9:98–107 (May–June 1955).

126. Bernard Chibnall, "The National Film Library Cataloguing Rules," *Journal of Documentation* 2:79–82 (June 1955); Robert L. Collison, *The Treatment of Special Materials in Libraries* (London: Aslib, 1957).

127. David Grenfell, "Standardization in Film Cataloguing," *Journal of Documentation* 15:81–92 (June 1959).

128. G. Crowther, "The Cataloguing and Classification of Cine Film at the Royal Aircraft Establishment," *Aslib Proceedings* 11:179–87 (July 1959).

129. David C. Fanning, "The Cataloguing of Film Material in the National Film Archive," *Library World* 62:280–82 (June 1961).

130. Robert S. Cox, "Is Your Film Library Ready for Automation?" *Audiovisual Instruction* 6:512–14 (Dec. 1961); Ellinor Archer and Shirley Gawaith,

"Cataloging a Film Library," *Australian Library Journal* 11–13:121–24 (July 1962).

131. Bernard Chibnall, "The British National Film Catalogue and Its Contribution to Information Work," *Aslib Proceedings* 15:141–45 (May 1963).

132. Carl T. Cox, "Filmstrips: Selection, Evaluation, Cataloging, Processing" *Wilson Library Bulletin* 38:178–82 (Oct. 1963).

133. L. R. Lindeman, "A Unique Venture in Joint Audiovisual Materials Cataloguing," *Educational Screen and A-V Guide* 43:84–85 (Feb. 1964).

134. Betty Stoops, "Cataloging and Classification Systems for Instructional Materials," *Audiovisual Instruction* 9:427–28 (Sept. 1964).

135. ———, "Film Title and Credits—Are They Adequate?" *Illinois Libraries* 48:83–89 (Feb. 1966).

136. Emily Jones, "The Background and Philosophy of Film Library Services," *Drexel Library Quarterly* 2:102–10 (Apr. 1966).

137. Robert Steele, *The Cataloging and Classification of Cinema Literature* (Metuchen, N. J.: Scarecrow, 1967).

138. *Film Reference Guide for Medical and Allied Sciences* (Atlanta: National Medical Audiovisual Center, Oct. 1969).

139. Fred and Mildred Winston, "Indexing and Cataloging the 8mm," *Instructor* 78:130+ (Jan. 1969).

140. Masaaki Ogi, "Pattern-matching Technique Applied to Indexing and Retrieving Films for Television Use," *Proceedings of the American Society for Information Science*, vol. 5, *Information Transfer*, pp. 89–93.

141. *Bowker Annual of Library and Book Trade Information*, 16th ed., p. 179.

142. Edah F. Burnett, "The Care of Phonograph Records," *Libraries* 31:22 (1962).

143. Irene F. Jaynes, "Springfield Lends Phonograph Records," *Library Journal* 58:86–87 (Jan. 15, 1933).

144. Ralph E. Ellsworth, "Phonograph Records in the Library," *Library Journal* 58:529–31 (June 15, 1933).

145. Music Library Association, "Code for Cataloging Phonograph Records," mimeographed (Washington, D. C., Public Library, 1941–42), p. 26.

146. Philip L. Miller, "Cataloging and Filing of Phonograph Records," *Library Journal* 62:544–46 (July 1937).

147. Guy R. Lyle and Rose Krauskopf, "Phonograph Collection in Antioch Library," *Library Journal* 59:266–67 (Mar. 15, 1934).

148. Sidney Butler Smith, "Simplified Procedures for Recordings," *Library Journal* 69:211–12 (Mar. 1, 1944).

149. Charles E. Stow, "Cataloging the Non-Musical Phonograph Record," *Library Journal* 70:20–21 (Jan. 1, 1945).

150. Inez Haskell, "The Cataloging of Records, Musical and Non-Musical, for a General Library," *Pacific Northwest Library Association Quarterly* 9:150–55 (July 1945).

151. Music Library Association, *Code for Cataloging Phonograph Records*, prelim. ed. (Chicago: American Library Assn., 1942).

152. Helen Maywhort, "All on the Card," *Library Journal* 71:806–8 (June 1, 1946).

153. "Audio-Visual Board," minutes of the ALA New York Conference (Chicago: American Library Assn., 1952), p. 123.

154. Beryl McPherson and Carolyn Berneking. "Phonorecord Cataloging—Methods and Policies," *Library Journal* 83:2623–24+ (Oct. 1, 1958).

155. Sister M. Edmund Lincoln, "Techniques for Handling Phonograph Records," *Catholic Library World* 27:107–10+ (Dec. 1955).

156. Chester K. Davis, "Record Collections, 1960: Lj's Survey of Fact and Opinion," *Library Journal* 85:3375–80 (Oct. 1, 1960).

157. Allen Cohen, "Classification of Four Track Tapes," *Library Resources and Technical Services* 6:360–61 (Fall 1962); Donald L. Foster, "Notes Used on Music and Phonorecord Catalog Cards," *Occasional Papers*, no. 66, Dec. 1962, Urbana: Univ. of Ill. Graduate School of Library Science.

158. Henry F. Currall, ed., *Phonograph Record Libraries: Their Organization and Practice* (Hamden, Conn.: Shoe String, 1963).

159. Carlos B. Hagen, "A Proposed Information Retrieval System for Sound Recordings," *Special Libraries* 56:223–28 Apr. 1965).

160. Sherman Anderson, "Cataloging the Contents of Certain Recordings," *Library Resources and Technical Services* 9:359–62 (Summer 1965).

161. Brian Redfern, *Organizing Music in Libraries* (New York: Philosophical Library, 1966); Hilary Hammond, "A Punched Card Gramophone Record Catalogue at Luton Central Library." *Library World* 68:168 Dec. 1966).

162. Roger B. McFarland and Caroline Saheb-Ettaba, *ANSCR: Alpha Numeric Scheme for Classification of Recordings* (Willlamsport, Pa.: Bro-Dart, 1968).

"Selection and Acquisition"

1. David O. Lane, "The Selection of Academic Library Materials: A Literature Survey," *College and Research Libraries* 29:364–72 (Sept. 1968).

2. Felix Reichmann, "Purchase of Out-of-Print Material in American University Libraries," *Library Trends* 18:332 (Jan. 1970).

3. Eugene A. Pringle, "Audiovisual Materials and College Objectives," *Choice* 3:1108 (Feb. 1967).

4. For suggestions on filing, *see* John K. Bertrand, "Media Reference Service: Neglected Step-Child of the New Era," *Audiovisual Instruction* 12:16–22 (Jan. 1967).

5. C. K. Ogden and I. A. Richards, *The Meaning of Meaning*, 10th ed. (New York: Harcourt, 1952), p. 50.

6. For some suggestions, see *Guidelines for Audio-Visual Services in Academic Libraries*, Audio Visual Committee (Chicago: Assn. of College and Research Libraries, 1968), p. 14–15.

7. C. Robert Haywood, "Old, Bold Librarians," *The Library-College Journal* 1:11–14 (Summer 1968).

8. Loran C. Twyford, "Educational Communications Media," *Encyclopedia of Educational Research*, 4th ed. (New York: Macmillan, 1969), p. 367.

9. Thomas Risner, "NICEM, Mediated Media Index," *Educational Screen and Audiovisual Guide* 49:15–17 (Jan. 1970).

10. C. J. Duncan, "A Survey of Audio-Visual Equipment and Methods," in *Media and Methods: Instructional Technology in Higher Education*, edited by Derick Unwin (London: McGraw-Hill, 1969), p. 14–15.

11. William H. Allen, "Media Stimulus and Types of Learning," *Audiovisual Instruction* 12:28 (Jan. 1967).

12. Frank Johnson, "Audio-Visual Aids," in *University Teaching in Transition*, edited by David Layton (Edinburgh: Oliver and Boyd, 1968), p. 126.

13. See *Review of Educational Research* 38:111–96 (Apr. 1968). This number is devoted to a review of the literature on "Instructional Materials: Educational Media and Technology" for the six-year period since 1962.

14. See *AV Communication Review* 16:333 (Fall 1968).

15. Charles F. Hoban, "Communication in Education in a Revolutionary Age," *AV Communication Review* 18:375 (Winter 1970).

16. Louis Forsdale, "8mm Film in Education: Status and Prospects—1968," in *To Improve Learning: An Evaluation of Instructional Technology*, vol. 1, edited by Sidney G. Tickton (New York and London· Bowker, 1970), p. 231–32.

17. William J. Quinly, "The Selection, Processing and Storage of Non-Print Materials: Aids, Indexes and Guidelines," *Library Trends* 16:275 (Oct. 1967).

18. Warren B. Hicks and Alma Tillin, *Developing Multi-Media Libraries* (New York: Bowker, 1970), p. 32.

19. Tickton, *To Improve Learning*, p. 50.

"Standards"

1. C. C. Certain, "A Standard Library Organization for Accredited Secondary Schools of Different Sizes," *Educational Administration and Supervision* 3:317–38 (June 1917).

2. National Education Association, Department of Audiovisual Instruction, *Quantitative Standards for Audiovisual Personnel, Equipment, and Materials in Elementary, Secondary and Higher Education* (Washington, D. C.: The Association, 1966).

3. ———, *Criteria for Educational Media Programs in Higher Education*, with evaluation checklist (Washington, D. C.: The Association, 1966).

4. American Library Association, Public Library Association, Audiovisual Committee, *Guidelines for Audiovisual Materials and Services for Public Libraries* (Chicago: The Association, 1970).

5. "Standards for College Libraries," prepared by the ACRL Committee on Standards, *College and Research Libraries* 20:273–80 (1959).

6. "Guidelines for College Libraries," mimeographed (Working draft of the Standards and Accreditation Committee, ACRL, approved for distribution Jan. 21, 1971).

7. "ALA Standards for Junior College Libraries," *College and Research Libraries* 21:200–6 (1960).

8. "AAJC-ACRL Guidelines for Two-Year College Library Learning Resources Centers," *College and Research Libraries* 32:265–78 (Oct. 1971). Superseded by "Guidelines for Two-Year College Learning Resources Programs," *College and Research Libraries* 33:305–15 (Dec. 1972).

9. *Standards for School Media Programs,* prepared by a joint committee of ALA and DAVI (Chicago: American Library Assn., 1968).

10. Association of College and Research Libraries, Audio Visual Committee, *Guidelines for Audiovisual Services in Academic Libraries* (Chicago: American Library Assn., 1968).

11. National Education Association, Department of Audiovisual Instruction, *Standards for Cataloging, Coding, and Scheduling Educational Media* (Washington, D. C.: The Association, 1968).

12. *Anglo-American Cataloging Rules,* North American Text (Chicago: American Library Assn., 1967).

13. Jean Riddle, Shirley Lewis, and Janet Macdonald. *Non-Book Materials: The Organization of Integrated Collections* (Ottawa: Canadian Library Assn., 1970).

14. *Standards for Cataloging Nonprint Materials,* rev. ed. (Washington, D. C.: Association for Educational Communications and Technology, 1971).

15. Glenn McMurry, "National Information Center for Educational Media," in Pearce S. Grove and Evelyn G. Clement, *Bibliographic Control of Nonprint Media* (Chicago: American Library Assn., 1972), pp. 184–86.

16. Katharine Clugston, "The Library of Congress and Nonprint Media," in Grove and Clement, *Bibliographic Control,* pp. 155–60.

17. Lenore S. Maruyama, "The MARC Project and MARC Records for Film Material," in Grove and Clement, *Bibliographic Control,* pp. 210–13.

18. *Films: A MARC Format:* Specifications for magnetic tapes containing catalog records for motion pictures, filmstrips, and other pictorial media intended for projection (Washington, D. C.: Library of Congress, 1970).

19. *Standard Book Numbering* (New York: Bowker, 1968). Also, *Supplement* (1971).

20. *Standards and the Education Consumer* (Washington, D. C.: Educational Media Council, 1973).

21. Jerrold Orne, "Standards in Library Technology," *Library Trends* 21: 286–97 (Oct. 1972).

22. John G. Veenstra, "Microimages and the Library," *Library Journal* 95:3443–47 (Oct. 15, 1970).

23. Allen B. Veaner, *The Evaluation of Micropublications: A Handbook for Librarians* (Chicago: American Library Assn., 1971), p. x.

24. "Preamble," *College and Research Libraries* 33:197–98 (July-Aug. 1972). A report of editorial standards for microfilm and hard copy facsimiles approved for circulation at a conference at the Lincoln Center Branch of the New York Public Library on November 20, 1971.

25. Marjorie E. Weissman, "Library Technology Program as a Service to Consumers," *Audiovisual Instruction* 16:32–34 (Sept. 1971).

26. "Data Communications Standards," *Information Retrieval and Library Automation Letter* 7:5–6 (June 1971).

27. National Bureau of Standards, *Federal Information Processing Standards Index* (U.S. Govt. Print. Off., 1971).

28. Douglas Knight and E. Shepley Nourse, eds., *Libraries at Large* (New York: Bowker, 1969), pp. 453 and 328.

29. Orne, "Standards," p. 296.

"Sound Recordings"

1. Peter Ford, "History of Sound Recordings: I. The Age of Empiricism 1877–1924," *Recorded Sound* 7:221 (Summer 1962).

2. Roland Gerlatt, *The Fabulous Phonograph: From Tinfoil to High Fidelity* (New York: Lippincott, 1954), p. 22.

3. Ford, "History of Sound Recordings," p. 204; Allen Koenigsberg, *Edison Cylinder Records, 1899–1912* (New York: Stellar Productions, 1969), p. xii; Gerlatt, *Fabulous Phonograph*, pp. 23–24.

4. Thomas Edison, "The Phonograph and Its Future," *North American Review* 126:527–36 (June 1878); "Editorial Comment," *Scientific American* 37: 384 (Dec. 22, 1877); "Mechanical Arts and the Library," *Public Library* 19:48 (1914).

5. Philip L. Miller, "Archive of Recorded Sound," *High Fidelity/Musical Americana* 15:40–41 (1965).

6. International Assn. of Music Libraries, United Kingdom Branch, *Gramophone Record Libraries* (London: Crosby Lockwood and Son, Ltd., 1970), p. 214.

7. Eric Cooper, "Gramophone Libraries in the United States of America," in *Gramophone Record Libraries*, International Assn. of Music Libraries (London: Crosby Lockwood and Son Ltd., 1970), p. 248.

8. E. T. Bryant, *Music Librarianship: A Practical Guide* (London: James Clarke & Co., Ltd., 1959), p. 185; W. Dawson Johnston, "Symposium on Music in Libraries: St. Paul Public Library," *Library Journal* 40:574 (Aug. 1915).

9. R. R. Bowker, "Music Selection for Public Libraries," *Library Journal* 40: 582 (Aug. 1915).

10. *Pierre Key's International Music Year Book, 1928* (New York: Pierre Key, Inc., 1928), p. 292–98.

11. Carnegie Corporation of New York, *Catalogue of College Music Sets, 1933* (New York: Carnegie Corp., 1933), p. v–x.

12. Robert MacDonald Lester, *Music Study Materials: Preparation and Distribution* (New York: Carnegie Corp., 1941).

13. William Carl Greckel, "A Study of Selected College and University Recordings Libraries" (Ph.D. diss., Indiana Univ., 1969).

14. Ibid., p. 10.

15. M. William Krasilovsky, "Problems in the Relationships between the Record Industry and Librarians of Recorded Sound," *Performing Arts Review,* vol. 1 (1970). A copy of the new law (Public Law 92–140), a definition of the terms used in it, a brief explanation of it, and samples of necessary forms for application may be obtained from the Copyright Office, Library of Congress, Washington, D. C. 20540, by asking for Circular 56.

16. American Library Association, *Anglo-American Cataloging Rules.* North American Text (Chicago: American Library Assn., 1967), p. 18–19.

17. *Music and Phonorecords,* Library of Congress Catalog (Washington, D. C.: Library of Congress).

18. See *Music: A MARC Format,* available from MARC development office, Library of Congress, Washington, D. C.

19. Information available from "Cards for Records," 310 West 86th Street, New York, New York.

20. Geoffrey Cuming, "Problems of Record Cataloging," *Recorded Sound,* vol. 3 (1961).

21. Gordon Stevenson, "Classification Chaos," *Library Journal* 88:3789–94 (Oct. 15, 1963).

22. P. T. Barkey, "Phonorecord Filing Systems," *Library Journal* 82:2514 (Oct. 15, 1957); G. A. Marco and W. M. Roziewski, "Shelving Plans for LP Records," *Library Journal* 84:1568–69 (May 15, 1959); James Coover, "Computers, Cataloging, and Co-operation," *Music Library Association Notes* 25: 437–46 (Mar. 1969); Stevenson, "Classification Chaos."

23. Bryant, *Music Librarianship;* International Assn. of Music Libraries, *Gramaphone Record Libraries.*

24. *Schwann Catalogs* including *Schwann Record and Tape Guide,* monthly; *Schwann Supplementary Guide,* biennial; *Schwann Artist Issue* (Boston: W. Schwann, Inc.).

25. *One-Spot Numerical Index, One-Spot Popular Guide, One-Spot New Release Reporter; Bielefelder Katalog,* biennial catalog of records available in Germany (West Germany: Bielefelder Verlangsanstalt KG); *Diapason,* annual with supplements, catalog of records available in France (Paris: S.A.R.L.); *The Gramophone: Classical Record Catalog,* quarterly catalog of records available in England; Francis F. Clough and G. J. Cuming, *The World's Encyclopedia of Recorded Music* (London: Sidgwick and Jackson, 1952); Library of Congress, *Music and Phonorecords.*

26. James Coover and Richard Colvig, *Medieval and Renaissance Music on Long-Playing Records,* Detroit Studies in Music Bibliography, Number 6 (Detroit: Information Coordinators, Inc., 1964); Victor Girard, *Vertical Cut Cylinders and Discs* (London: British Institute of Recorded Sound, 1971); Koenigsberg, *Edison Cylinder Records.*

27. Kurtz Myers and Richard S. Hill, *Record Ratings: The Music Library Association's Index of Record Reviews* (New York: Crown, 1956).

28. Mary D. Pearson, *Recordings in the Public Library* (Chicago: American Library Assn., 1963).

29. A. G. Pickett and M. M. Memcoe, *Preservation and Storage of Sound Recordings* (Washington, D. C.: Library of Congress, 1959), pp. 62–63.

30. Ibid., p. 45.

"Slides"

1. Louis W. Sipley, *Photography's Great Inventors* (Philadelphia: American Museum of Photography, 1965).

2. Betty Jo Irvine, "Slide Classification: A Historical Survey," *College and Research Libraries* 32:23–30 (Jan. 1971).

3. Wendell W. Simons and Luraine C. Tansey, *A Universal Slide Classification System for the Organization and Automatic Indexing of Interdisciplinary Collections of Slides and Pictures* (Santa Cruz: Univ. of California, 1970).

4. P. C. Beam, "Color Slide Controversy," *College Art Journal* 2:35–38 (Jan. 1943); J. M. Carpenter, "Limitations of Color Slides," *College Art Journal* 2:38–40 (Jan. 1943).

5. Richard Bibler, "Make an Art Slide Library," *Design* 56:105+ (Jan. 1955); L. B. Bridaham and C. B. Mitchell, "Successful Duplication of Color Slides: Results of Research at the Chicago Art Institute," *College Art Journal* 10:261–63 (1951); Shirley Ellis, "Thousand Words About the Slide," *ALA Bulletin* 53:529–32 (June 1959); Lester C. Walker, Jr., "Low Cost Slide Production for Teaching Aids," *College Art Journal* 13:39–41 (1953).

6. L. F. Perusse, "Classifying and Cataloguing Lantern Slides," *Journal of Cataloguing and Classification* 19:77–83 (Apr. 1954); Dimitri Tselos, "A Simple Slide Classification System," *College Art Journal* 18:344–49 (1958); Lester C. Walker, Jr., "Slide Filing and Control," *College Art Journal* 16: 325–29 (1957).

7. Phyllis A. Reinhardt, "Photograph and Slide Collections in Art Libraries," *Special Libraries* 50:97–102 (Mar. 1959).

8. B. W. Kuvshinoff, "A Graphic Graphics Card Catalog and Computer Index," *American Documentation* 18:3–9 (Jan. 1967); Elizabeth M. Lewis, "A Graphic Catalog Card Index," *American Documentation* 20:238–46 (July 1969).

9. Robert M. Diamond, *The Development of a Retrieval System for 35 mm Slides Utilized in Art and Humanities Instruction* (Washington, D. C.: Office of Education; Bureau of Research, U. S. Department of Health, Education, and Welfare, 1969).

10. Educational Media Council, *Educational Media Index* (14 vols., New York: McGraw-Hill, 1964); Olga S. Weber, ed., *Audiovisual Market Place* (annual, New York: Bowker, 1968); Audio-Visual Research Institute, *AV-Index: A Guide to Instructional Material Information in Selected Publications* (Detroit: the Institute, 1961); *Educational Screen and Audio Visual Guide,* complete annual listing of audiovisual materials (Chicago: Educational Screen, Inc.); *Educators Guide to Free Filmstrips* (20th annual ed., Randolph, Wis.: Educators Progress Service, 1968).

11. Celestine G. Frankenberg, ed., *Picture Sources* (2d ed., project of the Picture Division, Special Libraries Association, New York: the Association, 1964).

12. *A Guide to Films, Filmstrips, Maps, Globes and Records on Asia; Supplement Including a New Section on Slides* (New York: The Asia Society, 1967).

13. Elsy Leuzinger, ed., *Afrique: l'art des peuples noirs,* summary of the German work by Marga Anstett-Janssen, translated from the German by Adelheid and Alain Gascuel (Paris: Publications Filmées d'Art et d'Histoire, 1966), 83p., 21 slides in pockets. (Based on *Afrika: Die Kunst der Negervolker,* Baden-Baden; Holle Verlag, 1964).

14. National Art Education Association, *Slides and Filmstrips on Art* (Washington, D. C.: National Education Association, 1967); *Sources of Slides: The History of Art* (New York: Metropolitan Museum of Art, 1970).

15. Nancy Delaurier, ed., *Slide Buyer's Guide* (Kansas City, Mo.: College Art Association of America, 1972).

16. *A Handlist of Museum Sources for Slides and Photographs, or Everything You Always Wanted to Know About Buying Slides and Photographs* (Santa Barbara: Univ. of California, Art Department Slide Library, 1972).

"Film"

1. *Encyclopaedia Britannica,* 1965, S. V. "Motion pictures."

2. Lewis Jacobs, *The Rise of the American Film: A Critical History* (New York: Harcourt, 1939), p. 3.

3. Siegfried Kracauer, *Theory of Film: The Redemption of Physical Reality* (Oxford Univ. Pr., 1960).

4. "What? Color in the Movies Again?" *Fortune* 10:92–97+ (Oct. 1934).

5. George Kleine, *Catalogue of Educational Motion Pictures* (New York: George Kleine Co., 1910).

6. Fred W. Perkins, "A Twelve Year Trial of Educational Films," *SMPTE Transactions* 26:48 (May 1926).

7. *Encyclopaedia Britannica,* 1965, S. V. "Motion Pictures."

8. C.E.K. Mees, "A New Substandard Film for Amateur Cinematography," "The Cine Kodak and Kodascope," both in *SMPTE Transactions* 16:246–58 (May 1923).

9. T. E. Finegan, "An Experiment in the Development of Classroom Film," *SMPTE Transactions* 31:545 (Sept. 1927); idem, "The Result of the Experiment with Eastman Classroom Films," *SMPTE Transactions* 38:324 (May 1929).

10. National Education Association, *Audio-Visual Centers in Colleges and Universities* (Washington, D.C.: the Association, 1955).

11. Bronson Price, *Library Statistics of Colleges and Universities: Data for Individual Institutions, Fall, 1968* (Washington: National Center for Educational Statistics, 1969).

12. Nelson Associates, Inc. *Undergraduate and Junior College Libraries in the United States: A Report Prepared for the National Advisory Commission on Libraries* (Washington: National Advisory Commission on Libraries, 1968), p. 22.

13. Perrin E. Parkhurst, "A Comparative Analysis of Three New TV Storage Systems," *AV Instructor* 15:43–50 (Nov. 1970)

14. "Instructional Materials Selection Policy" (distributed by Univ. of California, Institute of Library Research).

15. James L. Limbacher, ed., *Feature Films on 8mm and 16mm: A Directory of 8mm and 16mm Feature Films Available for Rental, Sale or Lease in the United States* (2d. ed., New York: Educational Film Library Assn., 1968).

16. *Anglo-American Cataloging Rules:* North American Text (Chicago: American Library Assn., 1967), p. 282–93.

17. Jean Riddle, Shirley Lewis. and Janet Macdonald, *Non-Book Materials: The Organization of Integrated Collections,* preliminary ed. (Ottawa: Canadian Library Assn., 1970).

18. Joan C. Troutman, "Standards for Cataloging of Magnetic Tape Material," part 4 of the Final Report on Mechanized Information Services in the University Library, Phase I—Planning (Los Angeles: Univ. of California, Institute of Library Research, Dec. 1967); Brigitte L. Kenney, "Psychiatric Videotape Indexing: A Progress Report," *TV in Psychiatry, Newsletter and Progress Report* (Jackson: Univ. of Mississippi Medical Center, Department of Psychiatry, Dec. 1969).

19. Charles M. Bidwell, and Dominick Auricchio. *A Prototype System for a Computer-Based Statewide Film Library Network: A Model for Operation,* final report (New York: Syracuse Univ., New York Center for Instructional Communications, 1968).

20. Gerald D. McDonald, *Educational Motion Pictures and Libraries* (Chicago: American Library Assn., 1942) p. 78.

"Filmstrips"

1. Vera M. Falconer, *Filmstrips: A Descriptive Index and User's Guide* (New York: McGraw-Hill, 1948), p. 2.

2. Ellsworth C. Dent, *The Audio-Visual Handbook* (Chicago: Society for Visual Education, 1946), p. 84.

3. Dorothy Dent, *Landmarks in Learning: The Story of SVE* (Chicago: Singer, 1969), p. 38.

4. Ellsworth Dent, *Audio-Visual Handbook.*

5. Ibid.

6. Frances Hamman, "Bibliographic Control of Audio-Visual Materials: Report of a Special Committee," *Library Resources and Technical Services* 1:180–89 (Fall 1957).

7. Falconer, *Filmstrips,* p. 3.

8. Edgar Dale, *Audiovisual Methods in Teaching* (New York: Dryden Pr., 1969).

9. Falconer, *Filmstrips*, pp. 1–41.

10. Rudy Bretz, *A Taxonomy of Communication Media* (Englewood Cliffs, N. J.: Educational Technology Publications, 1971); Jerrold E. Kemp, *Planning and Producing Audiovisual Materials* (San Francisco: Chandler, 1963).

11. James W. Brown and Kenneth D. Norberg, *Administering Educational Media* (New York: McGraw-Hill, 1965), p. 104.

12. Carlton W. H. Erickson, *Administering Instructional Media Programs* (New York: Macmillan, 1968), p. 87.

13. Ibid., p. 327.

14. Ibid.

15. Ibid.

16. Ibid., p. 318.

17. Ibid., pp. 67–69; Brown and Norberg, *Educational Media*, pp. 72–77; Frank Holmes Laboratories, Inc., *Facts You Should Know About Filmstrips* (San Fernando: Frank Holmes Laboratories, Inc., 1965), pp. 13–16.

18. Mary D. Carter and Wallace J. Bonk, *Bibliography and Book Selection* (Metuchen, N. J.: Scarecrow, 1969).

19. National Information Center for Educational Media, *Index to 35mm Educational Filmstrips* (New York: Bowker, 1968).

20. Margaret I. Rufsvold and Carolyn Guss, *Guides to Newer Educational Media* (2d. ed., Chicago: American Library Assn., 1967).

21. Hamman, "Bibliographic Control," p. 188.

22. Susan G. Akers, *Simple Library Cataloging* (5th ed., Metuchen, N. J.: Scarecrow, 1969); Jean Riddle, Shirley Lewis, and Janet MacDonald, *Non-Book Materials: The Organization of Integrated Collections* (Ottawa: Canadian Library Assn., 1970); Evelyn J. Harris, *Instructional Materials Cataloging Guide* (Tucson: Univ. of Arizona, 1968); Warren Hicks and Alma Tillin, *Developing Multi-Media Libraries* (New York: Bowker, 1970); Association for Educational Communications and Technology, *Standards for Cataloging Non-Print Materials* (Washington, D. C.: the Association, 1971).

23. *Library of Congress Catalog: Motion Pictures and Filmstrips* (Washington, D. C.: the Library, 1966).

"Maps and Map Collections"

(NOTE: The Special Libraries Association Geography and Map Division Bulletin is listed as *Bulletin.*)

1. Edward B. Espenshade, Jr., "Maps for the College Library," *College and Research Libraries* 8:132 (Apr. 1947).

2. Alexander O. Vietor, "Faculty, Students Must Have Maps," *Library Journal* 75:456–58 (Mar. 15, 1950).

3. Lynn S. Mullins, "The Rise of Map Libraries in America During the 19th Century," *Bulletin,* no. 63 (Mar. 1966), p. 5.

4. Mary M. Bryan, "The Harvard College Library Map Collection," *Bulletin,* no. 36 (Apr. 1959), p. 4–12.

5. H. C. Badger, "Floundering among the Maps," *Library Journal* 17:375 (Sept. 1892).

6. Walter W. Ristow, "Maps in Libraries," *Library Journal* 7:1101–07, 1121–24 (Sept. 1, 1946).

7. "Development of the Collection of Maps at the University of Chicago," *Science* 79:176 (Feb. 23, 1934).

8. Special Libraries Association, Geography and Map Division, Directory Revision Committee, *Map Collections in the United States and Canada: A Directory* (2d. ed., New York: the Association, 1970).

9. Edward B. Espenshade, Jr., "Building a Collection of Maps," *ALA Bulletin* 30:206–15 (Apr. 1936).

10. Erwin Raisz, "Preservation and Cataloguing of Maps," in the author's *General Cartography* (New York: McGraw-Hill, 1938), pp. 342–45.

11. Lloyd A. Brown, "Special Reference Problems in Map Collections," *The Reference Function of the Library:* Papers Presented before the Library Institute at the University of Chicago, June 29 to July 10, 1942, edited by Pierce Butler (Chicago: Univ. of Chicago Pr., 1943), p. 146.

12. Frank T. Nicoletti, "U.S. Army Topographic Command College Depository Program," *Bulletin,* no. 86 (Dec. 1971) pp. 2–8.

13. Bill M. Woods, "Of Map Librarianship—A Very Personal Report," *Bulletin,* no. 76 (June 1969), pp. 4–6.

14. Dorothy Lewis, "Maps: Problem Children in Libraries," *Special Libraries* 35:75–78 (Mar. 1944).

15. Nordis Felland, "Some History: Of the Geography and Map Division," *Bulletin,* no. 76 (June 1969), pp. 2–4.

16. Special Libraries Association, Geography and Map Division, "Maps in the Library," *Library Journal* 75 (Mar. 15, 1950), entire issue.

17. ———, *Map Collections in the United States and Canada: A Directory* (New York: the Association, 1954), p. 1.

18. Nicoletti, "U. S. Army Topographic Command," p. 3.

19. Walter W. Ristow, "What About Maps?" *Library Trends* 4:123–39 (Oct. 1955).

20. ———, "The Emergence of Maps in Libraries," *Special Libraries* 58:400–19 (July-Aug. 1967).

21. Stanley D. Stevens, "A Short History of the Western Association of Map Libraries," *Western Association of Map Libraries Information Bulletin* 2:22–24 (May 1971).

22. Joan Winearls, "Map Libraries in Canada," *Cartographer* 3:163, 165 (Dec. 1966).

23. Helen Wallis, "Report on the Map Curators' Group," *Cartographic Journal* 4:11 (June 1967).

24. Nora T. Corley, "The Formation of the Geography and Map Libraries Subsection of the Section of Special Libraries, IFLA: A Canadian View," *Bulletin,* no. 80 (June 1970), pp. 40–45.

25. Walter W. Ristow, "International Map Librarianship, IFLA (Moscow), 1970," *Bulletin,* no. 82 (Dec. 1970), pp. 42–43; idem, "Geography and Map Libraries (Subsection): Report for the Year 1969–1970," and "Meetings in Moscow," in International Federation of Library Associations, *IFLA Annual 1970, Proceedings of the General Council, Annual Reports* (Copenhagen: Scandinavian Library Center, 1971), pp. 170–76.

26. Joan Winearls and Yves Tessier, comps., *Directory of Canadian Map Collections* (Montreal: Assn. of Canadian Map Libraries, 1969).

27. Western Association of Map Libraries, "Directory of Map Collections in Alaska, Arizona, California, Hawaii, Idaho, Nevada, Oregon, Washington, Alberta, British Columbia, mimeographed (Sacramento: California State Library, Government Publications Section, 1969).

28. Ristow, "Geography and Map Libraries," p. 175.

29. I. Mumford, "What Is a Map Library?" *Cartographic Journal* 3:9–11 (June 1966).

30. Jessie B. Watkins, *Selected Bibliography on Maps in Libraries: Acquisition, Classification, Cataloging, Storage, Uses* (rev. ed., Syracuse, N.Y.: Syracuse Univ. Libraries, 1967).

31. Bill M. Woods, *Map Librarianship: A Selected Bibliography* (rev. ed., New York: Engineering Index, Inc., 1970).

32. Frank J. Anderson, comp. and ed., *A Twenty Year (1947–1967) Cumulative Index to Special Libraries Association Geography and Map Division Bulletin (Numbers 1 through 70)* (New York: Special Libraries Association).

33. Special Libraries Association, Geography and Map Division, *Recent Practices in Map Libraries* (New York: the Association, 1971).

34. Jean Spealman Kujoth, *Readings in Nonbook Librarianship* (Metuchen, N.J.: Scarecrow, 1968).

35. Carlos B. Hagen, "A Brief Look at the UCLA Map Library," mimeographed (rev. 1969); Joyce Nelson, "LSU School of Geoscience Map Library," Louisiana Library Association *Bulletin* 33:87–90 (Fall 1970); Special Libraries Association, Geography and Map Division, "Map Collections in the United States and Canada," p. 43.

36. Louis Kiraldi, "Map Libraries in Michigan: A Survey," *Michigan Libraries* 35:4–6+ (Mar. 1969).

37. Robert L. Koepke, "Map Libraries in the Chicago Metropolitan Area," *Bulletin of the Illinois Geographical Society* 11:35–39 (Dec. 1968).

38. John V. Bergen, "Map Collections in Midwestern Universities and Colleges," *Professional Geographer* 24:245–52 (Aug. 1972).

39. U.S. Library of Congress, Geography and Map Division, *Annual Report 1971–1972.*

40. Special Libraries Association, Geography and Map Division, "Map Collections in the United States and Canada," pp. 27–30.

41. Ibid., pp. 83–84.

42. Arch Gerlach, "Potential Uses of Government Libraries for Geographical Research," *Journal of Geography* 52:32–40 (Jan. 1953).

43. Catherine I. Bahn, "Map Library Activities in the District of Columbia," *DC Libraries* 29:32–36 (Apr. 1958).

44. Richard W. Stephenson, ed., *Federal Government Map Collecting: A Brief History* (Washington, D.C.: Special Libraries Association, 1969).

45. Hildegard B. Johnson, "The James Ford Bell Collection," *Professional Geographer* 7:13 (Nov. 1955).

46. Ena L. Yonge, "The Map Department of the American Geographical Society," *Professional Geographer* 7:2–5 (Mar. 1955); American Geographical Society, Map Department, *Index to Maps in Books and Periodicals* (Boston: G. K. Hall, 1968), 10 v.; first supplement, 1971.

47. *Orbis Geographicus, 1968/72, World Directory of Geography* (Wiesbaden: Franz Steiner Verlag, 1970; Geographisches Taschenbuch, 1968/72, Sonderheft), pp. 288–301.

48. Mumford, "What Is a Map Library?" p. 9–11.

49. Robert C. White, "Map Librarianship," *Special Libraries* 61:233–35 (May–June 1970; D. S. Rugg, "Developing the University Map Library," *Journal of Geography* 66:119–29 (Mar. 1967); A. M. Ferrar, "The Management of Map Collections and Libraries in University Geography Departments," *Library Association Record* 64:161–65 (May 1962).

50. Stanley D. Stevens, "Planning a Map Library?" *Special Libraries* 63: 172–76 (Apr. 1972).

51. Carlos B. Hagen, "The Establishment of a University Map Library," WAML *Information Bulletin* 3:2–15 (Oct. 1971).

52. John Fetros, "Developing the Map Collection in Smaller Libraries," *Bulletin*, no. 85 (Sept. 1971), pp. 24–28; idem, "How to Win Administrative Support for a Map Collection," WAML *Information Bulletin* 2:14–20 (May 1971).

53. Nicoletti, "U.S. Army Topographic Command," p. 3.

54. Sandra Satterlee, "Sources of Free Maps from Central America, South America, and Africa," WAML *Information Bulletin* 1:41–47 (June 1970); John Fetros, [Bibliography from] "Free and Inexpensive Maps for the Public Library," WAML *Information Bulletin* 1:36–40 (Mar. 1970).

55. Stephenson, "Published Sources of Information About Maps and Atlases," *Special Libraries* 61:87–98, 110–12 (Feb. 1970).

56. Roman Drazniowsky, "Bibliographies as Tools for Map Acquisition and Map Collection," *Cartographer* 3:138–44 (Dec. 1966). Another version of this

article was published with the title, "Cartography," *Library Trends* 15: 710–17 (Apr. 1967).

57. Ristow, "Emergence of Maps," pp. 400–19.

58. Canadian Department of Energy, Mines and Resources, Departmental Map Library. *List of Map Sources* (2d ed., Ottawa: the Department, 1968; 3rd ed., 1972).

59. Watkins, "Selected Bibliography on Maps in Libraries," pp. 8–9; Edward B. Espenshade, Jr., "A Guide to Map Sources for Use in Building a College Map Library," *College and Research Libraries* 9:45–53 (Jan. 1948).

60. Association of American Geographers, High School Geography Project. Committee on Maps and Aerial Photographs, *Sources of Information and Materials: Maps and Aerial Photographs* (Boulder, Colo.: the Association, 1970).

61. Joseph W. Rogers, "Copyright Catalog Is Useful Tool," *Library Journal* 75:444–46 (Mar. 15, 1950).

62. *Bibliographie Cartographique Internationale* (Paris: Comité Nationale de Géographie et l'Union Géographique Internationale), annual.

63. Drazniowski, "Cartography," *Library Trends* 15:710.

64. Stephenson, "Published Sources," pp. 91–93.

65. Richard E. Harrison, "Evaluation of Modern Maps," *Special Libraries* 44:45–47 (Feb. 1953); Special Libraries Association, Geography and Map Division, *Keys to Map Evaluation* (Washington: the Association, 1953); James Patrick Walsh and S. Padraig Walsh, comp., *General World Atlases: A Comparative Analysis* (New York: Bowker, 1966); idem, *Home Reference Books in Print: A Comparative Analysis* (New York: Bowker, 1969), pp. 99–198.

66. Watkins, "Selected Bibliography," pp. 5–7; Anderson (comp.) *Twenty Year Cumulative Index.*

67. Ottilia C. Anderson, "No Best Method to Catalog Maps," *Library Journal* 75:450–52 (Mar. 15, 1950); idem, "A University Library Reviews Its Map Collection: The Cataloger's Point of View," *Library Journal* 70:103–6 (Feb. 1, 1945); Arch Gerlach, "Geography and Map Cataloging and Classification in Libraries," *Special Libraries* 52:248–51 (May–June 1961); Thomas R. Smith, "Map Classification and Arrangement at the University of Kansas Library," *Bulletin*, no. 22 (Dec. 1955), pp. 11–17; idem, "Map Collection in a General Library: A Manual for Classification and Processing Procedures," mimeographed (Lawrence: Univ. of Kansas, 1961); Mary Ellen Fink, "A Comparison of Map Cataloging Systems," *Bulletin*, no. 50 (Dec. 1962), pp. 6–11; Bill M. Woods, "Map Cataloging: Inventory and Prospect," *Library Resources and Technical Services* 3:257–73 (Fall 1959); Roman Drazniowsky, "The Need for Map Cataloging," *Special Libraries* 61:236–37 (May–June 1970).

68. Samuel W. Boggs, and Dorothy C. Lewis, *The Classification and Cataloging of Maps and Atlases* (New York: Special Libraries Association, 1945).

69. Thomas K. Hinckley, "Dewey Decimal Classification for United States Air Force Academy Map Collection," *Bulletin*, no. 82 (Dec. 1970), pp. 13–20.

70. Bertha R. Barden and Barbara Denison, "Maps," in *Guide to the SLA Loan Collection of Classification Schemes and Subject Heading Lists* (5th ed., New York: Special Libraries Association, 1961).

71. Ristow, "Emergence of Maps," pp. 406–7.

72. Ibid., pp. 408–9, 418.

73. *Maps: A MARC Format, Specifications for Magnetic Tapes Containing Catalog Records for Maps* (Washington, D.C.: Library of Congress, 1970); Walter W. Ristow and David K. Carrington, "Machine-Readable Map Cataloging in the Library of Congress," *Special Libraries* 62:343–52 (Sept. 1971); David K. Carrington and Elizabeth U. Mangan, *Data Preparation Manual for the Conversion of Map Cataloging Records to Machine-Readable Form* (Washington, D.C.: Library of Congress, 1971).

74. Mary Murphy, "Map Collection Prepares to Automate: The U. S. Army Topographic Command Library," *Special Libraries* 61:180–89 (Apr. 1970); Carlos B. Hagen, "An Information Retrieval System for Maps," *UNESCO Bulletin for Libraries* 20:30–35 (Jan.–Feb. 1966).

75. U.S. Board on Geographic Names, *Official Standard Names for . . . .* (Washington, D.C.: U.S. Dept. of the Interior, 1951–).

76. Lloyd A. Brown, *Notes on the Care and Cataloging of Old Maps* (Windham, Conn.: Hawthorn House, 1941).

77. William P. Cumming, *Southeast in Early Maps* (Princeton, N.J.: Princeton Univ. Pr., 1958); Carl I. Wheat, *Mapping the Transmississippi West* (San Francisco: Institute of Historical Cartography, 1957–63); Louis Charles Karpinski, *Bibliography of the Printed Maps of Michigan, 1804–1880* (Lansing, Mich. Historical Commission, 1931).

78. Library of Congress, *MAPS: A MARC Format;* Ristow and Carrington, "Machine-Readable Map Cataloging."

79. Mary Galneder, "Equipment for Map Libraries," *Special Libraries* 61: 271–74 (July–Aug. 1970).

80. Clara LeGear, *Maps: Their Care, Repair, and Preservation in Libraries* (rev. ed., Washington, D.C.: Library of Congress, Map Division, 1956), p. 10.

81. Ibid.

82. Barbara Mae Christy, "Critique of Pure Labeling [for Map Collections]," WAML *Information Bulletin* 1:12–22 (June 1970).

83. Ristow and Carrington, "Machine–Readable Map Cataloging."

84. J. Douglas Hill, "Map and Atlas Cases," *Library Trends* 13:481–87 (Apr. 1965).

85. Catherine I. Bahn, "Map Libraries—Space and Equipment," *Bulletin*, no. 46 (Dec. 1961), pp. 3–17.

86. Mary Fortney, "Relocation of Map Collection at Northwestern," *Bulletin*, no. 84 (June 1971), pp. 40–42; Alberta Koerner, "The New Map Room of the University of Michigan Library," *Bulletin*, no. 85 (Sept. 1971), pp. 33–38.

87. Howard G. Roepke, "Care and Development of a Wall Map Collection," *Professional Geographer* 10:11–15 (May 1958); James E. Collier, "Storing Map Collections," *Professional Geographer* 12:31–32 (July 1960); Arthur H. Doerr, "Map Collections: Another Approach," *Professional Geographer* 12:33–34 (Mar. 1960).

88. LeGear, "Maps."

89. Richard Daniel Smith, "Maps: Their Deterioration and Preservation," *Special Libraries* 63:59–68 (Feb. 1972).

90. Robert I. Boak, "Restoration and Preservation of Maps," *Bulletin,* no. 81 (Sept. 1970), pp. 21–23.

91. Helen Wallis, "Reference Work in a Map Library," *INSPEL* 4:85–88 (July–Oct. 1969).

92. Woods, *Map Librarianship: A Selected Bibliography.*

93. Bill M. Woods, "Map Information Reference Service," *Special Libraries* 45:103–6 (Mar. 1954).

94. C. B. Muriel Lock, *Modern Maps and Atlases: An Outline Guide to Twentieth Century Production* (Hamden, Conn.: Archon, 1969).

95. Walter W. Ristow, "Cartographic Exhibits," *Surveying and Mapping* 14: 18–25 (Jan. 1954); "Map Exhibits—Panel Discussion," *Bulletin,* no. 33 (Oct. 1958), pp. 11–14.

96. George R. Dalphin and Van H. English, "Geographical Exhibits," *Library Journal* 79:1466–68 (Sept. 1, 1954); Caleb D. Hammond, "Maps on Parade," *Library Journal* 83:1475–80 (May 15, 1958).

97. Marian D. Euler, "Introducing Librarians and Students to Maps," *Bulletin,* no. 87 (Mar. 1972), pp. 46–47.

98. Ena L. Yonge, "These Maps Are Essential," *Library Journal* 75:440+ (Mar. 15, 1950); Espenshade, "Building."

99. Carlos B. Hagen, "Survey of the Usage of a Large Map Library," *Bulletin,* no. 80 (June 1970) p. 27–31; Harry Bach, "Library's Map Room Enjoys Wide Use," *Library Journal* 74:268 (Mar. 1, 1949).

100. Walter W. Ristow, "Map Librarianship," *Library Journal* 92:3610–14 (Oct. 15, 1967).

101. "Current and Forthcoming Courses," *Bulletin,* no. 77 (Sept. 1969), p. 7–9.

102. Bill M. Woods, "A Continuing Need: Education for Map Librarianship," *Bulletin,* no. 81 (Sept. 1970), pp. 28–29; idem, "Training for Map Librarianship," *Special Libraries* 43:87–88, 102 (Mar. 1952); idem, "Map Librarianship," *Bulletin,* no. 23 (Feb. 1956), pp. 9–12; idem, "Map Librarianship," *Journal of Education for Librarianship* 7:9–12 (Summer 1966); Carlos B. Hagen, "Education and Training in Map Librarianship," *Bulletin,* no. 77, (Sept. 1969), pp. 3–7; Louis Kiraldi, "Courses in Map Librarianship," *Special Libraries* 61:496–500 (Nov. 1970).

103. Bill M. Woods, "Workshop for Map Librarians," *Professional Geographer,* 7:2–5 (Nov. 1955).

104. ———, "[Workshop at Free Library of Philadelphia]" *Bulletin,* no. 63 (Mar. 1966), p. 22; Hagen, "Education and Training," p. 5; "New Jersey Library Association Map Workshop [Reports and Papers]," *Bulletin,* no. 81

(Sept. 1970), pp. 20–29; Catharine M. Fogarty, "Report of the Map Workshop Presented by the Graphics Committee, NJLA History and Bibliography Section at Maplewood Public Library, March 21, 1972," *Bulletin*, no. 88 (June 1972), pp. 34–35; "LC Conference on Maps and Map Librarianship," *Bulletin*, no. 84 (June 1971), pp. 43–46.

105. Walter W. Ristow, "[Letters to the Editor]," *Bulletin*, no. 78 (Dec. 1969), p. 39; Carlos B. Hagen, "LC's Summer Special Map Processing Project [Letters to the Editor]," *Bulletin*, no. 79 (Mar. 1970), pp. 36–37; Harold M. Otness, "A Look at the Library of Congress Summer Map Processing Project," WAML *Information Bulletin* 3:16–19 (Oct. 1971).

106. Patricia G. Alonso, "Conservation and Circulation in Map Libraries: A Brief Review," *Bulletin*, no. 74 (Dec. 1968), pp. 15–18; Joan Winearls, "To Loan or Not to Loan," in *Proceedings of the Association of Canadian Map Libraries* (Fourth Annual Conference held June 1–3, 1970, Dept. of Geography, Univ. of British Columbia, Ottawa, 1971).

"Photographs, Pictures, and Prints"

1. Wolfang M. Freitag, "Art Libraries and Collections," *Encyclopedia of Library and Information Science* (New York: Dekker, 1968), vol. 1, p. 577.

2. John Austin Parker, "A Brief History of the Picture Collection," *Wilson Library Bulletin*, 30:257.

3. Ibid.

4. "Library of Congress Receives *Look* Magazine Photo Files," *Information; Part I* (Mar.–Apr. 1972), p. 78.

5. Freitag, "Art Libraries," vol. 1, pp. 586–89.

6. Norma O. Ireland, *The Picture File in School, College, and Public Libraries* (Boston: Faxon, 1952).

7. Merton B. Osborn, *Sources of Free Pictures* (Bruce Miller Publns., Box 369, Riverside, CA 92502, 1967), 17 p., Bruce Miller, *Sources of Inexpensive Pictures* (Riverside, Cal.: Bruce Miller Pubns.,); Bruce Miller, *Sources of Free Travel Posters* (Riverside, Calif.: Bruce Miller Pubns.).

8. Jane Clapp, *Art in Life 1936–1956* (New York: Scarecrow, 1959) and *Art in Life 1957–1963* (New York: Scarecrow, 1965).

9. Patricia P. Havlice, *Art in Time* (Metuchen, N.J.: Scarecrow, 1970).

10. Lucile E. Vance and Esther M. Tracey, *Illustration Index* (2d ed.; New York: Scarecrow, 1966).

11. Warren B. Hicks and Alma M. Tillin, *Developing Multi-Media Libraries* (New York: Bowker, 1970).

12. Minnie Earl Sears, *List of Subject Headings* (New York: Wilson Company, 1965).

13. Ireland, *The Picture File.*

14. William J. Dane, *The Picture Collection: Subject Headings* (6th ed., Hamden, Conn.: Shoe String, 1968).

15. *The UNESCO Catalogue of Colour Reproductions of Paintings Prior to 1860* (New York: Unipub, 1962) and *The UNESCO Catalogue of Colour Reproductions of Paintings—1860 to 1965* (New York: Unipub, 1966).

16. Margaret Bartran, *A Guide to Color Reproductions.* (2d ed., Metuchen, N.J.: Scarecrow, 1970).

17. New York Graphic Society, *Fine Art Reproductions of Old and Modern Masters* (8th ed.; Greenwich, Conn., The Society, 1968).

18. Isabel S. Monro, *Index to Reproductions of American Paintings* (New York: Wilson, 1948), 731 p.; *Index to Reproductions of American Paintings: First Supplement* (New York: Wilson, 1964), 480 p.

19. ——— *Index to Reproductions of European Paintings* (New York: Wilson, 1956), 668 p.

20. The annual "Purchasing Guide" issues of *Library Journal* list suppliers of framed reproductions.

21. Eugene Ostroff, "Preservation of Photographs," *Photographic Journal* (Oct. 1967).

22. Dorothy H. Dudley and Irma B. Wilkinson, *Museum Registration Methods* (Washington: American Assn. of Museums and Smithsonian Institution, 1968).

23. Carl Zigrosser and Christa M. Gaehde, *Guide to the Collecting and Care of Original Prints* (New York: Crown, 1965).

24. Dudley, *Museum Registration Methods.*

25. "The Slide Negative Pool of Taurgo, Inc., and Its Importance to College Education," *College Art Journal* 11:35–37 (Fall 1951).

)ue